Rolf Slotboom

Secrets of Professional Poker

1

Winning Strategies for Limit Hold'em, No-Limit Hold'em and Omaha

D&B
POKER SERIES

www.dandbpoker.com

First published in 2008 by D & B Publishing

Copyright © 2008 Rolf Slotboom

British Library Cataloguing-in-Publication Data

A catalogue record for this book is available from the British Library.

ISBN: 978 1904468-40-0

All sales enquiries should be directed to D&B Publishing:
Tel: 01273 711443, e-mail: info@dandbpoker.com,
Website: www.dandbpoker.com

Cover design by Horatio Monteverde.
Printed and bound in the UK by Clays, Bungay, Suffolk.

'Rolf always offers a fresh perspective on the game that's refreshing. His columns help readers think outside the box which is extremely important for any player looking to get to the next level.'

> Daniel Negreanu, *one of the world's leading authors. 4-times bracelet winner, 2-times WPT Champion, and over $10 million in live tournament earnings*

'There is not a single author who has caused as much irritation and aggravation as Slotboom has, yet who at the same time has such a refreshing and independent line of thinking. The author is not afraid to bite the hand that feeds him, and while he is very critical when it comes to the advice of others, he is also not afraid to ridicule or criticize his *own* plays at times.'

> Mel Judah, *one of the world's most consistent tournament players with numerous cashes and final tables at major events. Former bracelet winner at the WSOP*

'A collection of the good, accurate and sometimes controversial columns that Rolf has written over the years, completely revised to take into account the growth of online play and the no-limit hold'em boom. I highly recommend it.'

> Thierry van den Berg *(better known under his online handle BOKPOWER), one of the rising stars in tournament poker – with almost $800,000 live tournament winnings in just two years of play*

Poker books from D&B

Poker on the Internet
by Andrew Kinsman
978-1-904468-20-2, 208pp, $19.95 / £12.99

Advanced Limit-Hold'em Strategy
by Barry Tanenbaum
978-1-904468-36-3, 256pp, $24.95 / £14.99

Beginners Guide to Limit Hold'em
by Byron Jacobs
978-1-904468-21-9, 208pp, $19.95 / £12.99

How Good is Your Limit Hold 'em?
by Byron Jacobs with Jim Brier
978-1-904468-15-8, 192pp, $23.95 / £13.99

How Good is Your Pot-Limit Omaha?
by Stewart Reuben
978-1-904468-07-3, 192pp, $19.95 / £12.99

How Good is Your Pot-Limit Hold'em?
by Stewart Reuben
978-1-904468-08-0, 208pp, $19.95 / £12.99

Hold'em on the Come
by Rolf Slotboom and Drew Mason
978-1-904468-23-3 , 272pp, $19.95 / £12.99

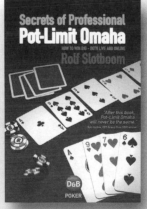

Secrets of Professional Pot-Limit Omaha
by Rolf Slotboom
978-1-904468-30-6, 240pp, $24.95 / £14.99

Limit Hold'em: Winning short-handed strategies
by Terry Borer and Lawrence Mak with Barry Tannenbaum
978-1-904468-37-0, 352pp, $24.95 / £14.99

Contents

Hold'em: No-Limit vs. Limit

Pot-Limit Omaha

Preface

Over the years, my columns have not gone unnoticed. Being someone who likes to explore new things, my writings have always reflected this attitude. I have always found it more important to come up with new and meaningful additions to poker literature rather than simply rehash old stuff written by others. For this reason, many of my articles have been called or labelled 'controversial' – something I have always taken as a compliment rather than as an insult. To me, it was always about exploring new territories, and even though I have not always been 100% right or accurate when it came to my recommendations, one could never accuse me of not thinking about the game in a deep, and rather unique manner.

Many of my columns have introduced concepts that were new at the time, often concepts that were heavily criticized at the time of publication. For instance, in my articles on seating position I recommended sometimes sitting to the maniac's immediate *right* rather than his immediate left (which was the common and 'correct' view at the time). Heck, I even called the seat to the maniac's left the 'Death Seat', something that went entirely against common wisdom. Also, I introduced a rather revolutionary short-stack approach for big-bet play at a time when everyone agreed that 'good players don't play short money', and that led to a whole bunch of 'Little Rolfs' shortstacking the online games. Plus, I had some articles that recommended extremely/overly tight folds in cash games, while at the same time I promoted an extremely loose-aggressive tournament strategy that included huge overbets and pushes with garbage. And last but not least, I wrote some rather influential columns about rules and behavioural issues that almost always were slightly different from the majority view.

All these columns have been put together in the two-volume *Secrets of Professional Poker* series, the first book of which you are reading right now. It includes the highly praised 14-part series on making the transfer to limit from no-limit, and the other way around – the series that were the foundation for my 'Rolf Slotboom's Winning Plays' 4 DVD-set. Of course, this book also contains the limit hold'em quiz with the – in the eyes of some – absolutely crazy recommendation to fold A-K before the flop against just a single raise. And finally, there are five or six pot-limit Omaha columns that did not make it into my *Secrets of Professional Pot-Limit Omaha* book, plus a whole bunch of new pieces.

Of course, all of these articles have been rewritten and edited to take into account all the changes that have happened to poker in recent years: the growth of online poker, the boom of no-limit hold'em, the success of tournament play, and the rise of shorthanded games.

The combination of all this should result in a highly interesting document, a collection of excellent, strange, renewing, controversial and almost always in-depth articles. I hope and expect that you will thoroughly enjoy them.

Rolf Slotboom,

Amsterdam,

August 2008

Limit Hold'em

Defending the blinds

When people analyse their game or try to explain why they have been losing, they will very likely come up with some kind of bad beat stories.
There are only a few players who try to discover what the leaks in their
game really are. It's a fact that every player loses money in the blinds,
which is logical since you're forced to put money into the pot without
looking at your cards. However, most people lose too much money when
playing the blinds; some even lose more than the sum of the blinds they
have already put in.

A lot of poker books have been written about hand selection as compared
to position relative to the button and I don't have much to add to what
Sklansky, Malmuth and all those others have already written. However,
whether or not to defend your blind is often less automatic than whether
or not to play a hand out of freewill, since in limit hold'em, if you're the
kind of player I hope you are (tight/aggressive), your tightness will invite
people to take a shot at trying to steal your blind. Obviously, you can't let
these people succeed in running over you. If you send the message that
your blind is up for grabs every time, everyone except for maybe the most
timid or frightened players will do exactly that: take it. Since at the limits I
play ($10-$20 and up) hardly anyone figures to make more than one big
bet per hour, it should be obvious that playing the blinds correctly can
have a huge impact on your hourly rate.

When I started playing poker for a living, I played very aggressively but
also extremely tight, which induced some players to take a shot at my
blind practically every time. Since it is clear that a free ride in the blind can
be very profitable in the long run, you don't want your blind to be raised
on every occasion. In deciding whether or not to defend, it is important
who you are up against: is your opponent a habitual stealer or a very tight
player, is the raiser in early position or near the button, and how does this
specific player view you? (That is: does he think he's able to outplay you
after the flop or to run over you and get away with it?) If the raise comes
from a solid player from early position and everybody else has folded, my
blind is his nine times out of ten. The only hands I would defend with are
wired pairs (since they play very easily after the flop – no set, no bet – and
if I hit, the raiser won't figure me for such a powerful hand) and A-K.
That's right, I'll fold hands like J-10s, Q-Js and sometimes even A-Q, suited
or not. My reasoning: the raiser figures to have a decent-sized pocket pair
or A-K a large percentage of the time, so I'm not going to chase him out of

position for a nothing pot to begin with.[1] On the other hand, if there are also two or three additional callers, I will call with a wide range of hands. I'll call with K-6s, 10-7s and sometimes even hands like 7-6o or 9-8o. However, I'll still fold hands which figure to be dominated by the raiser's hand. That is: hands like A-10, K-J and K-Q still go into the muck, unless they're suited. (One well-known author has claimed that if hands aren't worth playing offsuit you shouldn't play them suited. However, when in the big blind with trouble hands like this I think that being suited might be just enough to turn a fold into a call, especially in multiway pots.)

When in the blinds, it's important to figure out what the other guys might be playing, so you try to play hands that are opposed to theirs. (Therefore I sometimes defend with small cards, especially when the raiser has a tendency to raise with big cards rather than big pairs, so you might not have to hit twice to win.) More money is lost in limit hold'em by hands that are dominated (hands like A-J vs. A-K or K-10 vs. K-Q) than in any other situation. (When you flop top pair your kicker might not be good, and when you don't flop a pair you'll usually have to fold to any bets, since hitting one of your overcards on the turn may once again be more beneficial to the raiser than to you.) Therefore you should avoid playing offsuit big cards in raised pots!

When your big blind is being attacked by a late position, highly aggressive raiser, a totally different strategy is called for. Since the raiser figures to have something but the odds are against him having a powerhouse (raises with hands like K-9, Q-10 or A-8 or even worse are common), folding the trouble hands I just mentioned may be a costly mistake. In fact, hands like A-10 or A-J may become reraising hands in situations like this. (Beware of reraising with K-J or K-Q though – a lot of aggressive players have a tendency to raise with a 'bad ace' which will of course be good in a showdown. On the other hand, reraising with these hands may pave the way for a successful bluff postflop, for instance if the opponent has a small pair

---

[1]   This article was written in 2001, when more than nowadays, preflop raises tended to be done on solid values only. Especially early-position raises in full ring games were almost without exception the sign of a big hand. As nowadays, even good and solid players tend to open raise with a slightly wider range of hands that in the past, also from early position and even in full-ring games, this means that I will also *defend* a bit more loosely – and it will be much rarer than in the past for me to fold hands like A-Q or A-Js to a single raise.

and an ace flops. Because of your aggression and the fact that he might figure you for either a bigger pocket pair or two big cards including an ace, reraising preflop with your K-J type of holding could earn you a pot post-flop that you weren't entitled to based on the strength of your hand.) On the other hand, the small connecting cards or suited cards that I *would* defend with in a multiway pot will still have to be folded in heads-up situations like this, even if you suspect the raiser to be stealing. Make sure you're well armed before going to war! [2]

After the flop, don't automatically fold hands like A-10 or A-J when the board comes with rags in a situation where you are the big blind and have flat called a late-position raise. The raiser figures to have two (semi-) big cards also, so your ace might still be good; in fact, checkraising the preflop raiser on the flop in situations like this is often correct, and even check-calling an unimproved ace-high could be a good strategy if you are up against a somewhat overaggressive player who bluffs a lot. Also betting out on the flop, whether or not you have actually hit, might be a good thing once in a while. By doing this, you send the message that your blind isn't his *all* of the time, that you're willing to defend and even go to war once in a while, in short that you won't let him push you around. Still, you'll have to fold your big blind at least six or seven times out of ten, or you'll be giving too much action.

Folding your small blind should become second nature to you. I believe that most people lose even more money in the small blind than they do in the big blind. There are some otherwise good players who might complete the small blind without looking 'since it's only half a bet anyway'. You'll hear people talk about this being a 'discount', but just like in real life things aren't always what they seem. You'll be in the worst position throughout the deal; you don't have a lot of information about the other

---

[2]   If you do play the small suited connectors in this situation, it is some-times correct to reraise with them. By doing this, you take the initiative away from your opponent, with the goal of picking up all those small/default pots where you and your opponent both don't flop much. An added benefit is that your hand is very well-disguised, meaning that when you don't hit (big cards flop) you might make your opponent fold the best hand, whereas if you *do* hit, you could get a lot of action from your opponent's second-best hand or because the small cards on the board may have induced him to go for a bluff/try to bet you off your 'obvious' big cards.

people's hands since there was no preflop raise, and (especially in raked pots) being involved in pots with hands that don't really warrant it can become a costly habit.

In the small blind in a full-ring game, I fold more than 60% of the time. If there are only one or two not-too-dangerous limpers, I would rather raise than call with fairly marginal hands like A-10s or A-J to get the big blind out and to gain control over the hand. Weak hands like K-9, A-9, suited hands like K-7s or Q-8s and the small connecting cards like 8-7 or 9-8 are all rather marginal, but given the good price are usually worth a call here – especially if it looks like no really strong hands are out there, and thus you might be able to steal the pot postflop.

There are almost no hands I would call an early-position raise with in the small blind. I might call with a small wired pair if it seems like the pot is going to be five- or six-handed, but these hands and also hands like A-Js, A-Qs and sometimes even A-K all go into the muck if I see that there are no other players in the pot except for the raiser. If the raise comes from late position or from a loose open-raiser, then I usually treat this as a reraise-or-fold situation. I will rarely flat call a late-position raiser, as I want to isolate myself against the preflop raiser who doesn't need to have much, and because I don't want to give the big blind the chance to come in cheaply. Depending on the open-range that this raiser has, I will decide whether marginal hands like Q♣-J♣ or A♥-7♥ would require a fold or a reraise.

All in all, don't give in to the temptation of playing too many hands in the blinds since you've already invested 25 or 50 percent. You will be surprised how much good playing like this will do to your bankroll.

A limit hold'em quiz: part 1

You are playing in a typical $10-$20 limit hold'em game, fairly tight and aggressive, blinds $5-$10. The game is ten-handed and the rake is 5%, max. $3. You're playing in seat #10. There's a weak/tight player in seat #1, a professional player in seat #2 and a loose/aggressive player in seat #7. All other players can be considered average or a little below average.

The questions

1) You're in the small blind with K♥-8♥ and have completed the blind. No raises, six people see the flop J♥-8♦-5♦. Seat #2 bets and there is one caller. What do you do?

a) fold b) call c) raise

2) Same situation. This time everybody checks and seat #8 bets. What do you do?

a) fold b) call c) raise

3) You're under-the-gun (first to act), holding A♠-J♦. What do you do?

a) fold b) call c) raise

4) You're in the big blind with A♥-3♥. There have been no raises, so five people see the flop 10♦-8♥-5♥. You have played your nut-flush draw in a rather passive manner by checking and calling the flop (seat #4 has been the bettor), and all four remaining players have checked the turn (K♠). A third heart comes on the river (9♥) and the small blind comes out betting. What do you do?

a) fold b) call c) raise

5) You're in the small blind with 7♠-7♣. Four people call the initial bet and the button raises to $20. Since it looks like the hand is going to be played seven-handed (giving you the right odds in trying to flop a set) you call, as do all others. The flop comes 9♣-7♥-2♠. What do you do? (* the button being the most likely bettor)

a) check/if there's a bet*, fold

b) check/if there's a bet*, call (slowplay)

c) check/if there's a bet*, raise

d) bet/if there's a raise*, fold

e) bet/if there's a raise*, call

f) bet/if there's a raise*, reraise

6) You're in the small blind, holding A♥-K♠. Seat #2 has raised, everybody has folded. What do you do?

a) fold b) call c) raise

7) Same situation. This time you hold A♥-K♥. What do you do?

a) fold b) call c) raise

8) You're on the button with 3♥-3♣. Seat #7 has raised, like he has done the last four pots in a row. There are no callers. What do you do?

a) fold b) call c) raise

9) You're in the big blind with A♥-J♣. Seat #8 has raised to $20. There are no callers, the small blind also folds. What do you do?

a) fold b) call c) raise

10) You're on the button with A♦-K♦ and have raised before the flop. Six players see the flop J♦-10♦-3♠, giving you a gut-shot royal flush draw. The blinds check, as does seat #4. Seat #7 bets into you and gets raised by seat #8. What do you do?

a) fold b) call c) raise

11) You're on the button with 7♣-6♣. You have called before the flop only to see seat #1 (the small blind) raise to $20. Five people see the flop which comes 8♥-5♣-2♠. The small blind leads, seat #8 calls and it's up to you. What do you do?

a) fold b) call c) raise

12) Once again, you're on the button holding 7♣-6♣. Everybody has folded and it's up to you. What do you do?

a) fold b) call c) raise

13) You're one off the button with J♥-J♣. Seat #4 has raised to $20 and has been called by seat #6. What do you do?

a) fold b) call c) raise

14) You're in the big blind holding A♥-J♣. Seat #4 has raised to $20, everybody has folded. What do you do?

a) fold b) call c) raise

The answers/points per answer:

Listed in bold the original ratings from the quiz, and the original comments. I have put my current views in italics, taking into account the changed circumstances/different plays at today's $10-$20 and up limit hold'em games. If there are no comments in italics, then the preferred course of action has remained more or less the same.

1. a) 8 b) 4 c) 3

You've got no real (nut) outs here. The pro almost certainly has you beat. Even another eight or king coming on the turn or river may not win the pot for you (the pro might have K-J suited, the caller might have A-8).

> *This being a six-way pot, the pro is still likely to be betting a hand of real value. Of course, this could also mean a big drawing hand like the nut-flush draw. As we can almost close the betting (with just the big blind is behind us), since we've also got a backdoor flush draw and because there's at least the possibility that our middle pair could be good, I now tend to lean towards peeling one off. For someone who is not that good postflop, I would still recommend a fold though. My current ratings: a) 6 b) 7 c) 3.*

2. a) 6 b) 4 c) 7

Raising is your best option here. You've got a fair chance of having the best hand. You would like to play the hand heads-up against the late-position bettor. Still, there are so many draws possible that folding might not be such a bad idea after all.

3. a) 8 b) 5 c) 5

In a ten-handed game, A-J is not good enough to play under-the-gun. If you raise, you will only get called (or reraised) by hands that will be better than yours and on top of that you are out of position.

> *Play has become much looser now than it used to be in 2000/2001, and hands that used to be clear folds (8-7 suited, 10-8 suited and such) will now happily call a raise if they have position on you. One thing that has not changed: A-J offsuit under-the-gun is still a fold, although maybe not as clear-cut as the ratings suggest.*

4. a) 2 b) 8 c) 6

This is a good time to go for the overcall. The players behind you must have made something (small flush, straight) with the nine, hands that might be good enough for one, but not for two bets. The small blind might be bluffing, might fold against your raise or, if you get reraised, your hand might not even be good.

> *As in general, players have become a bit more tricky on the river, and have started making thin value raises a lot more than they used to, I don't like the 'overcall to induce action' as much as I used to. Nowadays, two-pair hands tend to call lightly even against a bet and a raise, any straight is likely to call the two bets as well, and some aggressive players would even three-bet in this spot with a non-nut flush. Of course, as people nowadays are more prone to make thin value raises, the chance of getting raised behind us if we flat call has gone up – heck, even just a straight may decide to raise for value in this spot. All in all, my ratings now would be: a) 1 b) 7 c) 9.*

5. a) 2 b) 5 c) 4 d) 2 e) 6 f) 8

This is the time to build a big pot. You flopped what you wanted, now bet your hand! Since the pot is big already, people might call your bet with just overcards and if the button decides to play back at you, you have the option to just call (to keep everybody in) or reraise. (There's so much money in the pot by now, you probably wouldn't mind to see backdoor flushes or inside straights fold.) Checkraising the button isn't a good play here: people with weak hands will just fold now without having put extra money into the pot, and if the button doesn't bet, someone who wouldn't have called your bet now gets a free card which might beat you on the turn, or which might create some backdoor draw that gets completed on the river.

6. a) 7 b) 5 c) 4

The raiser figures to have a high pair or A-K as well (remember – he's a professional player raising under-the-gun). Why get involved when your hand is an underdog to begin with? You don't know where you're at in the hand: if you flop a king, you might lose a lot of money; if you flop an ace when the raiser has in fact a wired pair, you might not get any action; if you flop nothing but he doesn't have anything either, he might outplay you and make you lay down the best hand.

Of course, this is the most controversial hand of the entire quiz, and one that has been hotly debated on many forums and newsgroups. (See also the articles that follow this quiz.) In the 10-handed games that I played in at the time, under-the-gun (UTG) raises were usually done only with quality hands; many good/winning players would not automatically raise in this spot with an A-Q, for instance. Also, as this article was directed at relatively inexperienced players and I valued the concept of 'staying out of trouble' very highly at that time, I recommended an in the eyes of some absolutely crazy fold. And indeed, nowadays I wouldn't make this fold anymore, and I also would not recommend it anymore – for a large part because of the reason that Mason Malmuth gives in the articles below. My current ratings would probably be: a) 5 b) 6 c) 7, and for those whose postflop play is in order and/or who have excellent reads, I might rate the preflop fold even a bit lower than a 5.

7. a) 7 b) 6 c) 4

The fact that your hand is suited isn't really important here. If your call induces a call by the big blind, then your hand might be playable. However, folding is still the best option – why invest a lot of money when there's nothing in the pot, out of position, when you know your opponent has a real hand?

> *I still agree that the suitedness of A-K should not be an overriding factor, at least not such a strong factor that it could turn a fold into a reraise. However, it does constitute a little more strength, meaning that it would add some value to calling and reraising at the expense of folding – meaning the ratings would be something like a) 4.5 b) 6.5 c) 7.5.*

8. a) 7 b) 5 c) 6

I don't like the play of reraising an aggressive player with a small pair, although you're a small favourite hot-and-cold if he holds two random cards. The fact is: the raiser might have a good hand (he doesn't always need to be in there with nothing), one of the blinds may wake up with a real hand (forcing you to pay four bets for a hand that may barely be worth one), or the raiser may in fact be playing two random cards, but receive help from the board. Still, if you decide to play, raising is better than calling, because you want to play the hand heads-up.

> *The fact that if you do reraise and both blinds fold, you will also have significant dead money, plus you have position with a hand that is probably not an underdog, I like the reraising option a bit more than I used to. This is especially true if you have a tight image and/or your opponent will only continue after the flop if he actually receives help from the board. Under those conditions, the 'powerplay' of reraising in position could be worth it, even though I still view the move as quite risky. New ratings: a) 6 b) 4 c) 7*

9. a) 3 b) 6 c) 8

Your hand is probably good: the button might very well be on a steal. You've got to show him your blind is not up for grabs all the time so reraising here might be best. Another option is to just call his raise and then checkraise on the flop or bet into him (whether the flop helped you or not).

10. a) 3 b) 8 c) 6

Although the flop has been pretty favourable to you, calling here is your best option. Every queen or diamond gives you the nuts. By calling you might be able to induce calls by the other players, giving you better odds in drawing to your hand. If you think no one has two pair yet, then reraising might be better (because any ace or king might then also make your hand a winner), but it seems likely that seat #8 has the J-10 or a small set already.

> *As play in general has become a bit more loose-aggressive than in the past, a bet and a raise in front of a preflop raiser don't necessarily mean two pair — they could be done on a fairly wide range of hands. For this reason, I actually prefer three-betting here with this big draw, not in the last place to maybe create some extra outs with a king or an ace. Even though flat calling to induce others/weaker draws to come in still has merit, we have a very big hand here, that probably deserves to be played highly aggressively. New ratings: a) 2 b) 6.5 c) 7.5*

11. a) 3 b) 5 c) 8

I rarely use the free-card play in hold'em, but in this case the situation might be right. The bettor might be in there with just A-K and since he's playing weak-tight, he will probably just call your raise and then check to you on the turn even if he does have a high wired pair. In fact, you might also bet the turn if you think the opposition is weak, if a scare card comes up (an eight, pairing the top card on the board), or if you receive some, but not a lot, of help (a six, seven, or club).

12. a) 7 b) 4 c) 5

I don't believe in trying to steal the blinds a lot. If there are often no callers before the flop in hold'em, or if pots are played heads-up all the time, I'll just go and find myself another game. Still, trying to steal the blinds here might work, especially since the small blind (the weak-tight player) will probably fold. Two problems: the big blind is a pro who knows what you're doing (he might reraise with nothing) and the rake makes playing for small pots unattractive (the rake is at its peak when the pot is $60).

> *Comments still hold true, although my ratings would probably be more like a) 6.5 b) 4 c) 6.*

13. a) 7 b) 5 c) 4

You figure to be up against high cards or, even worse, a higher pair (an under-the-gun raise usually means you're up against a quality hand). Even though you have a fine starting hand, you're not going to reraise here as any ace, king or queen on the flop would force you to give up your hand. In fact, this hand could prove quite expensive even if only low cards flop: you're going to play your hand, maybe even aggressively, hoping the raiser doesn't have A-A, K-K or Q-Q. The only way you can really like your hand is when a jack flops and the odds against that are 7.5 to 1. If you look at the situation like this, your hand isn't much stronger than a pair of deuces and folding here (don't show your hand to anyone!) might not be such a bad idea.

> *Again, not a move that I like much anymore, and that even at the time of publication of this quiz was probably a bit too tight. The fact that if we reraise here, there will probably be quite a bit of dead money from the blinds folding, and that we will be in position with the fourth-best starting hand in the deck, means that folding would be giving a bit too much credit here – or, to quote my critics, would be a weak-tight play. Especially as people nowadays open-raise with a wider range of hands, often including medium pairs, I would give 8 points for reraising now, 6.5 for calling, and only 4.5 points for folding – a rather different score compared to my views seven years ago. This doesn't mean that the jacks play easily after the flop, as they are still very hard to play especially if just a single overcard comes up and/or if we run into resistance with unimproved jacks. But having position, and especially if we have three-bet preflop, this should make our postflop decisions a little easier.*

14. a) 7 b) 4 c) 4

The raiser figures to have a high pair or higher cards than you. That is, if you flop a jack, he might have a higher pair; if you flop an ace you might be outkicked. You might decide to become aggressive with your hand if you think the flop hasn't helped your opponent, but most preflop raisers aren't going to give the blind credit for a hand and are unwilling to fold. Why get involved when you are taking the worst of it for a nothing pot to begin with?

> *I still don't like this type of holding against an early-position raise, exactly because of the reasons I gave in the original quiz. Still, I would probably change the ratings slightly to a) 6 b) 5.5 c) 4.*

Ace-king revisited: part 1

A while ago, while checking out the some of the poker sites for new information, there was a post on the 'Two Plus Two' forums that attracted my attention. It read:

Caro's advice...

A good player under-the-gun raises. I'm the small blind, and everybody folds. I have A-Ks or A-Ko. What's my action here?

This is a question from Mike Caro's online poker lessons, told me by a poker player who is a student there. Answer... clear fold, suited or not.

Is he right here? I doubt it, but I like to hear other opinions.

The first couple of responses were from people disagreeing with Mr Caro. Even though I don't post very often, in this case I decided to do just that. I wrote:

Mr Caro is right

I know most people will think: how can this be good advice? How tight do people expect me to play? But it's not about playing tight or loose – it's about having the best hand or not, and about risk vs. reward. For a more detailed analysis of this exact situation, I would refer to my first limit hold'em quiz where I describe the almost exact same situation, and also give the same recommendation.

When reading this, it's important to keep a few things in mind: I've been known as the 'Ace' for years – and for a reason. I was known as a super-rock when I started playing for a living. In fact, a lot of people claimed that I was not much of a player, that I was simply lucky to win as often (and as much) as I did with my tight play. For years, people have told me: 'How does he do this? When *I* raise with A-K, the flop comes with rags. But when *this guy* raises with it, an ace or king flops. And not just that; it's about the only hand he plays – but he always wins. How can this be?' When I stepped up to playing pot-limit Omaha, I heard the same type of comments – only this time it was the aces people were concerned with. Time and time, I've heard things like: 'How can this be? I cannot win with a flush or a full house. But this guy sits there for hours, waiting for aces. Then he is able to go all-in with them before the flop and he always wins – even with just a single pair. How is this possible?'

Well, what most people tend to forget here is that there is almost always a right or a wrong way to play a hand. You've got to adjust to the circumstances, the atmosphere at the table, the tendencies of your opponents and a dozen of other things. One of the reasons I still get action nowadays in pot-limit Omaha is that even though I hardly ever play a hand, I also 'gamble' with my opponents once in a while, especially with the loose players. Because I sometimes raise with hands that *they* wouldn't raise with, they sometimes raise me back before the flop, giving me the chance to get my whole stack in as a big favourite. Because I *give* them a bit of action occasionally with some funny hands, I get back a lot of action in return – sometimes also when I hold the nuts. Therefore, it's got nothing to do with luck when I win a big pot playing like this. Everything I do or say at the table, the amount of my early raises, all the chats I have with the gambling type of players, the overall image I try to create: all this is done to *get me* into these kinds of favourable situations.

The reason why I used to win with A-K so often when I was still playing limit hold'em exclusively, was because people saw me as a super-rock, and always assumed that I was in there with the nuts when I was in a hand. So, they folded when they should have called, called when they should have raised, gave free cards to me that would cause them to lose the pot etc. Yet, what people forget is that no A-K (in limit hold'em) or A-A (in PLO) is the same. In fact, I think there is not a single player in Europe who has folded A-K before the flop so often, even though I love the hand. I know there are people who *never* fold the hand and claim that 'if you cannot play A-K, what hands *can* you play?' However, their thinking is besides the point. It's not a matter of playing tight or loose, it's about having the best hand, or getting the right odds. Having said that, what possible reasons could there be to fold such a good hand before the flop?

♠ The pot has been raised or reraised, and you think there's a decent chance that you are up against aces or kings.

♠ Even though the (re)raisers don't necessarily need to have aces or kings, you figure your hand may be rather dead, i.e. the kings and aces you need are in some of your opponents' hands, and the way the hand has developed so far you know you will have to improve your ace-king to win.

♠ Even when your ace-king is in fact the best hand before the flop, you feel that the situation you are in right now is simply a bad one. If you flat call or reraise the players who have made the initial raise(s), you might get outplayed by them after the flop. This is especially true if even by reraising you cannot isolate one person, but you will have to play your ace-king in a three- or four-way pot against aggressive and experienced players. Knowing what type of hand you probably hold, they may be putting a lot of pressure on you in order to make you lay down the current best hand – for instance when the flop comes with rags. This is especially likely if you are relatively inexperienced, and are not really able to make the distinction between someone who truly has a good hand and someone who is only representing one.

♠ You are probably going to win a small pot if your hand is good, but lose a big one if it's not (reverse/negative implied odds).

♠ You are playing in a game with a high rake, which makes playing for small pots unattractive (this is the case in most of the places in Europe that I frequent).

♠ You are in a ten-handed game. In a ten-handed game, players in early position would need a slightly better starting hand to raise with than in a nine-handed game, simply because there are now seven players behind you who are still to act instead of six (once again, this is the case in most of the limit hold'em games in which I play).

♠ You are out of position, not knowing where you're at and whether your A-K is good or not.

Having said all this, you hardly ever fold A-K before the flop. Most of the time, you have a calling or (re)raising hand. You should keep in mind, however, that your A-K is *very* strong in position, heads-up against a loose goose, but not nearly as strong out of position against a solid, or even good, player who has shown strength – especially not if the person you are up against has high raising standards for the position that he's in.

Back to the thread. I got an interesting response from someone who claimed:

> *Well, I agree with what you say about this not being a too 'tight or loose' question, but I still don't like this fold. A solid player will raise with several hands even under-the-gun that A-K and especially A-Ks dominate. Finally, this is coming from somebody who has folded A-K before the flop plenty of times, and I even folded it out of the big blind once not too long ago, but I just don't think that this situation calls for a fold.*

Most posters agreed with this reasoning[3], claiming that I was wrong in my recommendation to fold the hand from the small blind for just a single raise, because of positive expected value (EV in internet parlance) the ace-king would have here. They claimed that there are a lot of hands the under-the-gun raiser could hold that would still give you a decent chance to win the pot, and that, in short, you would be getting the right odds to call

---

3   As should be clear, I nowadays indeed tend to agree with this reasoning myself – even though against extremely tight open raisers or against very good players, I think a large part of my comments/remarks from this article still hold true.

with your ace-king here.

I didn't agree with the people who claimed the A-K would have a positive expectation in the situation mentioned, and that the advice offered by Mr Caro in his online poker lessons (folding) was therefore wrong. I wrote:

> *OK, suppose you call. Now, how are you going to play your hand? If you are lucky enough that you still have chances (i.e. the UTG player doesn't have aces or kings but a lower pair), then you can win – if an ace or king flops. But your opponent sees that too. So what does he do? He's not going to give you action: you will win the money in the pot and that's it. But what are you going to do when only low cards flop? Are you going to call him down hoping he doesn't have a pair? (Playing like this will be very expensive in the long run.) Or are you going to fold, maybe. But what if your hand was good and the under-the-gun player did have one of these hands that you guys claim he might possibly hold (A-10s, A-J, whatever), then you get bluffed out. Either way, you are in bad shape after the flop, and your preflop call has got you into a lot of trouble. In my opinion, the situation is like this. You are out of position, with a hand that might be a dog to begin with, with nothing in the pot, and if you hit you win nothing, but if you don't hit you lose a bunch of extra bets. Or, if you hit an ace or king when your opponent has aces or kings, then you will lose even more bets, in fact you are going to be busted. Yet, you guys still think Mr Caro is wrong? Try to look beyond your own starting hand, because it is just that – a starting hand. Nothing more, nothing less.*

Things got even more interesting. Mason Malmuth himself got involved, and wrote:

> *'In my opinion, the situation is like this. You are out of position, with a hand that might be a dog to begin with.'*
>
> *Rolf, I don't want you to take this wrong, but I suspect that you are being influenced by your pot-limit play, since this is exactly the argument that a pot-limit player would make. You are overlooking the fact that your hand might also have the under-the-gun*

player in serious trouble.

Here's how I would usually play it. First, you must realize that the hand is playable. Now with that being the case, it is important to keep the big blind out, so it becomes imperative to make it three bets. This increases your chances of winning without improving. Now that you have made it three bets (assuming your opponent only calls), you can lead the betting on the flop and turn.

Notice that this strategy is much more dangerous in pot-limit than in limit, since in the pot-limit version you may look at a giant size bet or raise from a person who has position on you. So you must be much more cautious and folding may now be correct.

I responded:

Well, while it's true that most people know me as a pot-limit player, I still consider limit hold'em to be my main game. (I've been playing limit hold'em almost exclusively – and professionally – for almost three years before moving up to pot-limit poker.) Nowadays I play mostly pot-limit Omaha, but never pot-limit hold'em, so I have no opinion on how to play the ace-king in that game, and in the situation you mention. In limit hold'em, I am somewhat leery to play hands that I might be a big dog with, and I think that the A-K in this situation qualifies. I don't agree there are many hands you will be dominating with your ace-king. In my games (OK, not Vegas, and ten-handed) under-the-gun raises by solid players are almost always pairs eights and up or A-K – but in the Vegas middle-limit games things might be a lot different, so I cannot and should not judge on these games. (Also, keep in mind Mr Caro offered his advice to a Poker School student, and this student is not likely to be playing in aggressive middle-limit games.) Although I agree that reraising is an option, how are you going to play your hand when your opponent caps it (assuming three raises only), and three small cards flop. Are you going to call all the way assuming your ace-king is good? Or are you going to fold at any stage, when your opponent might have a lesser hand? In my opinion, chances are you will win a small pot when your hand is good, and lose a big pot when it's not – and this is not the most enviable position to be in when playing poker. Also, putting in a lot of bets in a small pot when it's unclear where you're at is something I try to avoid – even though it is possible that by doing this I will occasionally fold the best hand preflop.

Mr Malmuth then made a final response:

Rolf, you need to understand that if you are against someone who would raise with a pair smaller than kings, you certainly want to play A-K because of the blind money that is already in the pot. Granted, this is only a small profit situation, but it still has positive value. So being against someone who would raise with any pair 8-8 or higher should be incentive to play, not fold.

By the way, if you read our books, and this is consistent with the way I usually play, you usually call UTG with J-J, 10-10, 9-9 and 8-8. So when I think of a tight solid player raising under-the-gun, I am thinking of someone who is less desirable to play against than you are describing.

However, I am also thinking of someone, and again if you follow our advice you would do this, who raises UTG with A-Q. You seem to be thinking of someone who would not raise under-the-gun with A-Q. While in certain games it might be correct not to raise with this hand up front, the typical tight solid player (in my experience) will raise with it virtually every time UTG.

Now, as I have already stated in another post, I do agree that if A-Q is not a possible raising hand then this changes everything. Furthermore, I would also agree that even if you knew they were to raise with the additional pairs you mention but not raise with A-Q, the additional pairs would be enough to swing your A-K from a fold to a call.

Anyway, I think we have the answer. If the tight solid UTG player does raise with A-Q, folding A-K is clearly wrong. If he also raises with some other hands such as A-Js and K-Qs, and some additional pairs, it becomes even more wrong to fold the A-K. However, if the only non-paired hand he will raise with is A-K, then you should give it up when you hold A-K in the small blind.

So the question is whether the tight player who raised UTG plays as you describe or as I describe. In my experience they almost all play much closer to what I am describing than what you are describing. However, it's not how they play in general, but how this particular person plays. So I would agree that against a few people it might be right to fold the A-K. This would be the person who, as you say, you might be a big dog against. But also notice that this person is virtually never a big dog against you. If he can also be a big dog against you as well, then that changes everything.

Some final words

Interesting discussions like this one go on and on on the Internet. There's not just the Two Plus Two Forum, but also RGP, the Poker Pages Forum, the United Poker Forum and a few other (smaller) places where poker players interact. Most of the time you will get opinions – it is hardly ever a matter of right or wrong.[4] It's a great thing that some of the best players in the world are willing to share their knowledge for free. I would highly recommend anyone to visit some of these newsgroups and forums, to see poker from a slightly different point of view maybe.

So, was I right in my recommendations regarding A-K for this specific situation, or was I wrong? You just make up your own mind. Every game is different, every hand is different, every situation is different, and it's hard to come up with cut and dried answers all the time. I would say: take advantage of the fact that good or even excellent players are willing to share their opinions in public, even though they don't necessarily have to be right – and this includes me. (Even experts or proven champions can be wrong on occasion. However, because they *are* experts this will not happen very often, and most of the time when they *are* wrong they will be only *slightly* wrong.) Now, if you are able to make the right play a large percentage of the time, *knowing* why you're making that play, you've come

---

4   As it happened, in this case it might have very well been exactly that: a case of wrong or right. While in my own games, I had a high enough level of thinking to beat the games constantly and consistently, I *did* pass up some +EV situations on some occasions because of what could be called a slightly 'weak-tight' way of playing. And even though I didn't like to hear that, and even though the harsh criticism I sometimes received was not always nice or pleasant, it *did* help me to lift my own level of thinking – and as a result, also my overall play.

a long way; in fact, I guess you've come a lot further than maybe 90 or 95 percent of the poker players.

Anyway, in the second part of this article I will make a final analysis of what has become known as the 'ace-king-in-the-small-blind-problem', and I will dig into the matter a little deeper.

Ace-king revisited: part 2

In the first part of this article, I discussed a Two Plus Two Forum thread regarding the play of ace-king in the small blind, facing a raise from a solid (good) player in early position. In his *Poker School Online* lessons, noted poker authority Mike Caro had recommended his students to usually fold A-K in such a situation – suited or not – and in the thread that I discussed in the previous article the quality of this advice was being questioned. Most posters thought the advice given was wrong, and that calling or re-raising was better. I thought that in most cases a fold was in order, and that therefore Mr Caro's advice was right. (Also, when teaching people how to play well in poker, it is usually best to first teach them how to fold in difficult situations. Now if they prove to be good students, and have learned how to avoid marginal and/or difficult situations, then there might come a time when the merits of other options could be evaluated, like calling or reraising in the situation described here.)

Anyway, when my first limit hold'em quiz was published in the now demised *Poker Digest* magazine, a quiz that contained a rather similar situation regarding A-K in the small blind facing an under-the-gun raise, where I also recommended folding the hand, quite a few people were *outraged* by the advice I had given. Most of the people that were involved in discussions on RGP and Two Plus Two claimed that was wrong. Only a few people acknowledged that I might have a point, that maybe there was a bit of truth in my reasoning. Here, I will take a final look at the A-K problem from the quiz, and the way this hand could, or should, be played under the conditions mentioned.

> You are playing in a fairly standard $10-$20 hold'em game,
> ten-handed, with a 5% rake, max. $3. You're in seat #10.
> There's a weak-tight player in seat #1, a professional player
> in seat #2 and a loose-aggressive player in seat #7. All others
> can be considered average or a bit below average.

Problem No. 1

You are in the small blind, holding A-K♦. Seat #2 has raised to $20, and it's been folded to you. What do you do? a) fold b) call c) raise.

Problem No. 2:

Same situation, this time you hold A-K♠. What do you do? a) fold b) call c) raise.

In the quiz I gave points for every decision, ranging from 1 (terrible) to 10 (excellent/superb). Most decisions would get anywhere from 4 (bad) to 8 (good) points, as in this quiz I tried to touch a bit on borderline situations. After all, a quiz with questions like 'You are heads-up with the nuts on the end. Your opponent bets into you. What do you do?' wouldn't really get you to thinking deeper about the game, in my opinion. What's more, in quizzes of this kind it is not so much the total scores you should focus on, it's the reasoning behind the decisions that is most important. Having said that, after publication of the quiz I received more e-mails than ever before, mostly from people who hadn't done well in the quiz – and it was always the A-K problems that had cost them points. The answers/points per answer I gave were as follows:

Problem No. 1

a) 7 b) 5 c) 4

The raiser figures to have a high pair or A-K as well – remember, he's a professional player raising under-the-gun. Why get involved when your hand is an underdog to begin with? You don't know where you're at in the hand. If you flop a king, you might lose a lot of money; if you flop an ace when the raiser has in fact a wired pair, you might not get any action; if you flop nothing but he doesn't have anything either, he might outplay you and make you lay down the best hand.

Problem No. 2

a) 7 b) 6 c) 4

> *The fact that your hand is suited isn't really important here. If your hand induces a call by the big blind, then your hand might be playable. However, folding is still the best option – why invest a lot of money when there's nothing in the pot, out of position, when you know your opponent has a real hand?*

While the recommendations I gave may seem overly tight to most players, I still think that, for most players, it's the proper way to play the hand in the situation described.[5] Only truly excellent players who are capable of outplaying their opponents after the flop, top players who know exactly when to release a hand (if it's beat), when to check-and-call (to induce a bluff) and when to launch a bluff because the opponent is likely to be weak – only players of this calibre would be able to get a positive EV out of this situation, in my opinion. (For those who ever encounter me in a limit hold'em cash game, you can be sure that I don't just *recommend* these kinds of folds: I practice what I preach.) On poker forums and newsgroups, especially on Two Plus Two, there had been furious discussions for days on the folds that I had advocated, with people commenting things like 'Gee, this brings playing tight to an entirely new level. When all the smoke was cleared, I posted the following:

A-K revisited (long)

Guys,

There was a discussion on ace-king in the small blind, facing a raise, only two months ago in this place. Involved in this thread were, among others, Mr Malmuth and me. Most posters claimed that folding ace-king in the small blind against an early-position raise is wrong (i.e. has negative EV), and in some cases this may be true. In the case I described in the quiz (ten-handed game, max. $3 rake, under-the-gun raise by a professional player), it may seem extremely tight to fold your A-K here. However, in my opinion it's not a matter of playing tight or loose, it's a matter of having a positive expectation for the hand or not. While I agree that before the flop your ace-king may be in really bad shape only a

---

[5] 'Still think' at the time of writing this article. For my current views, see my revised 'A limit hold'em quiz' earlier in this book.

small percentage of the time (when the pro has aces or kings), I think this situation still calls for a fold. (I have to admit though, that I know lots of players who have never folded ace-king before the flop and still are long-term winners. Also note that in the quiz I give seven points for a fold and five or six for a call, so it should be clear we are talking about a borderline decision here.) In my opinion, the most probable situations look like this (I assume you'll tip half a dollar when you win; I'll also assume the big blind folds every time, whether you reraise or just call.)

Situation 1: You call the pro's raise

The problem is: how are you going to play your hand now? The pro knows you've got a quality hand, probably a big ace. If an ace or king flops, you might not get any action unless you're beat. If only small cards flop, you've got an even bigger problem. The only way for you to know if your A-K is good is to call your opponent down, all the way, with a no-pair hand. Now, if he keeps on betting, you might very well lose another $50, in addition to the $20 before the flop.

Situation 2: You reraise and the pro calls

If the flop comes with small cards and the pro does hold a weaker hand than you (A-Q for example), he will probably fold on the flop. The $70 pot will be yours, net win $36.5. However, if your hand isn't good (i.e. the pro holds a wired pair or has received help from the flop) you will lose either $80 (if he calls you down all the way, or maybe bets the river after you've checked) or $90 or $100, if he raises you on the flop or turn. In all cases, you cannot fold, because if you fold at any point in the hand the pro might have made you lay down a winner. If an ace or king flops and the pro holds a smaller pair, he will probably fold on the flop and, once again, you will win $36.5. However, if you get a lot of action after you've flopped an ace or king, be prepared to lose a very big pot. Even though it's mathematically unlikely that the pro holds kings or aces, this doesn't mean that he can't have them.

The point is: you can never make your opponent fold a winner, but he can make you fold a winner, or make you fold a split pot, *when he holds A-K also. In order to avoid this, you cannot possibly fold. If you are willing to lay down your A-K at any stage in the hand, you may get outplayed – remember, you are up against a pro who knows what he's doing. What this means, is that when your hand is good you will probably win a small pot (net win between $26.50 and $46.50), but when it's not you will lose a big one (net loss anywhere from $60 to $120, depending on how aggressive you are with your hand).*

Yes, it might seem like a big deal to fold A-K before the flop. However, in my opinion it is best to avoid situations where a) you're up against very good players, b) you're out of position, c) you don't know where you're at and d) the opposition has shown strength. In this case, you're up against a professional player, raising under-the-gun in a ten-handed game, and you're out of position with a hand that is very good, but not necessarily best – and even if it is, you might get outplayed after the flop. For all these reasons, I think a fold is in order here, even though I understand – and respect – anyone who thinks differently.

Some final words

A funny thing with discussing strategy in forums or newsgroups is that in most cases you don't know the people that you're talking with. In real life, you would talk strategy with players whose game you think highly of, or people that have at least the theoretical knowledge to play well. On the Internet, you talk with players you have never met, and therefore might be thinking on a totally different level than you.

Still, it is a good thing to be confronted with views and opinions that are opposed to yours every now and then, and sometimes you may actually be forced to re-evaluate your opinion. After all, just because you *think* your decision to play your hand in a certain way is the right one, doesn't mean that it *is*, or maybe someone comes up with an even better play than the one you chose, a play you hadn't even thought of. I would like to thank Jim Brier for starting the discussions regarding my quiz; not because he always agreed with me – quite the contrary, in fact – but because for all people involved in the threads, including me (and probably also for the people who just followed these discussions without participating), a lot of poker knowledge was brought into the open, which might have helped us in improving our games further.

A limit hold'em quiz: part 2

A while ago, I wrote my first limit hold'em quiz. After publication in the now demised *Poker Digest* magazine, I received more e-mails than ever before – both positive *and* negative. The negative comments were mostly from players who think that they play well, yet performed poorly, or from players who *do* play very well, but still had a bad score. The thing to keep in mind here is that most quizzes are aimed at the average or slightly below average player wanting to improve his game; they are usually not aimed at the excellent player wanting to become even more excellent. Quite a few (good) players thought that my recommendations were overly tight, that the folds I recommended would actually cost them expected value (EV). The truth is, that a few good or excellent players could indeed eke out some profit in the situations where I said folding was better, simply because their play after the flop is impeccable: they know exactly when they're beat, when it's best to release, when they might be able to bluff their opponent out, etc. However, it is my opinion that the extremely tight approach I recommend will serve the majority of the players best, especially the ones who are still moving up the ranks, as it keeps them from making (compounding) mistakes, and it helps them stay out of difficult situations that require lots of judgment – judgment that they don't have yet, or not enough.

Having said that, after having reread the quiz a couple of times, and after having discussed the advice with some good or very good players, online as well as in real life, I had to agree that some of the advice was rather questionable at times, and also that in some cases the reasoning behind the advice was a little too simplistic. And while some of the tight folds I suggested may have been correct for *some* players and in *some* games at the time it was written (1999), after the recent Internet boom it is clear that play has become much more loose-aggressive than in the past – which makes laying down some very good hands even more questionable than it already was. Still, please don't think I only *recommend* these tight plays: if you ever encounter me on a limit hold'em table, you will see that I practice what I preach. (It is my opinion that in limit hold'em it is best to look extremely tight, play extremely tight, and then steal some pots away from your opponents when they least expect it.) More than all this, I don't think your exact scores are that important. It is the reasoning behind decisions that is important, not whether your score suggests you are 'average' or 'below-average'. Anyway, here is my second and so far last limit hold'em quiz – I hope you enjoy it.

The concept has basically stayed the same. You are playing in a fairly standard $10-$20 hold'em game, ten-handed. An average of three to five players see the flop, so the game tends to lean a bit towards the looser side. The rake is 5%, max. $4, and there's a maximum of three raises (unlike Vegas, where four raises are allowed most of the time). You are sitting in seat #9. In seat #1 there's a rather weak-tight player, in seat #2 a professional player whose (tight-aggressive) play you highly respect, and there are two highly (overly) aggressive players in seats #6 and 7. All others can be considered average or a bit below average.

The questions

1) You are in the big blind, holding Q-Q. Seats #6 and 7 have called the initial bet, which is rather surprising: whereas they prefer calling over folding, they prefer raising even more. The small blind has also called. What do you do?

a) check b) raise

2) Once again, you are in the big blind holding Q-Q. This time, seat #2 has limped, as have seats #4, 6 and 7. The small blind has folded. What do you do?

a) check b) raise

3) You are on the button, holding A-10 offsuit. The field folds to seat #7, who comes in for a raise. What do you do?

a) fold b) call c) raise

4) You are on the button, holding 8♥-6♥. Seats #2 and 6 have called, seat #7 has raised and has been cold-called by seat #8. You have read that in position suited connectors can be played for profit, sometimes even against a raise, and especially when you're playing in a multiway pot. You also figure that you probably hold cards that are opposed to your

opponents, since seat #2, the raiser and seat #8 all might be playing big or semi-big cards. What do you do?

a) fold b) call c) raise

5) Even though in theory you have one of the best seats at the table (tight opponents to your left, aggressive opponents to your right), the players to your right keep on raising your blind all the time, and because of this you have thrown away a winner twice already. This time, you're in the small blind, holding J♥-9♥. It is folded to seat #7 who, once again, raises. What do you do?

a) fold b) call c) raise

6) You are on the button, holding J♥-10♥. It is folded to seat #8, who calls the initial bet. What do you do?

a) fold b) call c) raise

7) You are on the button, holding A♥-Q♥. Seat #2 has opened for a raise and, much to your surprise, everybody has folded. What do you do?

a) fold b) call c) raise

8) You are in third position, holding A♥-9♥. Seat #7 has raised blind (without looking at his cards), but it is not a live straddle: straddling is not allowed in the casino you play in. Seat #8 has folded and it's up to you. What do you do?

a) fold b) call c) raise

9) You are in the big blind, holding A-K offsuit. Seat #10 has limped, as have seats #3, 4, 6 and 7. The small blind has folded and you decide to vary your play by not raising here: you simply tap the table. The flop comes K-10-7, giving you top pair/top kicker, but also creating quite a few straight possibilities. It's up to you. Do you bet out or do

you go for the checkraise?

a) bet b) checkraise

10) You are on the button, and have called a raise before the flop with pocket fives in a six-way pot. Seat #2 has made it $20 and has been called by seats #4, 6 and 7. The small blind has folded and the big blind has called. The flop comes 7-6-4 rainbow. The blind checks, seat #2 bets, gets called by seat #6 and you decide to call as well. Three players see the turn, which is a ten of the fourth suit. Seat #2 bets again and gets called by seat #6. What do you do?

a) fold b) call c) raise

The answers/points per answer

1. a) 4 b) 8

With this (relatively weak) opposition there is no question that you should raise, as you figure to have the best hand by far. It is quite likely that the small blind will fold, giving you the chance to play against just the loose guys with a hand that can stand a lot of heat.

2. a) 7 b) 6

Even though you probably hold a better hand than all of your opponents do, you might gain the most by playing deceptively. Since the small blind is already out (which is good for you, as there is now no danger of the small blind betting through you after the flop), raising will not make anybody fold. (It is rare to find a player folding against a raise for one more bet, after having called voluntarily.) More importantly, raising will basically announce to everybody what you hold, making it tougher to defend your hand when the flop comes favourably (for example, when three small cards flop), and making it easier for your opponents to play well against you after the flop. A problem with not raising is that you don't know what the pro holds. If he is in there with A-A or K-K and the flop comes 5-2-2 rainbow, it will be hard for you to release your hand (this might have been easier if the preflop betting had marked him with a premium pair, i.e. if you raise and he reraises). If you do as I recommend (check), you will almost invariably go for the checkraise if the flop looks favourable, unless you think you might make more money by betting out – if you think that you can reraise an aggressive player by making it three bets. If you do raise before the flop, you hope to tie your opponents to the pot in case you flop a queen; you know that if you don't flop a queen, it will be easier for you to lose a big pot than to win one.

3. a) 4 b) 5 c) 7

Even though I don't like to play big offsuit cards against a raise, in this situation folding would be a bit too much credit to the raiser. The raiser is a highly aggressive player, who is the first one in, in rather late position. He doesn't need to have a big hand, and you quite likely hold the best hand here. On top of that, you have position on him. The blinds will almost certainly fold, unless they hold a big or medium pocket pair, A-K, A-Qs, and maybe A-Q, K-Qs or A-Js. If they fold, you will be able to play heads-up, in position with a hand that figures to be best – a favourable situation, to say the least.

4. a) 8 b) 6 c) 4

While you are right that you have good position, your cards may be live and small suited connectors tend to do reasonably well in multiway pots, and that therefore your hand might be playable even against a raise, there's a big problem here: your action doesn't close the betting. The pro in seat #2 has called under-the-gun, which is a sign of strength. He might hold a hand that he's willing to build a big pot with, and there's a decent chance he will make it three bets. Even if he just calls, there's still seat #6 who might reraise 'just for the hell of it' with the possibility of seat #7 capping it. The danger of this happening is too big to warrant a call, which might have been OK under slightly different circumstances. Also, the fact that you are in the pot with three aggressive players is bad for your type of hand. Small suited connectors are sometimes profitable because of implied odds, when initial costs are low and most players are passive; when there's not a lot of raising so that you can make your draws rather cheaply, and you will also get paid off if you make them. However, the aggressiveness of your opponents will not give you the chance of a cheap draw here.

5. a) 7 b) 6 c) 6

A case can be made for either one of these options. You may fold, simply because you don't figure to have the best hand, and you're out of position. You may call, because your hand does have some value, and because you may be able to represent a wide range of hands after the flop – so that you can put pressure on your opponent, who is probably not loaded for bear, either. Or you may reraise, to put even more pressure on him, and to show him that he cannot pick up the blinds all the time. In this case, you will bet the flop almost 100% of the time, to represent a very big hand, and you would win a lot of pots where both you and your opponent flop nothing. The reason I give seven points for a fold and six for the others, is that the rake makes playing for small pots unattractive: the rake is at its peak when the pot reaches $80.

6. a) 5 b) 5 c) 7

You would like to play heads-up all evening against someone who simply calls in the cutoff when he's the first one in. Your hand is fairly good and even if it's not, you should be able to outplay your opponent after the flop. If one of the blinds three-bets you, your hand still has some value. The reraiser will probably hold two very big cards or a wired pair and your cards are therefore probably live, in addition to the obvious straight and flush possibilities.

7. a) 7 b) 6 c) 5

Even though you have a fine hand, it doesn't rate to be better than the pro's: he probably holds a high pair or cards that are as big, or bigger, than yours. The fact that your hand is suited makes your hand slightly stronger, and you are also in position, which may allow you to gain – or save – a bet, or maybe to steal a small pot when the flop looks very dangerous to your opponent (8-7-6 of clubs for example, when he holds A-K of spades). Reraising is a power play that will sometimes work against a weak player, but not likely against a pro raising under-the-gun. Even though it is possible that your hand is as good or even better than the pro's, it is far from certain that this is the case here – especially if the pro is someone who has tight raising standards in early position. (In a ten-handed game, some pros will need a premium hand to raise under-the-gun; in fact, some of them wouldn't even raise with A-Q here. If you think that this specific player may have these kinds of raising requirements, it's all the more reason to fold.) With one or two callers in the middle, your hand would have been clearly playable, but now it's a bit borderline, and things depend a lot upon your view on the pro, how the hand will likely develop postflop, the hands that he may or may not give you credit for, and his willingness or unwillingness to lay down his hand after the flop, for instance an unimproved A-K.

8. a) 7 b) 5 c) 6

This is not as easy as it might look to some. Some would claim that reraising is best: you want to play heads-up, in position against a random hand. However, the people behind you know that you will try to isolate the raiser (since he raised blind) and will not fold their marginally good hands; in fact, they might even cap it with hands like A-J or A-Q. Calling will make you look very weak, and people will put you on exactly the hand you have: a suited ace or two semi-big cards. Even if the people behind you don't reraise, you will be sandwiched between an aggressive player on your right, who will almost certainly bet the flop, and a few random hands behind you who know you are weak – now, this is not an enviable position to be in. In late position, you would have held a playable hand, but with so many players still to act a fold is in order.

9. a) 6 b) 8

You played somewhat deceptively before the flop, by simply tapping the table with your ace-king. Your opponents probably won't figure you for this type of hand, so if you bet out, a hand like K-J or K-Q might very well raise to give you the protection you need. However, chances are equally likely that if you bet out all gutshots (A-J, Q-9, J-8 for example) will simply call, as will any pair (either top, middle or bottom pair, and maybe even a wired pair that will try to hit a set on the turn), in addition to the openenders that will probably call for any amount. This means that any turn card, except for a king, five, four, three or deuce will scare the hell out of you. So let's say you bet, three people call you and then a scare card comes up – I don't like your chances here with only one pair. To avoid all this, it would seem 'natural' to go for the checkraise on the flop, which is quite likely to succeed because you have not shown any strength yet, and especially with those two aggressive players near the button. You can charge your remaining opponents for two bets now, having put no chips into the pot yet – thus giving your top pair/top kicker the best possible chance to survive.

10. a) 4 b) 6 c) 7

There's no doubt you are still behind in this hand, as seat #2 almost certainly holds an overpair to the board. Most people would therefore simply call to try and make their hand, which isn't a bad play in itself. However, from the pro's perspective the board doesn't look too good when a solid player like you raises him on the turn – and this might very well be your best option. Because the pot has grown so big, it might be worth it to go for the semi-bluff raise, to try to make the pro lay down his hand. From his perspective, you might very well be in there with 9-8 for the nut straight, making him drawing dead, or you might have hit your pocket pair for a small set, making him drawing extremely thin. What's more, there is also another player in the pot who could have anything – who might have him beat already, or beat him on the river. Also, the chances that you are bluffing are rather small – exactly because of the presence of this third player. From your perspective, however, seat #6 might very well have a drawing hand like A-8 for example, having flopped a gutshot, and having improved to a double belly-buster on the turn. So if you can get seat #2 to fold and seat #6 calls, your pair of fives might even win the pot for you if you both receive no help. If seat #2 doesn't fold, you will simply need to improve on the river to win. There is no need for you to try to bluff him off his hand when all the cards are out: if he doesn't believe you on the turn, he will certainly not believe you on the river, so don't throw away that extra bet. However, if seat #2 calls your raise on the turn but seat #6 folds, your raise might have given you two extra outs: not only are you going to value-bet on the river if an eight or three comes for a straight (eight outs maximum), but also if a five comes up for a small set.

> Minimum points: 49
>
> Maximum points: 73

Some final words

It should be clear that if you have scored 68/69 points or more, you have a pretty keen insight on the way this game should be played – in my opinion, that is. Conversely, if you scored fewer than 62 points, you might want to re-evaluate your basic strategy to see if it is in need of improvement. However, what is most important here is the *reasoning behind the plays*. If you are able to understand the thought processes required for playing successfully at $10-$20 and up, and then translate these thoughts into making the right decisions at the table, then you may well have become a serious contender for the money.

A few flops in limit hold'em

In my article 'A few flops in pot-limit Omaha' (available in the 'Classic Articles' section of my book *Secrets of Professional Pot-Limit Omaha*) I described five different kinds of flops and how they can be of influence in the way you play. Since in pot-limit it is easier to defend your hand and therefore your opponents will be less likely to call you down, the (semi-)bluff has a better chance to succeed than in limit poker. On the other hand, your bluffs in pot-limit are also much more expensive than in limit if they fail. In limit poker, you might be able to steal a $140 pot with just a $20 bet, so the bluff has to succeed only a small percentage of the time to actually make a profit. Having said that, you're going to have to show the winning hand in limit most of the time; only occasionally will you be able to steal a pot away from your opponents.

Just like in all other flop type games, the flop is *the* decision point in hold'em; if the flop doesn't fit to your hand you will probably have to give it up. Of course, calling or raising on the flop doesn't mean that you should go all the way to the river with your hand. In fact, I will often fold my hand right away if people play back at me on the flop or turn after I have shown strength by betting or raising. If I think my opponent might have me beat on the flop, I am not going to try to outdraw him (that is, if I have some kind of made hand myself, rather than a draw). In limit hold'em the best hand holds up more often than in any other game, limit hold'em is a game where the made hand is king. If you are playing A-K against A-J with an ace on the flop, you figure to make a lot of money. More than that, on the flop just a hand like top pair/top kicker is the favourite to win the pot against even the best draws most of the time (unlike Omaha, where a premium draw can be the favourite with two cards to come, even against a hand as strong as the current nuts). In limit hold'em multiway pots are more common than in pot-limit Omaha, and because trying to make your draw is cheaper here than in pot-limit (the bet being so small), you will get goods odds most of the time (even though you're an underdog to make the hand). Now, let's take a look at a few flops in limit hold'em and how they influence the way you play your hand.

Flop #1: Q♦-J♥-9♦

This is a flop where you can expect lots of action, especially if there has been a raise before the flop. You can expect hands like flush draws, straight draws, top pair/kicker, two pair, sets and even A-K to continue here. Contrary to what most players do, I don't like to continue against a flop like this with less than a premium hand. I see lots of players play a hand like J-10 very aggressively here, but why would you ever do that? (Except of course when only two or three people have seen the flop or you are playing in a shorthanded game, then the hand can and sometimes should be played aggressively.) Although your hand *looks* good (open-ended straight draw + pair) I wouldn't be too thrilled about it, for the following reasons:

- ♠ You have an open-ended straight draw, but no draw to the nuts. Somebody may be in there with a straight already (even the nuts, K-10, may be out there, making you almost drawing dead) or have the same draw as you, so that if you make the hand you draw for you'll have to split the pot. If a king comes, you might not even split (someone might be in there with A-10).

- ♠ Your pair is pretty worthless. If there are three or four players still in the hand after the flop, a two-pair hand (Q-J, Q-9, J-9) or even a set is almost certainly out there. While your hand is in good shape when you're heads-up (having a multiway hand), against more than one opponent your hand isn't nearly as strong.

- ♠ There are two diamonds on the flop. Straight draws play very poorly when there's also a flush draw on the board. In fact, the flush draw's best friend *is* the straight draw[6]. Although you think you might have eight outs, you have only

---

[6]   For an extensive discussion on this subject, see my book *Secrets of Professional Pot-Limit Omaha,* and also Konstantin Othmer's *Seven Card Stud.*

six, and even if you make your hand on the turn, your opponents may redraw against you on the river (diamond for flush/pair for full/ten or king for higher straight).

Flop #2: 10-10-9 rainbow

Although in hold'em a pair on the board is not nearly as dangerous as it is in Omaha, you are usually not going to continue with anything less than trips against this board (assuming a multiway pot with quite a bit of action on the flop). Don't make the mistake of calling with Q-J in this situation: somebody may already have a full house (10-9, 9-9) or make a full at the same time that you make your straight (lots of players routinely play hands like K-10 or 10-8s). While it is sometimes possible to steal a pot when there's an open pair on the flop, you almost never try this when the board also creates possible straight or flush draws, that is: if it seems like the flop cards fit in with the hands your opponents might be playing.

If you've got the 10-9 yourself, well then of course you should bet the hell out of your hand! Don't slowplay here. Your opponents will give you plenty of action and will call or raise you with draws or weak made hands, thinking that they might win the pot if they make their draw, or suspecting that you're trying to steal the pot by representing a hand you don't have.

Flop #3: 7-4-2 rainbow

Now here's a flop where you sometimes *can* try to pick up the pot. If there have been no raises before the flop and you're in one of the blinds, the flop isn't very likely to have helped your opponents. Since it might very well have helped you (being in the blind), most players will fold overcards here (A-9, K-10) against a bet, the pot being so small. If one of them calls on the flop, a bet on the turn will probably get the job done. The only real danger is that one of the preflop callers might have a wired pair: if he has an overpair to the flop (8-8, 9-9) he will most likely raise on the flop, but he might also have made a set and decide to smooth call rather than raise. It's up to you to decide if a flop call means that your opponent has a real hand or is just taking off a card, trying to hit one of his overcards. Ill-coordinated flops (e.g. 8-5-2, Q-7-3 and K-8-2) are excellent candidates to try and pick up two or three pots a session (at the higher limits, that is; don't *ever* try this when playing $3-$6, and especially not against more than three opponents). Don't be too eager to try to steal a pot when there's an ace on the flop, because of the tendency that a lot of players have (even at the higher limits) to play weak aces.

Now, let's say you've raised before the flop with A♠-K♥ and the flop comes with three rags like the 7-4-2 rainbow that we have here. Whether or not to drive the hand after the flop depends a lot on:

♠ How many opponents there are left. (Don't try to bet more than two opponents off their hands; since you raised before the flop they will probably figure you for precisely the hand you have – A-K – and they will call or even raise you with any pair and sometimes even with nothing to just make you fold.)

♠ What hands these opponents most likely hold.

♠ How these opponents usually play. (Can they fold a marginal hand, will they let you win a showdown with ace-high, or will they try to bluff you out if you check, do they respect your play etc.)

A-K is a fine hand, but in multiway pots when you have not hit the flop, it usually is not much more than just a drawing hand – and sometimes it's not even that. If you're up against more than two opponents, it's unlikely to win the pot on its own, without any further improvement. And for this reason, automatically firing again to follow up your preflop raise is not always recommended.

Playing bottom two pair

As most readers of this column are probably aware, I play mostly pot-limit poker nowadays. After having played limit hold'em professionally for about three years, the beautiful game of pot-limit Omaha came my way. I was fortunate enough to be very successful there right from the beginning (winning a lot more than I was entitled to), and I put all my energy into improving my game by thinking and analysing – and practising, of course. Nowadays, I only play limit hold'em when there's no PLO game available, or if the limit game looks better than the big money game – which is hardly ever the case. However, unlike many other big-bet poker players who look down on limit hold'em (claiming that it's a mechanical game, invented by the casinos to make money, and played by grinders trying to eke out a living), I still like the game. Even though I agree that big-bet poker requires a lot more skill than limit poker (in addition to discipline and patience to wait for the best hand, other poker skills like heart, courage and playing the players are very important here), limit hold'em requires a lot of skill as well – even though it's on a different level.

In this article, I'll discuss a hand that can cause you quite some trouble when playing limit hold'em: bottom two pair. While a lot has been written about playing big cards before and after the flop, there is not much information available regarding this complex hand. The information that *is* available regarding bottom two pair goes something like this: 'When you flop bottom two pair, you should be very aggressive with your hand. You have to charge people to draw out on you and try to eliminate as many players as possible because, even though your hand is probably best right now, it is still extremely vulnerable.' If you ask any player about how to play this type of hand, almost everybody will say the same thing: bet the hell out of your hand. I disagree.

Situation #1: playing bottom two on or near the button (last to act)

You're in a standard $10-$20 hold'em game and you're on the button with 10♠-8♠. Three people limp, you call as well. Six players see the flop K♠-10♥-8♦. The blinds check, the under-the-gun player bets and gets called in two places. Now, what do you do? According to common poker wisdom, you should raise here, but I (respectfully) disagree. The problem for you is that many turn cards might cripple your hand. You don't want to see any ace, king, queen, jack, nine or seven coming off the deck. Even though it is likely that your hand is good right now (it would be fair to assume that the UTG player has top pair + kicker, A-K or K-Q for example), what will raising on the flop accomplish for you? The callers (who are probably on some kind of straight draw) will simply call your raise (assuming that the UTG does not reraise; if he does you may have to fear your bottom two pair might not be good after all). If they make their straight on the turn and bet, the pot is not big enough for you to call (you only have a maximum of four outs to improve to a full), meaning that your flop raise has cost you an extra small bet. My advice would be to simply call and see one more card before committing any further. If a dangerous card comes off, the action in front of you will dictate your course of action (raise/call/fold). If a safe card comes off, the UTG player will probably bet again, maybe one guy in the middle calls and *then* you raise. The thing you do is you wait one round before committing fully. Then, when you think you are still good on the turn, you make your opponents pay the maximum, giving them the worst possible odds in trying to improve. When you raise on the flop, you will have to survive *two* cards to have your hand stand up, and investing too much on the flop will only entice your opponents to stay until the river – which is *not* what you want with a hand this vulnerable. [7]

Situation #2: playing bottom two pair in the blinds (first to act)

If you're a decent player, there are only two spots where you can flop bottom two pair: in the blinds or near the button. If you regularly play hands like 10-8, J-9 or 8-7 in early or middle position, you might want to take another look at your hand selection. However, you're very likely to come up with these types of hands in the blinds, especially in unraised pots. Let's take the same hand as before, 10♠-8♠. You have completed your small blind and, once again, six[8] players see the flop K♠-10♥-8♦. You might be tempted to go for the checkraise here; I know this would be the first thing *I* would consider with this hand and this flop. However, going for the checkraise is not automatic. If you figure the under-the-gun player for two big cards and he's fairly aggressive, you might choose to bet out, hoping that he will raise and thereby put a lot of pressure on the other players: they will have to call two bets cold (unlike in situation #1 where they already had one bet in). On top of that, there is the danger to them that you might pop it again, so they will need a fairly strong hand to continue in the pot.

If you do decide to check on the flop rather than bet out (which would seem 'natural', being in the blind), you do not necessarily have to raise right now. I would only checkraise a bet from late position (to try to force

---

[7]   As play has become more and more loose-aggressive in recent years, and many flop raises on the button are almost automatically perceived as semi-bluffs/free-card plays/attempts to take initiative, I would nowadays be more inclined to make the obvious flop raise with my bottom two. This because in a multiway pot like this, even a hand as weak as K-Q may decide to three-bet here in order to shut out the field – and this would of course be to my benefit.

[8]   Not very likely anymore. Except for maybe at the lowest levels, six-way unraised pots don't occur very often anymore. As play is more loose-aggressive, two- or three-way pots with everyone in for two or three bets have become the norm.

the other players out and play the hand heads-up); if the UTG player is the first bettor and there are two or three callers already when the action gets back to me, then I would opt for the same play as in the first example: simply calling to see the fourth card cheaply. Once again, when a danger card comes on the turn, you will simply check and let the action behind you decide your best course of action; when another king comes (counterfeiting your bottom two pair) you simply check-and-fold. When a small card comes, the UTG bettor will definitely bet again, maybe one or two people call and *then* you raise, putting a lot of pressure on all remaining players, and just as importantly: maximizing your expectation. The UTG bettor will have a hard time calling your checkraise with just one pair, especially because he's sandwiched between you and the player(s) behind him, who might or might not call as well. You have now got your money in as a big favourite, and you will need to survive only one more card – the infamous river card.

Some final words

Bottom two pair is a difficult hand to play well and requires a lot of 'feel', judgment regarding possible future actions, and the ability to put your opponents on a hand. It's silly to invest a lot of money on the flop by raising when a lot of turn cards will force you to lay down your hand[9], especially when some of your opponents already have put money in. Having said that, if it's possible to get the hand heads-up against either top pair + kicker or against some kind of straight draw, well then of course you should do everything you can to eliminate the other players, and then you *should* bet the hell out of your hand – just as common wisdom says you should.

---

[9]   Again, not 100% true anymore. While many years ago, playing in the games where I used to know every player well, and where a turn bet into my flop raise was almost never a bluff, nowadays people seem to have become a bit more creative. Because (compared to my 'old' game) a higher percentage of bets by the opposition are not exactly what they are representing, I don't fold my bottom two pair as easily – not even when faced with a scare card. And because I don't fold this bottom two on the turn as easily anymore as in the past, this means that flop raising to get more money in the pot may actually have started to become my preferred choice, at the expense of the creative 'wait one more card' play that I suggested.

What to look for in starting hands: part 1

In this series, I will discuss a few starting hands, and the conditions under which these starting hands may, or may not, be profitable. I will discuss a few limit starting hands that are often misplayed by average and even above-average players, hands that require a lot more situational/circumstantial analysis than they are given by a lot of players. Note that I'm not discussing any of the 'Group 1' hands like aces, kings or ace-king here. A lot of poker writers (most notably David Sklansky and Mason Malmuth) have devoted so much time to discussing the play of premium hands, and have written so much excellent material on the subject, that there's nothing much for me to add. What's more, it is my experience that in hold'em most players know how to play the premium cards fairly well – it is often the not-so-premium hands that cause them trouble. I will take a short look at some of these not-so-great hands, and discuss the best way to play them before and after the flop – taking into account situational and circumstantial factors. (By the way, a lot of excellent material *has* been written on this subject, also by the authors mentioned. It is just that even a lot of serious players still seem to have trouble adjusting the value of their hand to the current situation; they simply play their own hand, regardless of, and oblivious to, whatever action has taken place – or might take place. If you think your play fits into this category, this series might be of help in improving your overall poker-playing ability.)

Hand #1: 7-7

Analysis

Now this is what I call a 'situational hand'. Under certain circumstances, you might make it three bets with your wired sevens, whereas under different circumstances the hand might not even be worth a call. In loose-passive games where lots of players see the flop for one bet, you get excellent odds in trying to flop a set, and the hand can often be played for profit – even from early position. Unfortunately, at the limits I play ($10-$20 and up), the games are like this only a very small percentage of the time. In these games, players prefer raising and calling over folding, and your hand is therefore not automatically playable anymore.

Early position (EP)

In a ten-handed, loose-passive game my percentage 'folding-calling-raising' in EP would be something like 5-85-10, in tougher games maybe 55-25-20, and in tougher, shorthanded games it might be more like 15-10-75. Always take a close look at the texture of the game, your image, the atmosphere at the table and your position relative to your weaker opponents (the ones you want to make money from) and the strong ones. (Are they likely to call or even raise you, and what does this mean for the quality of your hand?) Try to predict how your fold, call or raise might influence future action and act accordingly.

Late position (LP)

In late position, your hand is almost always playable if the pot hasn't been raised yet. If there are no callers, you might choose to raise yourself. If there are lots of callers, you might also raise, to try to tie the limpers onto the pot, and to win a huge pot in case you get lucky and flop a set. However, most of the time calling would be natural with your pocket pair, as you will need to receive help to win.

Against a raise

If a tight, unimaginative player has raised from early position and there are no callers, there's usually no need for you to get involved unless you are on the button and have a very good read on this player. (Then flat calling may be your best option, especially if this player will hold specifically A-K or A-Q a high percentage of the time, meaning that it should be quite easy to make the correct postflop decisions against him.) If there are a few callers in the middle when the action gets to you, then calling the raise is definitely worth it, as you might win a big pot if a seven flops (the odds against that are about 7.5 to 1). Whenever the raise comes from a maniac in late or middle position and you are sitting somewhere to his immediate left, *and* if the players behind you respect your play and are capable of folding even reasonably good hands, then an isolation-reraise might be your best option. By doing this, you try to play your relatively small pair heads-up, in position against a random hand. Most of the time, the way you play your pocket pair after the flop is fairly easy and straightforward. In the situation mentioned here, you would almost always bet after the flop, and the board will have to get *very* scary for you to lay down your hand at any point. (Remember, you made the three-bet because you labelled the raiser as a maniac – now please don't make any expert laydowns after the flop because just maybe, he might have you beat.) In the multiway situation described above, you would almost always need to flop a seven to continue with the hand (even though there are exceptions), and you should be able to play your hand mistake-free here without too much thought. However, *before the flop* your best decision isn't always easy and you will need to judge closely and accurately to see if folding, calling or raising is recommended for the specific situation.

Some final words

In the next article, I will discuss three more hold'em hands that may cause the average player problems. To be more specific, I will analyse the following hands: A-5s, 10-9s and K-Jo. I will discuss if, when and how these hands can or should be played for profit.

What to look for in starting hands: part 2

In the last article we discussed some of the important factors that influence the strength and the profitability of a relatively small pocket pair (7-7). Here, I will take a look at three more 'situational hands': hands that are not always automatically playable, but that in some cases can actually be played for profit, whereas they may cost you money under different circumstances.

Hand #2: K-Jo

Analysis

Also known as the 'problem hand', king-jack offsuit is the type of hand that can easily make you second best – and unfortunately, there are no prizes for second place in poker. I'm not really fond of the hand in any type of game, not even in loose-passive games. Actually, the way I handle a hand like king-jack offsuit is this: I usually muck, *unless there is a clear reason not to*. Most players do exactly the opposite: they usually *call* unless it's very obvious (raises and reraises) that folding is better. Still, this type of hand does have some value in some cases, especially in late position when there's been no raise. And of course, in shorthanded games the hand is actually quite strong, simply because it is much less likely that you are dominated.

EP

In a ten-handed ring game, I fold the king-jack more than 90% of the time. When there are fewer players, the hand might become playable and maybe even worth a raise, especially if it looks like the players behind you seem ready to throw away their hands.

LP

If there have been no callers when the action gets to you, you might have a raising hand – if the people who are still to act don't view you as a habitual stealer, that is. Also, keep in mind the game conditions. If the rake makes playing for small pots unattractive (for example, you are playing $10-$20 with a max. $4 rake), then you might not be giving away all that much by simply folding your hand. However, even in that case K-Jo as the first one in on the button or cutoff is a rather mandatory raise, of course.

Against a raise

Against a raise, you have no hand, period. That said, if you're in the big blind and you get raised by a very aggressive player on the button, then you would be giving up too much by folding (for more, see my article 'Defending the blinds in limit hold'em').

Hand #3: A-5s

Analysis

Ace-little suited is one of the most overrated hands in limit hold'em, especially by inexperienced players. It has a lot of value in loose-passive games, but almost none in the tougher games that are the rule in the limits $10-$20 and up. Some, even experienced, players call raises cold with this hand on a regular basis and quite often they get away with it, but most of the time they are making a big mistake. (Sometimes, it is correct to call a raise from late position with this hand if you know that you can easily outplay your opponent postflop. In this case, you would be calling not in the first place because you think your A-5 may be good, but because you know that after the flop you could possibly bluff your opponent out of the pot if the board gets scary – in addition of course to those times when postflop you actually *do* have the best hand and get paid off.) In tighter games, ace-little suited in late position might be good enough to try to steal the blinds with, and in short-handed games, you even hold a pretty decent hand most of the time.

Hand #4: 10-9s

Analysis

The ten-nine suited has been the cause of plenty of discussion, controversy and disagreement. (For more on this, visit rec.gambling.poker, or better the Two Plus Two Forums, where there has been a lot of debate on this specific hand involving Mr Malmuth, among others.) A lot of players love the hand ('I always play suited connectors – I just love them'), and call regardless of position, opponents, betting actions or the texture of the game. Even though I play mostly pot-limit Omaha nowadays, I still play my former main game limit hold'em quite frequently (on a yearly basis, I would say at least 500 hours). Because the rake in limit hold'em is so high in most of the places I frequent, I play a lot tighter than almost all other players, and even tighter than most experts suggest. A high rake simply doesn't give room for many fancy plays, or plays that might have a slight positive EV (expected value) under normal, better, game conditions. Therefore, I will need a very good reason to enter the pot with a speculative hand like this. (In the higher-limit games that have a time charge, this is obviously less true. Even though the time charge per hour may be higher than in most places in the US, there are no extra costs when you win a pot. Therefore, plays with just a slightly positive EV should not be abandoned anymore, because they *will* add to your hourly rate, even though it may be only slightly.) When the rake is a bit lower, a bit more reasonable, however, you might play this hand a bit more often. You might occasionally play it from early position (in the somewhat tougher games, for deception mostly, or in the looser games, for its multiway value), and you might even raise with it from late position, once in a while. Always keep in mind what you hold, though; suited or not, a ten-nine is still a ten-nine and you will need a lot of help from the board to turn your hand into a money-maker.

Trying to find a solution for some common low-limit problems

Just like all other poker writers, I usually try to respond to reader questions or comments within a couple of days. Because I appreciate any feedback I get *and* because I genuinely want to help readers of the various magazines to improve their play (most of all the guys who look at *my* columns first, of course), I take a serious look at any questions I get. I try to answer each and every one of those questions as well as I can, and try to help where I think help is needed. Most of the time my solutions come down to this: stay calm, cool and disciplined, take your time and move up slowly, never ever give up learning, do not overestimate yourself or underestimate your opponents, try to keep things in perspective, and stay critical towards yourself but also have fun – things like that.

Here, I will share with you a concrete example of this advice. It is from an e-mail discussion I had with someone (John) who was having a bit of a bad run, and wanted advice on how to solve a few problems he sometimes encountered at the tables.

Mail No. 1

Rolf,

You are probably a very busy person. However, if you could take the time to answer a few questions (the second and third questions are in mail no. 2), it would be so much appreciated. I consider myself a 7, maybe 7.5 out of 10 player. I am on disability so I get paid once a month. I play mostly $3-$6 hold'em. I like and can play $5-$10, but there seems to be more action in a $3-$6 game, and $10-$20 I could afford but if I take a bad beating I'm in trouble the rest of the month. OK, here's my question.

A guy sits down, buys in for $30 and raises 90% of all preflop hands, then continues to bet or raise at the later streets. Because he was not winning many hands, I was only able to see his cards twice (6-4 suited and a 9-7 offsuit, both for a raise). When he had gone all-in, he would buy in for $30 more, then again $30, then again... anyway, you get the picture. Now I know that it's time to tighten up with all this aggression and to simply play solid hands. But many times, five to be exact, I had a hand that I could have *played but didn't, when in fact it would have won. Also, the table consisted of mostly ignorant players in addition to the bully (no one knew or used the checkraise, for example), so I got pretty frustrated that I kept on folding winners – so frustrated, in fact, that I decided to quit.*

Rolf, I have learned a long time ago that if you are nervous, upset or worried, then it's best not to play and to wait for another night. I know that what this player did was legal, and he is not the first I see who plays like this. Now, how do I handle this type of player? I don't gamble for 'fun'; I am there to win money. I only live 20 minutes away from the casino, so I only need to win a little and there's always tomorrow. Please help me to mentally cope with this type of gambler – if there is a way to do this, in fact.

Mail No. 2

This one is more mental. This does not happen often and depends upon the amount of money in the pot and the size of my stack. I am dealt ace-king suited and get reraised; so far, no problem, happens all the time. Now the flop comes A-K-x, turn is a blank, river queen. No problem here, until I get raised on the river; obviously trip queens, and so it was. I am mad as hell, even though I don't show it in any way. I don't cuss or throw things; as far as anybody is concerned I am my jolly, fun-loving self – however, I am burning inside. And Rolf, I swear I am telling you the truth, when this happens, after I get a beat like the one here, my cards turn to crap immediately, and for a really long time (K-5, J-3, K-2, you get the idea). I take breaks, then come back but I keep getting the same old crap. What should I do? Also, regarding the situation above with the queens: do you think it is best to call or fold? It may be a stupid question, but in my casino, in the $3-$6 and $5-$10 games, raises on the turn or river represent a very strong hand most of the time; I would say that in 95% of the cases the raiser holds what he's representing.

On a different note, let's say someone raises before the flop and after the river I have a pair or better (even a pair of deuces), I will call every time an ace or king has not hit the board. You would be amazed at the amount of money I have won by doing this, what do you think: is this the right or the wrong way to play?

Finding a solution for these (for low-limit, rather common) problems

All in all, two rather extensive mails with some concrete questions. My answers were as follows:

Hi John,

I read both your mails and here is how I look at things. The situation you described in your first mail is in fact a rather common occurrence. If a maniac/highly aggressive player comes to your table, you indeed need to tighten up, and you will be folding a lot more hands that would have been winners than usual. While you will also win a lot more on your good hands than usual, the swings will be huge and if you're on a short bankroll then playing in games with maniacs may not be a profitable situation for you, because of the danger of 'playing scared'. (This is especially true when taking into account your emotional state of mind whenever you lose a pot. If you want to become a good player, you will simply have to get your emotions out of the way here, and stop thinking in terms of 'this and this guy put a beat on me'. You should actually be happy if someone calls you without having the proper odds, because this is exactly how you make money in the long run. Also, the correlation you make between getting a good hand cracked and not getting a proper starting hand in a long time is a mystery to me, and must be in your mind only. Cards run in cycles, and there's no need to complain when you're not getting the hands you're 'entitled' to; the cards have no memory and what's more, you cannot change them – so why worry about them?)

In my opinion, you will just have to look for soft, passive games where people aren't that aggressive or are in fact rather predictable. Until you are financially (and mentally) ready to get into these exciting-but-dangerous games, you should just try and find yourself the softest game in the house.

Regarding question no. 2. While it may be true that your good hands get cracked quite often, it might also mean that your basic game is simply not good enough yet. It is my experience that a lot of players who still think in terms of 'good' and 'bad' starting hands often lack certain 'feel' for the game that makes the good players really good. Of course, if you are playing low-limit games your good hands get cracked all the time. Still, if your ace-king wins 30% of the time when five players go all the way to the river, then your hand will lose 70% of the time – but you will still make money! It might also mean that your hand selection is not as good as you think: if you're in a very loose game then your A-J or K-Q offsuit will not make you a lot of money, whereas volume hands (suited aces, suited connectors and pocket pairs) will.

Regarding question no. 3. I know it's true that you will often catch your opponent with just two unimproved big cards on the river and that simply calling your opponent down with any pair might therefore have made you quite a lot of money. Still, I wouldn't recommend playing like this too often. You will be in danger of becoming a calling station and while playing like this won't be that horrible at the lower limits – because a lot of your opponents will be oblivious to the way you play anyway and will just keep on betting their unimproved big cards when rags flop – at the higher limits calling stations simply don't stand a chance. If people catch up on what you're doing (which they inevitably will), they will start to value bet on the river with just one pair or else just check on every street – and you will lose a lot of money playing the way you do.

More in general, I would recommend this to you: don't be too re-sults-oriented. Poker is a beautiful game and you should enjoy it even when you're down. It is my experience that people who really love the game perform much better than the people who just think in terms of money made/money lost.

Anyway John, I hope my answers may be of benefit to you. Take care – and good luck.

A poker correspondence: part 1

I have a friend, Marc, who is still relatively inexperienced when it comes to playing poker.[10] However, he is very eager to learn, and in a short period of time he has been able to become rather successful at the middle limits.

---

[10]   Inexperienced *at the time of this writing*. In fact, Marc has worked his way up to becoming a highly successful middle-limit player, who has even cashed in two consecutive years at the *World Series of Poker* Main Event.

While this may for a large part be because of the very weak opposition in his home country, it is nonetheless a good achievement on his part.

Every once in a while, Marc sends over some hands or situations for me to analyse. With his kind permission, I have reproduced our exchange of ideas. My thoughts/comments are in italics.

Hand No. 1 (limit hold'em $20-40):

I get pocket queens in the small blind, there is one limper (a relatively tight player) and I raise. The big blind calls, as well as the limper. The flop comes J♠-9♠-6♣. I bet with my overpair, the big blind raises me and the limper cold-calls. I decide to just call. When a red three comes on the turn, I check, the big blind checks, and the limper bets. I put him on a jack and raise him. The big blind folds and the limper calls. River: 2♦. I bet, the limper calls and shows me a set of nines. Actually – as he told me later – he respected my raise so much that he was scared to play back at me even with a hand this strong. I guess my fault was that I hadn't really paid attention to the fact that he had cold-called on the flop after a bet and a raise. I would be glad to hear your thoughts.

> *Well, I guess you played it well. You did what you had to do and based on your description of the situation, I might have put him on a jack as well, or on a pair + flush draw maybe. Also, your image seems to be good, because he respected/feared you so much that he didn't even reraise you on the turn – a very weak play on his part. Even though you lost, you did what you had to do to defend your vulnerable overpair against the most likely hands (pair of jacks, pair of nines, straight or flush draw). In fact, you played the hand exactly as I would have.*

Hand No. 2:

Meanwhile, it is eleven-handed now that a couple of live ones have entered the game. As a result, play has changed from loose-passive to loose-aggressive. But in this hand there are four limpers to me and I'm in the cutoff with ace-jack suited. I raise and everybody calls, including the button and the blinds. Eight people see the flop A-5-5 rainbow. The small blind, a very, very loose and bad player, comes out betting, there are two callers to me and I raise. My reasoning: I want to know whether or not he's got that five, which is not an unlikely card for him to hold. (I have seen him play a 6-2 offsuit in early position once.) He three-bets, one loose player in the middle calls and I call too, hoping to catch another ace. Now, when the turn comes a seven, the small blind bets again, gets called by the loose player and I muck. The river is another seven and the small blind wins the pot with A-Q vs. A-9. Any thoughts?

Hmmm. When the main motive for your raise is to see what the other player holds, then his response should be fairly reliable. In this case, you raised to gain information, yet the information you got was wrong. All in all, I can understand your play, though. With so many players in the pot and so much money in the middle, your flop raise was probably right; after all, you cannot let gutshot straight draws, small pocket pairs and backdoor flushes outdraw you for free. Also, raising helps clear the field, making it easier for you to see who is holding what, and how the hand will probably develop. But then, with all this money in the middle and the small blind being the weak player you describe, I cannot see why you would fold on the turn. Remember, weak players who flop three of a kind are often much more likely to be going for the checkraise (either on the flop or on the turn) than to be betting out. Of course, they are wrong in doing so, but the fact remains that quite often these types of player will not come out betting when they flop three of a kind. All in all, I would say that there is a fair amount of doubt as to whether or not the small blind does indeed have the five, and folding the current best hand (or even a hand that could become the best hand or that has the potential for a split pot) would be a catastrophe. I think you should have called on the turn, and possibly on the river as well. One just cannot afford to fold a possible winner in this type of situation.

Hand No. 3:

I get pocket jacks in early position and raise. One loose caller, the big blind calls as well. Flop: A♠-6♦-3♦. The big blind checks, I bet, and both the mid-position player and the blind call. When an offsuit deuce comes on the turn, everybody checks. The river is the ten of diamonds, putting a possible flush on the board. The big blind checks, I check and then the mid-position player bets, with the big blind folding. It is now up to me. Even though this player is very loose in his starting hand selection, he is fairly experienced, and isn't out of line *very* often. Somehow I don't believe him and I call. He shows me K♦-7♦ for a flush. I think that apart from the flush, I should have given him credit for at least an ace. I called because I had the feeling that he had stolen a pot from me earlier, and I didn't want to let him succeed a second time.

> *Well, I think you made the correct decision to pay off. The pot is fairly big, and the person last to act finally bets after having been checked to twice. An ace seems unlikely (he would probably have bet the turn), and a flush is not probable either, as he would have to have played his flush draw very passively in a shorthanded pot like this. A bet with just a ten or even a total bluff seems just as likely as either one of these hands, and for this reason (if you make the wrong decision by calling it will cost you a bet, if you make the wrong decision by folding it will cost you the pot) I think your call is correct. Having said that, I think I would probably have bet the turn to protect my jacks in the (far from unlikely) case that none of my opponents holds an ace.*

Some final words

In the second part of this article, I will analyse three more hands of another one of Marc's sessions.

A poker correspondence: part 2

In the first part of this article, I discussed a few hands that Marc, a good friend of mine, had sent over to me for review. Here, I will analyse three more limit hold'em hands that Marc played in another session. My thoughts/comments are in italics.

Hand No. 1 (limit hold'em $30-60):

It is a full game with two good players (James and Jack), one average player, a couple of weak players and a maniac whom I've seen four-betting with 5-4 suited. I get A-3 offsuit in the big blind. The average player (AP) raises in middle position. Everybody folds to the small blind who calls the raise, and so do I. Flop: Q-6-3 rainbow. We both check to the AP who bets, the small blind folds, I checkraise, the AP three-bets and I call. The turn is another three. I once again checkraise the AP who just calls now. The river is a six; we both check and my A-3 is good. In hindsight, I think I definitely wimped out on the river and missed a bet. What are your thoughts?

> *Well, I don't like calling raises with weak aces, especially if your opponent is the type of player who likes to raise with big aces. (Quite a few average players fit this description.) I would say that your flop checkraise is rather creative and your turn checkraise very good. Even though you won the hand, from the way it was played it looks like you're up against A-Q, meaning that both before and on the flop you were drawing extremely thin. Your evaluation of your river play is correct: You should definitely have bet for value here.*

Hand No. 2:

I get Q♦-J♦ in the cutoff and raise after five limpers. Everybody calls. The flop comes J-10-6 with two spades. An early-position player (EPP) bets into me, there is one caller and I raise. Only the EPP calls, all other players fold. When the turn is an offsuit queen, the EPP once again bets into me, and I just call with my top two pair. Another queen on the river gives me top full. The EPP bets once more, I raise and he calls, showing Q-9. In hindsight, I think I should have raised him on the turn, but I'll be honest: I was afraid that he had the straight.

> *I think that you probably did the right thing by just calling. You are in position, and you don't need to raise to force out the other players/possible draws, as they are out already. Just call, and if a blank comes on the river simply call him if he bets, or bet if he checks. This might be the best way to play the hand from a maximizing wins/minimizing losses point of view. By the way, I don't like your opponent's play one bit. On the flop, he sort of tries to semi-bluff you, when it should be clear that both you and the other players will probably like this flop. Not just is he likely to be up against top pair, an overpair or even a set, if someone has A-Q*

(quite likely in a multiway, raised pot), he is drawing to just a gutshot. On the turn, he bets into you once more, but a board of Q-J-10-6 with two of a suit doesn't look that great to me when you're heads-up against someone who has shown strength both before and on the flop. (Other than against specifically A-J or K-J, there was no way he could be in the lead; against a probable hand like A-K he would even be drawing dead.) However, his turn bet is not nearly as bad as his flop bet. Now, he lost exactly the same by betting as by check-calling, and in case you just have a jack then by betting the turn he avoids giving you a free card. Even though it is probable that his hand is no good, with so much money in the pot he cannot afford the mistake of folding the winner; after all, he does have top pair + an open-ended straight draw, so whether he bets or not, it is clear that his hand is good enough to take to the river. All in all, I would say: you could have raised the turn, either a) because you think you have the best hand, or b) to represent A-K for the nut straight, to slow down your opponent in case he's got a small straight like 9-8, in order to get a free showdown. But flat calling might be just as good – or even better, because if your opponent does have the straight and your raise doesn't slow him down, then you will lose a lot more money than would seem normal with this type of hand.

Hand No. 3:

I get K♠-Q♦ in late-middle position and raise after four limpers. Jack calls from the small blind, as do all others. Flop: K♣-Q♥-4♣, a beautiful flop indeed, apart from the two-flush of course. I get checkraised by Jack, an AP cold-calls, and all the others fold. I three-bet, Jack folds(!) and the AP calls. Turn: 9♣, a card that completes two of the most probable hands the cold-caller can have (J-10 for an open-ended straight, or two clubs for a flush). With this death card staring me in the face, and up against someone who has checkraised me before, I respond to his check by checking it back. He swears and bets out after a rag comes on the river. I make a crying call and he shows me jack-ten offsuit for a straight. Would you have folded top two pair in this case? I think I played this hand pretty fine?!

First of all, I don't think that king-queen offsuit is a raising hand after four limpers. It is usually better to just call, hoping you will

*flop top pair with a good kicker, a good but vulnerable hand that is
often easier to defend in an unraised pot. This is because someone
with top pair/weaker kicker might now bet into you, and if you
raise then you will be putting a lot of pressure on your opponents
to try to outdraw you, and they probably will not be getting the
correct odds because the pot is still relatively small.*

*After you got checkraised on the flop, with the cold-caller in the
middle, you decided to raise back immediately, while I would
probably have delayed this action until the turn. (First flat call to
give Jack the impression that he is in the lead, and if Jack bets
again after a blank comes on the turn, raise him then, a) to put
more pressure on the probable drawing hand in the middle, and b)
to simply get more money in the pot with the current best hand.)
Having said that, when you did three-bet and then that dangerous
card fell on the turn, you deduced correctly that the AP might
have been planning a checkraise. Since top two pair is too good to
fold here, but has only four outs to improve, I like your check, and
I also like your call on the river: The pot is simply too big to fold,
especially since your opponent could conceivably be betting a
weaker hand than yours. For instance, he might have a smaller
two pair or even just one pair of kings that he thinks might be
good. Heck, he might even be making a desperate bluff with something like A-J or A-10.*

Some final words

I hope you have enjoyed these descriptions of the hands that Marc played,
and also my views and recommendations in this respect. Even though a
proper analysis isn't always easy (a lot of decisions are based on what you
'feel' the other player holds, and if you are not present in a game then it
often hard to come up with more than just some general guidelines), I
hope that these two articles have given you some insight into the thought
processes that are needed to become a successful middle-limit hold'em
player.

And about Marc: well, he still has a lot to learn of course. Also, the fact that
he is doing so well may have more to do with the weak play of his opponents (just look at all the limpers!) rather than his own excellence. Nonetheless, he's got one great thing going for him: his willingness to learn.
This alone may be enough to put Marc way ahead of the majority of the

poker players who don't have that same drive, and who are not willing to invest as much time and effort into improving their play.

Choosing the best seat versus a maniac

A lot has been written about some of the difficult situations you will encounter when there's an extremely aggressive player, a maniac, at your table. Most poker writers have claimed that you should try to sit to his immediate left, so that you will be in position to isolate him. That is: when he raises before the flop, you can reraise with your good hands to shut out the entire field and play heads-up, in position, with a hand that figures to be best. In my opinion, choosing this seat is not necessarily the best way to neutralize the maniac's power. In fact, I think that for quite a few games the advice given might even be dead wrong; I would contend that in some cases the seat to the maniac's immediate left might be the *absolute worst seat at the table*. (Note that I said in *some* cases, not in *all* cases.) In this article, I will take a closer look at some of the problems you might face, seated to the maniac's immediate left.

The best seat in limit hold'em

Of course I know that most poker literature is aimed at limit hold'em[11], and that the advice given (sit to the maniac's immediate left) is meant for that game and not necessarily for pot-limit Omaha as well. However, even in limit hold'em I usually try to avoid the seat to the maniac's immediate left, for the following reasons:

♠ In the games I play in, most of my opponents tend to adjust their play to special circumstances fairly quickly. If they see me sitting to the maniac's immediate left, they *know* I will try

---

[11]   Not true anymore. In response to the huge popularity of no-limit hold'em, also the majority of the new book releases concern no-limit hold'em. Because it is a bit harder to analyse no-limit hold'em well (as it is less mechanical than limit, less math-oriented if you will, and therefore more decisions are player-related, and based on specific tendencies and weaknesses of the opponents), I think not a lot of no-limit books are yet of the same level as the best limit books.

to isolate him with any decent-looking hand; they know I won't need aces or kings to three-bet before the flop in this situation. If someone is sitting behind me with a relatively marginal hand like A-Q (which he would fold for three bets under normal circumstances), he will probably not fold now – in fact, he will probably cap it at four bets (and if he doesn't, the maniac might). What happens now is that you are sandwiched between a highly aggressive player who will bet after the flop with anything, and a serious player behind you who has shown strength – now, this is not an enviable situation in which to be.

♠ Most players know that if there's a maniac in your game, you should tighten up considerably, simply because it will be more expensive than usual to see a flop. (This is common knowledge, and I generally agree with this reasoning.) Now, if you are seated to this maniac's immediate left, you will be seeing even fewer flops than that, *exactly because of the seat you have chosen*. When you have a hand that looks good enough to play, you will usually three-bet to shut the others out and to give your hand the best chance to hold up unimproved (hands like A-Js, 7-7 or even K-Qs come to mind). However, if you get any action behind you after you have three-bet with hands like these, you are in deep trouble. In fact, you will have paid three or four bets with a hand that clearly has negative EV for this situation: the player behind you almost certainly holds a better hand than you do. This doesn't mean that your three-bet was wrong; based on the information you had, it seemed like a reasonable play (your hand was quite likely to be best on this given deal). However, this does not change the fact that you have now paid three or four small bets for a hand that may barely be worth one, and in the long run your hourly rate will suffer. But flat calling with these types of hands I mentioned is not an option either. If you get any callers behind you, you are in the same (bad) situation as described above: sandwiched between a highly aggressive player who will bet with anything, and players behind you who may or may not have received help from the flop.

♠ In limit hold'em, the expert player is able to make or save money because of the information he gets from his opponents' betting actions. If serious players have raised or re-raised when the action gets to him, he will almost certainly pass a hand like A-Js, while this same A-Js might have been a calling or raising hand for him under different circumstances. When sitting on the maniac's immediate left, you will not have a lot of information to rely on. Had you taken the seat I usually recommend for limit hold'em (three or four seats to the maniac's left, preferably with some weak callers in the middle), you would have had more information available to you in making your decisions. Also, you will have this information on exactly the type of hands where you need it most (pocket pairs, suited connectors), in the position where you are most likely to play them: the last four positions. By choosing the seat I recommend, you will have neutralized the maniac's power to a large degree, while still having position on him on the hands that count most (on or near the button). Now, because of the actions of the players in the middle, you will know whether or not you have the right odds to play your 10-9 suited, and if your pair of sixes might be profitable or not. Seated to the maniac's immediate left, you would have had no other choice but to fold these – potentially profitable – hands.

♠ The other people in the game will certainly adjust their play to the presence of the maniac. Almost all players, even the ones that aren't usually very imaginative, will try to check-raise the maniac on a regular basis, and by doing this they will be bagging you as well. Therefore, isolating the maniac *after the flop* will not be easy either. If everybody checks to the maniac who bets, you are once again in the middle. You will have to fold a lot of your marginal hands that may in fact be good, simply because you don't know if the checks by the other players mean 'I have nothing' or 'I am waiting to trap the bully'.

♠ Not only will you play very few hands, the pots you win will also be relatively small. On top of that, you will probably be risking three or four bets instead of the usual one or two. Unless you are fortunate enough to pick up kings or aces, you will also *lose* a rather high percentage of the hands you three-bet against the maniac, simply because he receives help from the flop and you don't, or when he *does* have a better hand than you. (The fact that he raises so often, doesn't mean that he cannot hold aces or kings now – even a maniac is entitled to his fair share of premium hands, just like any other player.) There's a lot of luck involved in hold'em once the flop comes and while it's not easy for him to outdraw aces, it is not that difficult with some of the other hands you might three-bet with (A-K, A-Q, A-Js, K-Qs, for example). Also, if the maniac raises and you three-bet, he knows the type of hand *you* are probably holding, but you know nothing about *his* hand. If the flop comes A-K-Q, he will definitely fold to your bet if he has nothing, but what do *you* do, having three-bet with A-Q, when three small cards flop and he comes out betting? Remember, there is hardly a maniac who is highly aggressive before the flop, but timid after. Most likely the maniac will put a lot of pressure on you when the flop is unlikely to have helped you. By playing the way he does, you will of course make money off him when you have him beat, but he will also force you to lay down the best hand every now and then, and he will often get paid off generously when he has a real hand.

Some final words

What all these points illustrate, is that the seat to the maniac's immediate left isn't necessarily the best or most profitable one. I know that equally valid points can be made *in favour of this seat*, and I think that in some cases (especially when your opponents respect your reraises and fold all but the very best hands) choosing this seat *will* be profitable for you. However, in quite a few of the games I have played in, the problems associated with this specific seat outweigh its benefits by far, and I guess that in your game they might too. Therefore, I suggest you take a closer look at the exact type of game you're in, at the tendencies of your opponents, at the atmosphere at the table, and in pot-limit games also at the stack sizes of the various players, including the maniac. You should take all these factors into consideration when choosing your seat and then use this seat as a starting point to a) neutralize the power of the maniac and b) to exploit his weaknesses.

The trouble with maniacs

In the previous article I explained the trouble you can get into because of highly aggressive players, even – and especially – if you're in the position that quite a few people think is best: sitting on the immediate left of the maniac (i.e., having the maniac on your immediate right). One of the big problems that a good player will face in this type of situation occurs when the players behind you don't respect you when you three-bet the maniac. Let's say the maniac raises as the first one in, you three-bet with a hand like A-Q or 9-9 (you would definitely reraise with these hands to isolate the maniac, wouldn't you?), and now someone behind you cold-calls or even caps it. After the flop, you will find yourself sandwiched between a highly aggressive player who will bet with anything and someone behind you who may or may not have you beat – not a very enviable position to be in, to put it mildly. This is especially true if the flop has not helped you, but may in fact have helped your opponents.

Let's analyse a concrete example of this type of situation and look at the betting patterns and possible thought processes before, and after the flop.

Before the flop

Situation

The maniac has raised in early position as the first one in. Why is he a ma-niac? Well, he raises something like six or seven hands out of 10 before the flop, and after the flop he will usually keep driving by bluffing and semi-bluffing, yeah sometimes even by betting with the best hand. Note that I said he will *usually* bet after the flop, *but not always*. This maniac *does* change gears every now and then. He knows how to put pressure on peo-ple, senses weakness very well and just feels when the opposition may not be that strong (meaning that he might be able to bully them out of the pot).

Your hand

J-J

Analysis

You have a very good hand that is almost certainly better than the raiser's.

In fact, you should probably give the raiser credit for not much more than a random hand, since he raises before the flop so frequently. In this case, you have an almost automatic three-bet. If the people behind you fold, you will be able to play heads-up, in position, with a hand that is likely to be best by far – a highly profitable situation.

Actions

The cutoff cold-calls behind you, the big blind calls and the maniac caps the betting. Everybody calls, and you take the flop four-handed.

After the flop

Situation

The flop comes K-8-4 rainbow. Now the big blind bets out, and immediately gets raised by the maniac. It's up to you. What do you do?

Analysis

This is one of the most common problems when there's a maniac in your game. You have invested four small bets before the flop with what may very well – though not necessarily – be the best hand, and now that the flop is here your opponents are piling the pressure on. Knowing that the maniac will probably try to bully you out, the big blind bets into him, expecting that he will probably raise. The blind knows that if you hold a hand like 9-9, 10-10, J-J or Q-Q you will have a very hard time calling, and therefore he might be betting a relatively weak hand like A-8 to make you lay down the current best hand. You know that the blind might hold a hand like this, and you also know that the maniac doesn't need to have anything in this spot. On the other hand, there is someone behind you still to be heard from (someone who has cold-called your reraise before the flop, and who might very well hold ace-king, king-queen or some other hand that has you beat). Plus, if you call – and thus show weakness – the hand may get three- and four-bet to put even more pressure on you, and if someone *does* have just a simple king, you will be putting in four small bets on the flop while drawing to a mere two-outer. And that is just the flop: The same type of betting sequence might occur on the turn as well, where the betting doubles. However, if you decide to fold but indeed you were holding the best hand, this can be considered a catastrophe, the pot being so big, and your opponents willing to go all the way to the river with hands as weak as just middle pair or maybe even ace-high (in the case of the maniac).

Actions

It is hard to tell if folding, calling or reraising would be best in this situation with you holding the jacks. If you think that by reraising you might be able to make someone lay down a king then this might be your best choice. However, this scenario is highly unlikely considering the amount of money in the pot, and the fact that people know you may simply be trying to isolate the bully. So, it is imperative to know your opponents here, but even then you will make the wrong decision every now and then: either folding the current best hand (i.e., the big blind holds A-8, the maniac holds a hand like 5♥-4♥ and the cutoff holds something like A-Q), or calling or even reraising when at least one player has you beat.

Some final words

Now, this is the trouble with maniacs. If your opponents keep playing their normal game, then having one maniac in the game can be very profitable to you. You can isolate the maniac with your good hands, having good position on top of that, meaning that you give your hand the best possible chance to hold up. But usually, your opponents *won't* be playing their normal game. They will be waiting for the maniac to bet or raise, and will not respect your raises and reraises as much as they usually do, because they *know* you will try to isolate the maniac whenever you can – they know you won't need aces or kings to do that. If you're in this type of situation, you may well get forced into making the wrong decisions after the flop, because people know how to use the maniac's tendencies against you. This is even more so because of your position: you will often find yourself sandwiched between the maniac who will bet into you with anything and the players behind you who are also in the hand. And with all the bets you have paid before the flop and *will* pay after, and with the pots being much bigger than usual, any wrong decision you will make here can be considered a terrible, or even horrible one.

24 vices in limit hold'em

When playing limit hold'em, it is important to have a couple of strengths working for you. For instance, if you have better knowledge of odds and percentages than most of your opponents, you have an edge over them – at least, in that specific area. That said, it is my experience that *lacking* in certain areas will often *cost* you more than being proficient in them can ever make you. Example: a few otherwise good and capable players go on tilt quite frequently, and it is this characteristic alone that makes it impossible for them to win in the long run – despite the fact that they *are* good players, and may have more knowledge about the game than any of their opponents. At the same time, when you are able to always play your best game, and you never, ever tilt, this strength alone will not allow you to be a long-term winner if it's the only edge you have over your opponents. However, if your basic strategy is good already, and especially if you are also somewhat game-/table-selective, then this ability to always stay calm may be an important factor in maximizing your results, and in beating the games.

Here I am going to give you a list if 24 vices, 24 areas in poker where some players simply lack compared to others. I will rate every one of these areas on a scale from 0 to 100, the figure indicating how much your overall results will be harmed if you lack considerably in that specific area. (Example: by giving 90 points to discipline, and only 47.5 to table image, I am saying that in my opinion lacking in discipline is much more harmful to your results, than not having the right image.) Of course, this list of vices is somewhat arbitrary, and the ratings I give are not much more than an indication only, assuming a fairly standard, full-ring low- to middle-limit hold'em game.

Vices in limit hold'em (in alphabetical order)

1) Not *adjusting* enough to changed or changing circumstances
Points: 75

One of the factors that separate the break-even players from the winners. Knowing what to do *in general* is important, but not as important as applying it correctly to the current, specific situation.

2) Not *aggressive* enough/not maximizing wins

Points: 72.5

While it is true that in order to win you have to play tight, you also have to play aggressively, and push your edges when you have the best of it.

3) Playing with not enough *chips*/buying in for an insufficient amount

Points: 42.5

While quite a few poker writers emphasize the importance of playing a large stack (mostly because of the intimidation factor), I don't think in limit poker it is that much of an issue. If you have enough in front of you to play out every hand until the river, taking into account raises or reraises that you might want to make in case you flop a monster, you don't need any more. If you're a winning player, your opponents will notice – regardless of the chips that may or may not be at the table. (This is even more so when you play regularly against the same group of players. You won't fool them into thinking you are a big winner, just because you have a lot of chips in play.)

4) Not *disciplined* enough (in the broadest sense of the word)

Points: 90

Those who read my articles know that I view my discipline as one of the main reasons for my success, and still as one of my major strengths in the game. In my definition, discipline is a combination of extreme patient, non-tilting behaviour, and the ability to stay cool and calm under all circumstances – not just in the game, but also in your personal life, off the table. Without discipline, you stand no chance playing (limit) poker.

5) Not capable of *folding* when hand turns sour

Points: 77.5

If you are incapable of folding aces against a board J-10-8-8 with a bet and a raise in front of you, then you are costing yourself a lot of money. It is imperative to know when you're beat, and have the ability to make your decisions accordingly.

6) Not capable of creating a healthy *gambling atmosphere*

Points: 70

An area where quite a few grinder-type of players could improve considerably. Creating a healthy gambling atmosphere will make winning easier – and more pleasant, too.

7) Not enough *heart*/courage/determination

Points: 80

An intangible factor. Why do some very talented players, having all the knowledge needed to be a consistent winner, perform significantly worse than players with less natural ability and/or less knowledge of odds and percentages? It's the heart to do whatever it takes, the determination to be the best, and the courage of one's convictions (regardless of results, adversity or bad luck one may or may not have had).

8) *Knowing* the right play, but not always making the right play

Points: 75

Another intangible factor. Why do some players *know* what to do, yet don't always do it? Whatever the reason, always playing your best game and making the right plays is what gives you your edge, what makes you the pro – so this is what you should do.

9) Not *loving* and/or enjoying the game enough

Points: 72.5

Love for the game should be the driving force, the main reason for turning pro. When the thrill of playing poker has gone, it will be very tough to keep a positive expectation, especially when you are playing full-time.

10) Having poor *money management*

Points: 62.5

Playing above your bankroll can easily wipe out years of hard work. Once you have built a healthy bankroll, by all means protect it. It is only the extremely good and talented player who could afford to fluke in this area, as he might be capable of simply rebuilding the bankroll he has lost – because of his excellence in the game, or his ability to get staked. (And even for him, it would be a waste of talent to be negligent in this area of poker, as it will harm him considerably on his way to the top.)

11) Not knowing the exact *odds*/percentages

Points: 67.5

Any serious player should know the odds of making his hand, and be able to calculate the pot odds he is getting, an important guideline when making decisions. People who don't know the exact odds often base their decisions on a few rules of thumb (don't draw to an inside straight, unless the pot is big), and in limit poker they often guess their way into the right, or only slightly wrong, decision.

12) Not enough *patience* in waiting for the right hand/situation

Points: 87.5

Playing limit hold'em for a living requires an enormous amount of patience. If you are not (always) patient enough, you just cannot beat limit games – it's that simple.

13) Playing your own cards only, lacking in *playing the players*

Points: 70

Not as important as in big-bet poker, but still important. It is this area in poker where you can outperform other good and winning players, who are just playing solid, 'percentage' poker.

14) Lacking in *preparation*

Points: 67.5

From the moment I started playing poker for a living, I have given this subject considerably more attention than most other pros. Preparation means: coming in the right frame of mind to play poker, and also checking out games, tables, and the general atmosphere in your cardroom – so that you *know* what to expect before taking a seat. With so many distractions in casinos, it is not always easy to stay focused on your task at hand, and preparing yourself the right way will help you accomplish just that.

15) Not performing well under *pressure*

Points: 70

Quite a few players snap under pressure, especially when the pots get big, or when they are up against top players. This is even more of a factor in big-bet games.

16) Not good enough at *reading hands*

Points: 80

If you don't know what type of hand you may be up against, how could you possibly know the right course of action? All top pros take pride in their reading abilities. Reading hands properly will enable you to steal some pots and to gain or save bets, so that you can maximize your edge, and improve your hourly rate. Still, because of the fixed betting in limit hold'em and the enormous odds that you are often getting on a call, the premium on an expert read is not as big here as it is in pot- or no-limit play.

17) Lacking in *seat selection*

Points: 77.5

When going to the 24/7 casinos that are the rule in the US, most of the time you simply get assigned the first available open seat, and often you have no other choice than to take it. Where I play, casinos usually open and close at fixed times. Because I'm always there long before the poker room opens, I am generally able to pick the most profitable game – and the best seat. Having position on aggressive and/or dangerous players, while giving position to the ones who will not take advantage of it anyway, will improve your results considerably, so you should not be negligent in this area.

18) Lacking in the selection of *starting hands*

Points: 85

The foundation of your game. Without a solid basis, you stand no chance playing this game.

19) Lacking in *table/game selection*

Points: 80

The importance of choosing good tables, and picking the types of games that are best suited for your style of play, is habitually underestimated by a lot of fairly good players. Doing everything in my power to choose the most profitable game available has been one of my biggest edges over almost all other, in theory equally skilled, players, and one of the main reasons why my results have been so good.

20) Bad *table image*

Points: 47.5

If people view you as exactly the type of player you are (i.e., they view you as tight/unimaginative and that's exactly what you are), this will cost you money. However, at the lower and middle limits quite a few people just play their own hand, oblivious to everything else, so your image might not be that big a deal here.

21) Lacking in *talent*/natural ability

Points: 55

While I think that being talented and having a natural ability for the game are very important to make it in poker, this is not necessarily the case for limit hold'em. This is because limit hold'em is a rather mechanical game where the betting is fixed, and the best play is often fairly obvious. In value-driven games like limit hold'em, and even pot-limit Omaha, being very talented is of less importance than in games like five-card stud or no-limit hold'em, where this area of poker is often *the* deciding factor whether you'll be successful or not.

22) Vulnerable to *tilt* and steaming

Points: 87.5

In middle-limit poker, making one big bet per hour is considered quite an accomplishment. The players who steam off 10, 15 or 20 big bets in one session can never beat the games, even if they go on tilt only a small percentage of the time. In limit hold'em it is the tight, disciplined, non-steaming player who takes the money – not the one who plays well 85 out of 100 sessions, but loses big time because of tilt in the other 15.

23) Not *tricky* and/or creative enough

Points: 55

Low- and middle-limit hold'em rewards good, solid poker. Creative and tricky plays become increasingly important at the higher limits, in big-bet play, or when playing against very good players.

24) Being plain *unlucky*

Points: 35

Of course, in the long run there is no such thing as luck. However, those who are familiar with my works know that I believe firmly in conditioning my opponents into *thinking* that I am lucky. I believe that as a result they will be more apt to make mistakes against me, which in turn will reaffirm my lucky image, get my opponents even more off-balance, and increase my edge further. (Still, this is not the same as *being* lucky or unlucky.)

Playing the blinds: part 1

Top pair/no kicker in a multiway pot

As readers of my works may know, I am known as a very tight player. In fact, I play a bit tighter than even most experts suggest, and I will usually need a very good hand *and* a potentially profitable situation to enter a pot. Having said that, I sometimes defend my big blind with hands that other people would fold, especially when the preflop raiser is a rather weak and/or predictable player. I will be especially likely to defend with a marginal holding if my opponent has a tendency to raise with all big offsuit cards, while often playing his wired pairs a bit less aggressively. Because in full-ring play, quite a few players (especially the ones who *think* they play well) will always raise with hands like A-K, A-Q and A-J, sometimes even from early position, but will just call with all medium pairs, this will influence the way *you* should play your blind. Against people with these types of raising standards, I will often fold hands other people would call with, and call with hands some people would fold. To be more concrete: in the big blind against someone who is more likely to be playing two face cards (A-K, A-Q, A-J) than all other possible holdings combined, I will usually fold hands that might be dominated by the raiser – hands as good as ace-jack or king-queen offsuit. I will occasionally defend with hands like

9-8, 8-6, small suited connectors and even hands as weak as K-7 suited, especially if other players are in as well. I will do this only if:

- ♠ The raiser is rather predictable in his pre- and postflop play.
- ♠ His raising standards are as discussed above.
- ♠ The other players in the hand are not especially tricky and/or aggressive.
- ♠ Just as the raiser, these players are more likely to be playing (semi-) big cards, rather than hands like suited connectors or a wired pair.

Even though I will probably have the worst hand going in, I call because after the flop it will be fairly easy for me to make the right decisions *and* because I think I can lure my opponent(s) into making the *wrong* decisions. I can safely fold when the flop is likely to have helped the others, and if this is not the case then I will be able to put a lot of pressure on them – even when holding a relatively weak hand myself. Because of all this, I believe that defending with these types of holdings can actually give you a positive expectation for the hand – or to be more precise, a less negative expectation than simply folding would give you. Note that if you play as tight as I suggest, people will not expect you to be defending with the types of hands mentioned above, especially because *they* would never defend with them, and you might therefore get a lot of action if you happen to catch a perfect flop. (Lots of players *would* defend with hands like king-jack offsuit, even – and especially – in heads-up situations, but they wouldn't even *dream* of defending with 8-6 in a three-way pot. Because *they* play like this, they don't expect a tight player like you, who is known to fold against a raise so often, to be playing crummy cards like these on occasion.)

In this five-part series, I will discuss a few blind defence situations, and the recommended plays before and after the flop. Quite a few of these plays may be somewhat unconventional, and some of the strategies I will discuss have never appeared in print before, to the best of my knowledge. Having said all this, it is important not to use this series as an excuse to play a lot of extra hands from the blinds. If you play as I suggest, you will still be folding your big blind to a raise about six or seven times out of ten. If you fold less often than that, you are simply giving too much action with bad hands, or in unprofitable situations – and probably both.

Top pair/no kicker in a raised pot

A somewhat predictable player has raised from early position and gets called by two rather weak players, who call raises with any hand that they were intending to play anyway. You are in the big blind, holding K♥-2♥, and you decide to defend. Now, the flop comes K-10-7 rainbow, no hearts. What do you do?

Note that the raiser, and the callers, might all very well have received help from the board (two flop cards being in the 'playing zone', as Bob Ciaffone and Jim Brier call it in their book *Middle limit hold'em poker*). In fact, one of the most likely hands for an early raiser to hold is ace-king, and you would be drawing dead to your kicker then. A case can be made for betting into the raiser (to see where you stand, and to put extra pressure on him), but I would simply check, to see how things develop. If there's a lot of action, like a bet and a raise, you simply fold, knowing that you're almost certainly beat. But if the preflop raiser bets (which is to be expected: preflop raisers will often bet whether or not they have received help from the board), and one or two players call, but you somehow sense that no one has a king…well, then it's OK to continue in the hand for instance by taking off a card, and make your move if a safe card comes on the turn. Or, if no-one bets on the flop and it gets checked around, then you know with almost absolute certainty that your hand is best now. Unless the raiser is slowplaying a monster (which is not just unlikely, but also very unwise, taking into account the draw-heavy nature of the board), he almost certainly cannot beat your hand. And after the definite sign of weakness from the preflop raiser checking, the two players behind him still couldn't bet – meaning that they are unlikely to have a king, ten or even a seven. Now, this seems like an ideal situation to go for the checkraise on the turn, if a blank comes. Any preflop raiser will try to pick up the pot here, after all the weakness his opponents – you included – have shown. You can expect him to bet in this type of situation almost 100% of the time – and even if *he* doesn't bet, one of the callers may decide to stick it in after all this checking that's been going on. Now, in the most likely scenario (preflop raiser bets the turn, gets one call behind him from a hand like J-8 or Q-9, only to see you checkraise from the blind) you will have created quite a big pot with your rather marginal top pair/no kicker – which by now should be a solid favourite to win, though.

Some final words

When in the blinds, it is important to realize that your opponents will almost always assume you hold nothing. So, when you call a raise before the flop and then check on the flop *and* turn, there will almost always be someone to try to pick up the pot here, because you have not shown any strength yet. (This is especially true at the middle and higher limits.) Now, if you can recognize this type of behaviour, or simply 'feel' that they are betting without proper values, then it is possible to win a rather big pot by becoming aggressive on the flop or turn with a relatively weak holding yourself. Remember, defending with marginal holdings is profitable only if:

♠ You know how to maximize your hand when it is best (as described above).

♠ You read your opponents well enough that you don't have problems folding a reasonable hand even against only moderate action. (For instance in the case with your K-2, when you would simply 'know' by the way the betting goes that your opponent must hold a better hand than you, and thus you are capable of folding your top pair on the flop or turn.)

If you are unable to lay down top pair when it's clear that you're beat, or if you're simply too scared to check twice and go for the checkraise on the turn when that is undoubtedly the proper play, well then you should stick to a tighter blind strategy than I recommend here. If your postflop play is not strong enough, or if your reads are often way off, then playing marginal hands from the blind in the way I describe will actually *cost* you money.

In the second part of this series, I will discuss another top pair/weak kicker, this time in a heads-up situation against a possible steal raiser.

Playing the blinds: part 2

Top pair/weak kicker against a possible steal raiser

In the previous article, I discussed the play of top pair/no kicker in a four-way pot, having defended with K♥-2♥ against an early-position raise. This next hand may seem quite similar (because once again you flop top pair with your king, and once again you are the first to speak), but there are a lot more differences than may seem obvious at first glance. Because situational factors are not the same as in the other hand, the recommended play is different as well.

The situation

This time, you are in the big blind, holding king-nine offsuit in a full ring game. Everybody folds to the button, who raises. The small blind folds, and it's up to you. What do you do?

You have played with the button player lots of times, and know that he doesn't need to have premium values in this spot. You know that he's an aggressive player who likes to play his position, and who thinks that because you fold before the flop so often you may well be an 'easy blind'. You decide to defend (rather than fold or reraise), keeping in mind that you might even hold the best hand at the moment. This means that you are not automatically willing to surrender your hand after the flop, even when you receive little to no help.

Once again, the flop comes K-10-7 rainbow. So, you have flopped top pair with a relatively weak kicker. Even though the raiser *might* have you beat (because hands like K-Q or K-J would be common raising hands in this spot), in a heads-up situation like this you will not automatically give the raiser credit for having top pair with a bigger kicker – in fact, you will probably assume that *you* hold the boss hand. However, this does not mean that you should automatically take the lead to defend your hand. Since a pair of kings is not that easily overtaken in a heads-up situation, there's nothing wrong with letting your opponent do the betting for you – especially with the pot being so small. When you check, he will bet close to 100% of the time – whether he holds a great hand like K-K, a good hand like K-Q, a drawing hand like J-9, a marginal hand like Q-7, or a horrible hand like 5-4. In fact, he is much more likely to be bluffing or semi-bluffing than to be betting a decent or even good hand. Checking is therefore clearly better than betting out or even checkraising, because then you would not be giving your opponent enough room to bluff off his money.

So, checking and calling would seem like the natural course of action on the flop, slightly better than checkraising. (In this situation, I think I would bet into the raiser about 5% of the time, check-call 55% of the time, and checkraise 40% of the time. If this player is very overaggressive and will bet on the flop with a wide range of hands to keep the initiative, I would checkraise around 65% of the time here. This is especially true if he thinks you could be checkraising with a draw or a marginal made hand – and thus he may get further with a marginal hand than would seem reasonable against a checkraise.) If indeed you check-call the flop, well then because you have not shown any strength yet other than by responding to his bets by only calling, he will bet again on the turn a very high percentage of the time, whether he is bluffing, semi-bluffing, or simply betting the best hand.

While it may seem right for you to pull the trigger on the turn and check-raise (because you *are* quite likely to be holding the best hand), I think that check-calling once again might be the superior play – *but only if you are willing to bet into your opponent on the river*. If, say, an offsuit four comes on the river which looks like a total blank to your opponent, and you suddenly come out betting (make sure this is a hesitant bet!), you will have your opponent totally confused. He will probably think that you were drawing and have now missed – for instance, you've got the 9-8 and are now on a stone-cold bluff – but you may also have been bagging a monster, like a flopped set. Because you make it seem like an either/or situation (you either have a monster, or are bluffing), your opponent will probably react to your bet as follows:

- ♠ With a relatively weak holding like ace-high or a pair lower than kings, he will probably call you, because you might very well be bluffing. Had you checkraised him on the turn, he would probably have folded, so you now get an extra bet out of him (which is very meaningful, with the pot still relatively small).

- ♠ With a hand like A-K or K-Q, he doesn't like you betting into him on the river, although he probably thinks his hand is still best. So, your bet can never make him fold, but he will probably not raise either, fearing that you either have a very strong holding (in which case you will reraise), or are bluffing (in which case you will fold and he makes no extra money).

- ♠ With a busted hand himself, or even a total bluff, your hesitant bet might convince him that you are now bluffing yourself.

This is especially likely when taking into account the board, and your sudden, highly suspicious, bet on the end. Your opponent might be tempted to go for the bluff-raise on the end, because with this strange betting of yours he might get away with a re-bluff, to make you lay down your higher 'nothing'.

By checkraising on the turn, even though you will often win the pot there and then, your opponent will probably figure you for exactly the type of hand you have: top pair. This means that he is likely to make the right decisions at this stage: laying down any hand lower than that, including his bluffs, and reraising with all other hands. But *you* may now be forced to pay him off (after all, he *is* a highly aggressive player, and he might still be playing his position, or continuing a semi-bluff), meaning that you will lose a lot more money than would seem natural with this type of holding. If you play your hand in the unusual manner I recommend, he is less likely to make the right decisions against you. Plus, you will often gain an extra bet (when he pays you off on the end with a relatively weak holding), and sometimes even two (when he falls for your trap, and goes for the bluff-raise on the river). What's more: not only are you maximizing your wins rather well, just as importantly you will also minimize your losses in case your hand is *not* good. Say your opponent holds a king with a better kicker, by checkraising the turn you might have lost four bets (by paying off your opponent's reraise and also his bet on the end), while you might lose only two bets now if your opponent responds to your bet as I have described.

A few words of caution

While it is important not to go for the fancy play too often, there's nothing wrong with making an unusual play once in a while. Especially in situations like this (a small pot, where your hand, if good, is likely to stay good, but if second-best, is likely to end second-best), there's nothing wrong with playing your hand in the manner described here. A few words of caution though:

♠ Don't get carried away with checking and calling, as it is almost always a very weak play. I know almost no people who check-call on a regular basis, and still beat the games.

♠ Even though late-position players often bet or raise on light values, you should not *automatically* assume that a late-position raiser holds nothing. If you take any pair to the river in this type of situation, regardless of player characteristics, betting patterns and/or the texture of the board, you will be standing on the rail sooner than you can imagine.

♠ When making decisions, you should always take into account your opponent's playing knowledge and experience, his level of aggressiveness and his evaluation of your play. These factors are very important when putting a play on someone, because you will have more information available on how your opponent will react to a bet or raise by you.

Now, if you take all these words of caution to heart, you might be able to get away with an unusual but effective play every once in a while – which in turn may add a little to your hourly rate and to your overall results.

Some final words

In the third part of this series, I will discuss the play of yet another marginal blind hand, the 6-5 suited, and how to play this hand in various situations, against various flops.

Playing the blinds: part 3

Six-five suited

In the first two parts of this series I've told you that in the big blind, I often fold hands that other people would defend with, and call with hands that other people would fold. A hand type I occasionally defend my blind with is the small suited connector. Contrary to what some writers will tell you, I will sometimes do this even in a heads-up situation, especially if the pre-flop raiser is more likely to be holding two high cards than any other holding. When you are in this type of situation – playing cards that are opposed to your opponent's – you know when he is likely to have received help from the board, you know when you can therefore put pressure on him, you know how you can maximize your win when you do catch a good flop, *and* you will know if there's an opportunity to make your opponent lay down the best hand – by representing a hand that he cannot possibly hold. Because of the combined chances of all this happening, defending your blind here with this type of hand might well be worth it. But don't forget the impact of the house cut here. You should be less inclined to defend your blinds in raked games than in time games, especially if it's just you and one other opponent. The rake that's being taken out of a heads-up pot will almost always turn your slightly positive expectation into a negative one – possibly even for the both of you. (This would be the case when playing low- and middle-limit poker in some of the casinos in Europe that have a very high rake.) And, perhaps just as importantly: In order to make this call profitably, you not only need to read this player well – he also needs to be slightly predictable, with exploitable weaknesses.

The situation

OK, so you're the big blind, a $20-40 hold'em game with time collection, holding 6♥-5♥. A mid-position player has raised, everybody has folded, and it's up to you. Now, you know that this player usually raises as the first one in with any playable hand – he just doesn't like flat calling if no one has voluntarily entered the pot yet. Playable hands for him in this type of situation would include any hand containing two paints, and pairs fours and up – but with aces or kings, he will often just call to induce some more calls from the players behind him who are still to act. Because you are up against a player who is a lot more likely to be holding high cards only than a large pocket pair, *and* because this person tends to play his hands in a rather predictable manner, there's nothing wrong with calling his raise to see the flop. If there are cards on the flop that the raiser figures to like, for instance when the flop comes with two paint cards, then you're out of there – even if you flop a six or five yourself. It is simply too likely that the raiser holds a better hand than you, and there's not enough money in the pot to go chasing. But now, let's say we change the flop to…

Flop No. 1: 8-4-2 rainbow

If your opponent holds a higher pair than the cards that are on the board, he will be very pleased to see this flop, and he will certainly bet or raise, being in a heads-up situation against just the big blind. However, from a mathematical point of view he is a lot less likely to be holding a high pair than to have two big or semi-big cards. What's more, even if the raiser *does* have a high pair, your double belly-buster straight draw will get there almost one time in three (31.5% of the time, to be precise). This means that you can put a lot of pressure on your opponent to make him lay down the current best hand, because even if you are wrong, and your opponent *does* hold the hand he's representing, you still have a pretty good chance to beat him. This means that you should probably become aggressive from the flop onwards, and let the subsequent actions of your opponent dictate your best strategy from there on. Let's say you bet on the flop, he raises, you reraise, and now he reraises again, well then you can be fairly sure he's got more than just ace-king. This means that from that point on you will probably play your hand in a passive manner, unless you make your straight, or catch (from his perspective) a scare card like a six or five. (In this case, you might go for the checkraise on the turn, to try to make him lay down the best hand once more, while still having a lot of outs if called.) But if you come out betting on the flop, and your opponent just calls, with what seems like just overcards… well, then it seems only logical to fire another barrel to semi-bluff him off his hand. Remember, if he holds a hand like K-Q, it will be very hard for him to call you on every street with just king-high. What's more, with two cards to come, you actually have a pretty good hand when you are up against just overcards: not only will a seven or a three give you a straight, also catching a five or six may be good enough to win the pot.

Flop No. 2: Q-5-4 rainbow

With this type of flop, the best play is somewhat less straightforward. Against people who respect your play, it might be best to simply come out betting. With this type of rainbow board a bet by you represents a queen. Now, if the raiser holds a hand like A-10, A-J, K-J and maybe even A-K or pairs sixes through jacks, and if he knows you don't mess around too often in situations like this, then it might be possible for you to win the pot uncontested. And if he *does* raise you, he is quite likely to be holding exactly the type of hand he's representing (A-Q, K-Q), so it should be fairly easy for you to make the right play from here on.

If the raiser *doesn't* respect you, however, his response to your bet is a lot less reliable (he might have that same A-10 and raise you now), so in that case betting out would not be wise. Your options are then limited to check-fold, check-call or checkraise, based upon what you think the raiser is likely to hold. If you check, I think it is best to let your gut instincts dictate your actions from there on. Because I often 'feel' if someone is making a play at me, I might use this information to for instance check-call the flop and then checkraise the turn with just a pair of fives. Or, I might call the flop and then bet out on the turn, or even check-call on all streets with just one pair to give my opponent the chance to bluff off his money. Having said all that, if you don't have this feel or if you are someone who likes to *convince* himself the opponent is always bluffing, then playing the types of hands discussed here will actually cost your money rather than add to your hourly rate. If you fit this description, it might be best to do what most writers would recommend in these types of situations: fold before the flop and take your loss, rather than try to battle things out in a situation that requires a lot of judgment.

Some final words

In the first three parts of this series, I have discussed a few marginal hands that might actually give you a profit if you play them a) well, and b) under the right circumstances. For those of you who have problems analysing these circumstantial factors, or who don't know how to adjust their decisions to their opponent's actions, it will be best to simply avoid these types of situation – which means that you should not be getting involved in the first place.

Playing the blinds: part 4

A few examples

In the first three parts of this series on blinds defence I discussed some very marginal hands that, when played under the right circumstances, can actually add to your hourly rate. Here I will give a few more big blind hands. I will discuss the type of thinking the big blind should be doing when facing a raise, and how he should translate these thoughts into making the right play.

Example hand No. 1: A-9o

When holding a hand like this, it is important to see *who* the raiser is, and the *position* the raiser is in. In a full ring game, an early-position raise by a serious player almost always means a good hand, most likely a big pair or two very high cards.[12] Either way, you are in bad shape, with a hand that is likely to be dominated. What's more, if you call the raise and then hit part of the flop, it will be very hard to get away from your hand, and if the raiser takes his hand to the river with you, you are likely to lose quite a few bets. For instance, if an ace flops and you get action, you have no kicker, and if you flop a nine for top pair/top kicker you must be a hell of a player to lay it down at any stage – even though, if your opponent goes to the river as well, your hand is probably no good.

So, in the situation described, with a serious player raising in early position and everyone else folding, you should simply give it up before the flop, rather than call and hope to get lucky. But even with one or two additional callers, I think you should still fold, because you are *still* likely to be dominated, *and* because an ace-nine offsuit simply does not perform well in a four-way pot, out of position. Treat the ace-nine offsuit as I have always done: usually fold, unless you have a *very* good reason not to. Note that many players would do exactly the opposite: they will usually *call*, unless it is pretty obvious that this would not be wise – for instance, when they face not just one, but two raises.

Example hand No. 2: 7-5o

Quite a few people in my regular game can be considered fairly decent players. They tend to play tight/aggressive, know Sklansky's hand rankings by heart, and know pretty well how to play from the flop onwards. But they don't know how to play the blinds. Time and time again, I have seen fairly good players call raises from serious players with hands like king-ten offsuit. At the same time, I have seen them fold hands like small connectors in a three- or four-way pot when it is pretty obvious everyone else in the hand is playing paint cards. This lack of understanding how to

---

12   Nowadays, there are also some players who sometimes raise from early position with small suited connectors. You should know who these players are, and adjust your calling/reraising requirements accordingly – for instance, by rating 7-7, 8-8, 9-9 and 10-10 a little higher than against the tighter open-range that did *not* include the occasional small suited cards. (These pairs 7-7/8-8/9-9/10-10 are not necessarily up against two overcards or a higher pocket pair anymore. They may also be up against two *undercards* now, and this improves the overall equity of these medium pocket pairs considerably.)

adjust to changing circumstances when you have to call 'only' one more bet, is one of the major leaks in the game of lots of otherwise good players.

As readers of this column know, I *will* occasionally defend with this type of holding (small connectors, preferably – but not necessarily – suited), but I will do this only if the situation is right. Thus I will only do this if:

- ♠ The raiser is a predictable player, over whom I have good control.

- ♠ He is more likely to be raising with high cards only, rather than with a big pair.

- ♠ The callers in the middle are not particularly aggressive and/or tricky.

- ♠ They probably hold big or semi-big cards as well, rather than a slow-played high pair or some small or middle suited connectors.

- ♠ My call closes the betting, i.e., I cannot face a reraise from someone who is still to act.

Only if *all* of these factors apply to a certain degree, a call is in order, and *only* if you know how to play this type of holding when getting some help from the board (rather than no help or a lot of help). I have won quite a few big pots with hands like 7-5o, because my opponents have a hard time figuring me for this type of holding in a raised pot – me being such a tight player – and because they see me folding my big blind against a raise at least six or seven times out of ten. They cannot understand that I am occasionally willing to defend with these small, connected cards – that they would never play – while I will easily throw away hands that they would not *dream* of folding (like semi-big offsuit cards).

Some final words

It is important not to carry these types of thoughts too far when playing small connectors, and start using my remarks as an *excuse* to play more hands. For instance, if you are faced with a raise, even when it's coming from a light raiser in late position, but there are no other players in besides you and him, then you should still fold. Why? Well, I would say because you have nothing. Even though your opponent doesn't need to have a premium hand either, you hold a seven-high only, out of position, not knowing what you're up against, and not knowing if hitting a seven or five will be enough for you to win the pot. But in this same situation (a late-position raiser who is known to raise on light values), your A-9 from before may now have become playable; in fact, I even think a three-bet should be considered. Even though in general an ace-nine is very marginal, in this case it is likely to be the best hand by far. Therefore, taking away the initiative from your opponent might be your best option – also to send him the message that your blind is not *always* up for grabs. Every once in a while, I make a play like this (three-bet with a far from premium holding facing a late-position light raiser), but only if:

♠ The hand I hold is clearly playable in this situation, and folding would therefore be wrong.

♠ It seems that the raiser doesn't need to have a premium hand, either.

♠ By representing more strength than I actually have, I will be able to take the initiative away from my opponent, so that I can pick up some pots when we both flop nothing.

I will continue these thoughts in the next article, the fifth and final part of this series on blinds defence.

Playing the blinds: part 5

Some more examples

In the last article, I discussed that it is sometimes correct to three-bet a late-position raiser before the flop with a rather marginal holding, under the following circumstances:

♠ You are in the big blind. (Make this play from the small blind with a marginal hand only *very* occasionally. It is very expensive play to make from the small blind, and even though it generally signals a stronger hand than a reraise from the big blind, there is a lot more risk involved because of a third party who is still in the hand: the big blind.)

- ♠ You were planning to call anyway, i.e., your hand and/or the situation seems too profitable for a fold.

- ♠ The raiser often raises on light values, especially in position.

- ♠ He respects your play, and does not think you are particularly tricky (that is, he will give you credit for a hand when you three-bet).

- ♠ You think that by three-betting you will be able to take the initiative away from your opponent (so that you can expect to pick up the pot when both you and your opponent flop nothing).

Hands like ten-nine suited and queen-jack suited are excellent candidates for making this kind of move every once in a while. To fully understand the strength of this play, you should put yourself in your opponent's shoes. If you have read him correctly (for a steal or semi-steal), he might well hold a hand like A-8o/K-9o or something like J-8s/8-7s – possibly even worse than that. How do you think he will feel when he gets popped before the flop, holding these types of hands – and not just by *someone*, but by *you*, a very, very tight player who hardly ever enters a pot. I guarantee you that he will actually be *looking for reasons to fold his hand after the flop*. If your image is correct, he will not only fold if he receives *no* help from the board, but also if he receives *some* help. Now, knowing that it is 2-to-1 against someone holding two random cards to flop a pair, if there's also the added chance of him folding when he *does* flop a pair, then it should be obvious that three-betting in this type of situation can be a very powerful play indeed.

Example hand No. 3: A-A

Now, the reason this can be such a powerful play to reraise with a fairly marginal hand is that your opponent fears that you might have aces or kings – or at least, a very strong holding. (Remember, a late-position player who raises as the first one in, is always scared of someone waking up with a real hand behind him, especially because the players in front of him obviously didn't hold much. This is called the *bunching effect*, meaning that at least in theory there might be relatively more high cards left in the deck, now that so many players have already folded their hands.) Now, let's say that you *do* have aces in the big blind and once again, a late-position player comes in for a raise. Should you trap by just calling, or play straightforwardly and three-bet? Well, actually in this case there is something to be said for just calling. After all, your call closes the betting, as there are no players behind you that you will either have to force out, or make pay for the privilege of seeing the flop. So, just calling may allow you to trap your only opponents on the later streets, as he will probably give you credit for all types of hands, but not aces.

Having said that, I usually like to play my aces straightforwardly. Because I sometimes play my hands in a manner *as if I have aces*, I don't think it would be right to do things differently when I finally get them. Your opponents will certainly notice if you are someone who likes to play his premium hands deceptively, so the next time you will try to represent aces, they will be less likely to fall for it. Even though quite a few good players I know do things differently than I do, I *always* raise with aces before the flop – in any type of situation, in any position, regardless of the action in front of me. After all, so many situations come up where you would play a hand like ace-queen or even ace-jack as if you held aces. For instance, when you three-bet an early raiser who is on your immediate right – and who is known to open-raise on light values – with A-Q or so, or even A-J. You three-bet, hoping to get rid of all the players behind you – including the small pocket pairs that are currently favoured over your two big cards – to play heads-up, in position, with a hand that figures to be best against the open raiser. Because in this situation, you are trying to represent a little more strength than you actually have, I think you should also play your aces like aces, and raise and reraise with them wherever you can. (Continuing with the A-Q/A-J from above. If players know that you are *less* likely to make this three-bet play with aces or kings, they may call or even four-bet you with fairly marginal hands like 9-9 or A-Q – hands that they might have folded if they figured aces or kings were a more integral part of your reraising range. Now, you definitely don't want this to happen. You don't want to be sandwiched between an aggressive player who might bet with anything, and someone behind you who has shown strength, and who may or may not have you beat. You don't want this: you want all the players behind you to simply fold.)

I always treat pocket aces for what they are: the best possible starting hand in the deck, and I will therefore try to get as much money into the pot with them as possible. Because your opponents will often hope you have ace-king or ace-queen rather than aces, and thus will call you down after the flop with any pair, I think it is best to *always* bet the hell out of your aces –

even though in some cases, like in this example hand, there is something to be said for just calling to make your move later.

Example hand No. 4: J-7o

Contrary to what most people do, I usually don't even complete my small blind with these cards in unraised pots, let alone defend my big blind with it against a raise. Regardless of the situation and whether or not the raiser is likely to have a big hand, if he catches me in the blind with this type of holding, the pot is his. The jack-seven offsuit is not just a bad hand out of position in a heads-up situation; in a multiway pot it is equally bad. This is: a) because you cannot make the nuts, and b) because you are holding cards in the playing range of your opponents – and on top of that, slightly worse. It is for this reason that the J-7 type of hands often have *negative implied odds*: you are simply more likely to *lose* money after the flop with these cards, than to win some additional money with them.

Some final words

In this series, I have discussed the subject of blind play, and shared with you the considerations and reasons why you should defend or not – and if you do, how you should continue from there on the later streets. Even though lots of writers don't like to focus on blinds defence (because it is so 'personal', and requires 'feel' more than anything else), I have done my best to give you some sort of guide map, a reference to rely on when facing the question: should I defend or not?

A semi-bluff succeeds

It's one of those nice and quiet Sunday afternoons. Usually, this would be my day off, because on Sundays there are no big pot-limit games in my regular cardroom. But because I haven't played any long limit hold'em sessions in quite a while, I head to the casino to play a little $10-$20 hold'em, which is the biggest limit available.

The game is unusually soft on this day. There are quite a few weak, easy-to-manipulate opponents, and I am up close to $500 for a way-above-average win. It needs to be said that I have been rather fortunate. In five hours of play, my aces and king have both held up, and I have flopped a set twice – meaning that I have played six hands, and won four of them. (I have also picked up two pots from the blinds while holding absolutely nothing, but my opponents have no clue that in both cases I was on a stone-cold steal.)

Now, a new player enters the game. Well, this player is not actually new; I have played with him on numerous occasions. When I had just started playing for a living, he was one of the regulars. This player – let's call him Johnny – does play rather tight, but he is also very tricky. He likes to push small edges and often bets with marginal hands if he senses that the opposition may be weak. At the same time, he isn't afraid to fold even reasonably good hands if it seems likely that someone holds a better one.

As I said, Johnny and I have been at the same table very often, but because he has moved abroad he doesn't play in my regular game anymore. Johnny still remembers me as the super-rock who only plays ace-king, and who would never continue in a hand with less than top pair. After all, that's how I played when I just started out: rock-solid, ultra-disciplined and very tight. Of course, over the years I have improved my game considerably (by occasionally semi-bluffing and even bluffing, and by making my tight image work by stealing a few pots here and there), but he doesn't know that. For him, I am still the tight, unimaginative player that I used to be.

Now, that is the crux to the play that I'm sharing with you here. It is the fact that Johnny still viewed me as someone who would never bet or raise without holding the goods. There were also some additional factors that, from his perspective, made it highly unlikely that I was making a move to make him lay down the best hand, not to mention the fact that by the way I played my hand, I was able to disguise my actual holding. Here's what happened.

The play

A waitress has just brought a delicious meal to the table. Even though I usually don't like to eat while playing, the game is so good that I simply don't want to take a break. The food is good too: I have a spicy, delicious combination of steak and green vegetables in a rich, thick Oriental sauce. I'm in the big blind with K♣-9♣. Five players have limped, including Johnny who is in the cutoff, so I get a free play. The flop comes J♣-6♦-3♣, meaning that I've got a king-high flush draw in addition to some (but not a lot) high-card and backdoor straight potential. Even though I often play my flush draws aggressively, because I have been quite active from the blinds earlier this session, I decide to simply check to see how things develop. It gets checked around to Johnny who bets in his unusual, strange manner.

Now, as I have said, this Johnny is a tricky player. He likes to play deceptively, and often checks when most people would bet, and bets when most people would check. For instance, while most people would almost always slowplay monsters like quads or top full, this player loves to simply come out betting in situations like this. In this specific hand that was going on right now, it seemed to me that he had a genuine hand, though – even though it was unclear to me if he was betting a genuine *made* hand or a genuine draw. All in all, I didn't like his bet, as he might well be pushing an ace-high flush draw, leaving me drawing dead or close to it.

Both the button and the small blind flat call his bet, and now it's up to me. While often in multiway pots like this I would have gone for the check-raise with my flush draw, in this case I decide to just call and maybe lure the two players behind me into the pot as well. My reasoning? Because most people in this game know that I often play my four-flushes aggressively, I might now be able to make quite a bit of money if I hit it, especially because of my passive play all throughout the hand. (A second reason for not raising was of course the threat that a higher flush draw than mine may be out there.) After all, because I have given no sign of aggression whatsoever (being in the big blind in an unraised pot, having checked-and-called on the flop in a six-way pot), I was fairly certain that I could get some of my opponents to pay me off generously in case I hit my flush, with hands as weak as one pair maybe. Anyway, there is one more caller, so five people stay for the turn, which is the 5♥. Now, this is an interesting card, knowing that it may well have helped one of my opponents. After all, with five people seeing the turn, and with people routinely playing hands like seven-four suited in this game, I know that this card might have given one of my opponents considerable help.

Everyone checks to Johnny, who once again makes a bet. Now, he is just about the only player in this pot who *can't* have a seven-four because, as I said, his preflop standards are rather tight. The most likely hands for him to hold would be top pair, second pair + ace kicker or, also still possible, the ace-high flush draw. He can also hold a set, but I usually read him very well, and I don't sense this much strength in him. In fact, I sense fear in Johnny, fear that this five may very well be a bad card for him.

So, when both the button and the small blind fold, and when I see that the remaining player behind me doesn't seem very interested either, I decide to make a move. I checkraise Johnny as a semi-bluff, to make him throw away his one-pair hands that currently beat my king-high, and also to pave the way for a river bluff in case he *does* hold a bigger flush draw than me. The player behind me indeed throws away his cards, and now Johnny goes into the tank. You can see him thinking: does Rolf have the seven-four here, or is he making a move? But then again, what kind of move could he be making? Because if Rolf *is* making a semi-bluff here, what could he conceivably have? With a flush draw, he probably would have checkraised on the flop or even bet out, and he isn't the type of player to make *any* move without the flush. In fact, he hardly ever makes a move! Plus, it is clear that Rolf *can* easily hold the seven-four here. After all, he *is* in the big blind, and with six players in the pot and relatively little raising, calling one bet on the flop with a gutshot may well have been the proper play – even for a tight player like him. Should I call? Should I fold? Does he have it – or doesn't he?

Johnny looks again at his cards, he looks at me, at my huge pile of chips, and at the food that is there waiting for me. It is clear that he just doesn't want to fold, but basically everything seems to indicate that he is up against a straight, or at least some other very strong holding. He knows that I almost never bluff (at least, that is his perception of me), I'm in front (usually, people who are in front are less likely to make any moves than people who are losing), I am eating (people who have just gotten food usually bet and raise only when they've got the goods), and the way I have played the hand is *exactly* how someone with a straight draw would play it: check-call while drawing, and then checkraise when it gets there.

After long deliberation, Johnny finally decides to throw away his cards, showing king-jack offsuit. I would have been drawing to nine cards only, if he had called me. Now, I win a good-sized pot while holding just a draw, and I have been able to make my opponent lay down a fairly strong hand, a hand *way* stronger than mine. I stack my chips, and feel warm inside. I have used perfect timing for this semi-bluff to succeed and have chosen the ideal opponent to execute it, knowing that probably more than the other players, this specific player would give me credit for having the best hand. I go back to my steak with the Oriental sauce and the green vegetables. It tastes even better than before, now.

A bold play

It was once again one of those nice and quiet Sunday afternoons. Knowing there are usually no big pot-limit Omaha games available on Sundays, I headed to the casino to play some limit hold'em, even though the stakes are relatively small (especially when you compare them to our regular pot-limit game). But because I rarely get to play any long sessions of limit hold'em anymore, I sometimes choose to play on one of these Sundays, because then the cardroom opens early – meaning that I can log in quite a few hours and practice my discipline probably more than anything else.

Now, it was three or four weeks after my article 'A semi-bluff succeeds' had been published in *Card Player* magazine, and quite a few of my opponents in the game have read that piece. In the article, I described this exact Sunday afternoon game, and analysed a hand that I stole from my one of my opponents, in addition to one or two other moves I had made. Possibly because of this piece, people seem to focus on this alleged 'stealing' and 'bluffing' of mine much more than usual, so I know that I have to make the necessary adjustments, and will have to come up with a real hand every once in a while.

The $10-$20 table that I'm playing at is not as soft as on an average Sunday, but it is still quite a good game. Having said that, I haven't won any pots in the first three hours of play, and I'm down almost $300. That's when the following hand develops. Everybody folds to a lady player two off the button who calls as the first one in, a loose/aggressive player in the cutoff calls as well, and I'm on the button with a queen-jack offsuit. Even though this is typically a hand I would limp with, because there are two relatively tight players in the blinds, and I want to get the chance to play against the two somewhat looser players only, I decide to raise. Indeed, both blinds fold, so three players see the flop A-Q-10 rainbow.

Both players check to me, I bet, and they both call. The way they call it looks to me like they are both rather weak. Even though some players like to check-call with a pair of aces (especially a weak ace, when they fear the raiser might have A-K or A-Q or so, but still want to keep him honest), in this case I think they don't even hold that much. So, when the turn is an offsuit six and they both check again, I fire $20, confident that indeed my pair of queens/jack kicker is the best hand right now.

The lady player hesitates and then finally calls. Knowing this player, she would have called instantly with an ace or even a queen, and the way she calls it seems to me that she isn't drawing but has a weak made hand. I put her on a ten, something like 10-9 or 10-8 probably. The other player, who is aggressive but rather inexperienced and way too loose, now calls rather quickly, and his body language suggests that he probably has a queen – in which case my jack kicker is undoubtedly good. (With king-queen, he probably would have raised preflop, and with any other paint card he would now have made two pair, and I don't sense that much strength in him.) It is possible that he's got a Q-J as well, but something like Q-9, Q-8 or even a queen-small suited are all just as likely, as this person would play all these hands in this type of situation.

Now, the river comes another six, making the final board A-Q-10-6-6. Once again, they both check, and with my now rather weak Q-J (my kicker doesn't play anymore, meaning that I will have to split with any queen – and anyone with an ace, six or even a K-J beats me easily), it would seem normal to simply check it back. After all, usually in this type of situation I will only get called by someone who has me beat or who has the same hand as me, so there would be no value in betting – right? Well, not really. If my read on both players was correct, and knowing both their tendencies, I was pretty sure that I could get the lady to pay me off with just one ten, and after this much strength (with a tight player like me betting on every street against this scary board, *and* the lady paying me off three times) the inexperienced player with the queen might then reason that at least one of us had to have an ace or better. And yes: this is exactly what happened: The lady with the ten called, and the third player then folded showing a queen, meaning that instead of a split I now won the entire pot.

The inexperienced player showed both surprise and disappointment at the outcome, because he is not someone to throw away a marginal hand easily, but now he had done just that and it turned out to be wrong! Well, of course he was correct in folding his hand, because in this situation where I *knew* I was going to get called, there was no chance whatsoever that I could be bluffing, and the way the betting went I was almost certain to have a big ace or better here. But because both players had basically given away their hands by their betting patterns, their predictability and their body language, they had made it very easy for me to make a 'shot for nothing' by making a bet that, if my read was correct, was basically free of risk – and fortunately, it paid off well for me.

After that, I was fortunate enough to win a couple more pots, having raised before the flop with some *very* marginal cards. First, I raised from the small blind with just a K♣-8♣, once again to force out the big blind, and to compete with the same two players again. This raise of mine happened to make the eventual winner fold, and instead of losing quite a few bets, my top pair of kings now won a decent-sized pot because of the contributions of the aggressive player, who called me down with second pair. And then, on the very next hand, I raised from the button with just an ace-nine offsuit, got three-bet by the small blind, and ended up winning a very big pot by making the nut flush on the turn. This meant that I had booked quite a good result for the day without getting *any* decent starting hands, and by winning three decent-sized pots with hands that were fairly marginal at best.

A few minutes after that, the two weaker players left and the table suddenly became shorthanded, as just some of the tighter players remained. With me having shown nothing but garbage in the last two or three pots, I decided to call it a day as well, because I knew that the tight players would *never* give me credit for a real hand anymore after all this previous aggression of mine with – in their eyes – crummy cards. Now, in a shorthanded game you simply cannot afford to wait on premium cards and you have to steal a lot, but after all the events on this day, I didn't think I could get away with any more thievery. So, this being the only game available on this day, I decided to simply go home and do some writing instead.

Still, I was pleased with the way I had played this session, in particular in the Q-J hand mentioned. It doesn't happen very often that you have an almost perfect read on not just one but two players, and that from there you can basically predict their actions and lure the worst hand into calling and the same hand as yours into folding. It was a bold play that's for sure, a play I might not make again in a *very* long time – but it sure felt good.

Plugging some leaks

In this article, I will give a short overview of some common limit hold'em leaks, an analysis of mistakes that are quite common and that can easily be solved. I will try to come up with some quick solutions to problems that especially somewhat inexperienced players may sometimes encounter.

Leak No. 1: Calling with overcards

The problem:

You've got two big cards in a raised pot. The flop comes with rags and there's a bet and a call. Should you call?

While quite a few players would almost always call in this situation unless there's been a raise, I think that in this situation it is often correct to fold. Of course, the quality of your opponents' play, the exact texture of the board, your position and the characteristics and habits of your opponents (especially those of the bettor) are all very important here. I would say that the people who habitually call with overcards in multiway pots like this are probably making a mistake, for the following reasons:

1) The pot has been raised (probably by you) and now, in a multiway pot, someone is betting into you. While the bettor may have 'only' top pair, he might actually have much better than that.

2) Even if you hit one of your overcards on the turn, someone may have improved to an even better hand; for example your pair of aces/good kicker may now face someone with aces-up.

3) If you hit and your hand is good, you might not make much more money (especially if your preflop play has marked you with A-K), but if your hand *isn't* good – for instance when you're up against a set – you will lose a lot. However, because the pot is big already, this may not be an overly important consideration.

4) Even if your hand is good at the moment you hit it, your opponents may have straight/flush/two-pair redraws on the river. This being a multiway pot, it is likely that even if you hit your six-outer on the turn *and* it is actually the best hand at that moment, you might still lose the hand on the river 35%, 40% or even 50% of the time (depending upon the exact board and your opponents' hands).

Now, all of this doesn't mean that you should *never* call with just overcards. What it does mean is that you will need to have a very good reason to do so, and avoid doing it 'because you only get so many playable hands, that when you finally get them, you have to stick to them'. Also, the comments above apply mostly to low-limit hold'em games where lots of people see the flop, and where someone betting into the raiser actually *means* something. In bigger, more aggressive games someone might simply be trying to bet you off the kind of hand that they think you might hold (un-improved overcards), even when they don't have a pair either. Now, obviously if you think that this might be the case here, then it would be a big mistake to fold too liberally, so you will often have to call or even raise in situations like this.

Leak No. 2: Failure to bluff on the river with a busted draw

When a weak calling station, someone who is known to bet with good made hands only, holds 10♥-9♥ and flops something like 8♥-7♥-2♦, then even someone like him is usually not afraid to bet or raise on the flop with his premium draw. In fact, some of these weak players will even have the courage to bet again on the turn, even when that card was of no help to him. But on numerous occasions, I have seen players like this suddenly shut down on the river after having once again received no help, when a bluff would have had a fairly good chance of success. Say that the final board looks something like 8-7-2-2-3, with no flushes possible, and you are up against just one or two opponents. Because you have been betting all the way (representing a good made hand), and your opponents have been calling all the way (indicating that they may very well be drawing themselves), there is a fair chance that one flat bet on the river might win you the pot. But time and again, I have seen players like this simply give it up on the river only to lose to an ace-high, king-high or even jack-high, hands that would never have called the final bet. Remember, if you bet $20 in a $200 pot, your bluff doesn't have to win you the pot very often to still have a positive expectation. If you think you might win the pot more than one time in ten, you will be making money with your bet, and against this specific board and the way the betting has gone, it should be clear that the chances of getting away with your bluff are *way* over 1 in 10.

In big-bet poker, this river bluff is even more of an issue, simply because you can put more pressure on your opponents here. Not only will you be able to make your opponents fold a busted draw (that still beats your busted draw though), often you will also be able to make them throw away some good-but-not-great made hands. If in pot-limit Omaha you bet the pot on the turn with a board K-Q-J-6, get called and you think you are probably up against a set of kings, then if a blank comes on the river you might very well win the pot with a big bet, simply because your betting on the previous streets has indicated that you may well have a straight. Of course, while a bluff on the river has a much better chance of success in big-bet poker than in limit, it is also much more expensive if it fails, so it pays to know your opponents here. Some people can easily be bluffed out of the pot even when they hold a near-nut hand, while other players are simply incapable of folding even relatively marginal hands on the end, no matter how much you bet.

Leak No. 3: Not changing your hand selection when there's a loose raiser in your game

Most starting hand tables analyse correctly the way you should adjust your hand selection when a very tight player raises – which means that in general, you should tighten up considerably, and fold lots of hands that you would otherwise have called or even raised with. But how does having one or two loose raisers in your game change things for you? Well, they change things considerably. Late-position calls with hands like 10-8s often cannot be made anymore now that the pot has been raised, and with small pocket pairs you would also prefer a multiway unraised pot – which is not the case now. So, you will need to adjust, meaning that you will often have to fold hands that would have been playable without the raise, and in some cases – especially if no one has entered the pot other than the raiser – you should reraise to isolate the light raiser, even while holding a relatively marginal hand yourself. (Hands as weak as A-J or 8-8 may qualify for a three-bet if the conditions are right.)

What you should definitely *not* do is something that quite a few people tend to do: play exactly the same hands as they would have without the raise 'because this person's raise doesn't mean a thing anyway'. People who claim things like this tend to forget that there are other things to consider with regards to hand selection that just the quality of the cards. Things like the number of players, the price you are getting on a call and your position relative to the raiser – things like this will be seriously affected by the aggressive actions of this player, regardless of whether or not he is in there with a good hand. Also, just the fact that someone is a light raiser doesn't mean he cannot hold a good hand *right now*. After all, if this person is not a total maniac, he will probably be raising with many hands that are a bit marginal, in addition to all of his good hands *and* possibly all of his great hands as well. This means that if you routinely call him with marginally playable hands like K-Jo or Q-10o, you may be behind more often than you might think, especially if there are also other players in the hand besides just you and the raiser.

Leak No. 4: Failure to see circumstantial factors in a hand

When discussing and analysing poker hands, quite a few players seem to be able to focus on just one or two aspects of the decision process, while failing to take into account other important factors. I will illustrate this with a limit hold'em example. In the first situation, you are in the big blind with Q-Q, two utter maniacs in late position have just called now, and the small blind has also called. In the second situation, there have been two early-position limpers, including an excellent and highly aggressive professional, then the same two calls by the maniacs, and this time the small blind has folded. (You hold the same Q-Q as before.) Now, when discussing the proper way to play the queens with some of my poker friends and students, quite a few of them didn't see much difference between the two situations, and recommended raising in both cases – after all, you hold an excellent hand and you will have to charge the weaker hands to draw out, they argued.

Well, in my view there *is* a lot of difference between the two situations. In the first situation, with this relatively weak opposition, there is no question that you should raise, as you figure to hold the best hand by far. It is quite likely that the small blind will fold to your raise, giving you the chance to play just against the loose guys, with a hand that can stand a lot of heat. But in the second situation, even though you may still hold a better hand than your opponents, you might gain more by playing deceptively. Since the small blind is already out, raising will certainly not make anyone fold. (It is extremely rare to see a player folding against a single raise, after having called the initial bet voluntarily.) More importantly, raising will basically announce to everybody the type of hand you are probably holding, making it harder to defend your hand when the flop comes favourable (say, when you flop an overpair to the board), and making it easier for your opponents to make the right decisions against you after the flop.

There is one problem with *not* raising though, and it has to do with the fact that you don't know what the pro holds. He may very well have limped with A-A or K-K, expecting the maniacs behind him to raise, so he can pop it again and try to build a huge pot with the current best hand. Now, if you don't raise and the flop comes something like 5-2-2 rainbow, then it will be very hard for you to give the pro credit for a bigger pair than yours, and you are probably going to lose quite a few bets to him. This is because he may well have a medium pair that he thinks might be good, for instance because he doesn't give you credit for a deuce and *certainly* not for a bigger pair than his nines, tens or jacks – after all, with a bigger pair you would probably have raised, right? The only way you could possibly have given the pro credit for a bigger pair than yours is if after your preflop raise he were to three-bet (and you know he would only do this with a premium hand), and then he continued his aggression later in the hand with this same kind of flop. But even then, it would have been hard to label him with exactly aces or kings, and with all this money in the pot *and* with at least two outs to improve to the winner, it would still not be easy to release a hand of this quality.

So, if in this second situation you do as I recommend (check), you will almost invariably go for the checkraise if the flop looks favourable, unless you think you can make more money by betting out – if you think you can reraise an aggressive player by making it three bets. If you *do* raise before the flop, you hope to tie your opponents onto the pot in case you flop a queen: You know that if you *don't* flop a queen, your raise may have made it much harder to defend your hand, and chances are that if you win the pot it will be a medium-sized one, and if you lose the pot it will be a huge one.

Now, all kinds of factors like this come into play when you're involved in a pot, and you should know all these things well in advance, well before you make that seemingly simple decision to either check or raise. Because if you are someone who looks only at the most obvious factor in the hand (the quality of your cards) while neglecting some other important circumstantial factors, it will be almost impossible for you to make the optimal decision, both before *and* after the flop.

Leak No. 5: Losing money with ace-little suited

A lot of weak players, and also quite a few average ones, lose a lot of money because they have the tendency to play any ace, suited or not. Better players know that ace-rag is usually a money burner, but they often don't have the strength to fold a *suited* ace – even when the situation is clearly unprofitable for that type of holding. In full ring games, I usually treat the ace-little suited like this:

Moderately tight games

Early position	Easy fold.
Middle position	Usually fold, in some cases raise to steal the blinds, occasionally call if, say, two people have limped in front of you.
Late position	With a couple of limpers in front of you, call. If you are the first one in, either raise or fold. Don't *always* raise here, as many players seem to be doing. Especially in heavily raked games, simply throwing away your hand is not all that bad, but if you decide to play (which would seem normal most of the time), then you should bring it in for a raise.

Loose games

Now here, the ace-little suited is a profitable hand, and can be played for a profit, sometimes even from early position. (This is especially true when the game is loose-passive, as opposed to loose-aggressive.) In loose-passive games, you can almost always call from middle position and sometimes even from early position as well, and in late position you might even raise every once in a while to create a volume pot. However, games this good are very rare and almost non-existent at stakes of $10-$20 and above.

More than all these preflop recommendations, the ace-little suited will be profitable only if you know how to play well after the flop, only if you are able to make the right decisions then – for instance, if an ace flops rather than the flush draw you were hoping for. If you are not capable of making the right decisions here, you should probably stick to the hands that require less judgment after the flop: the premium pairs, the suited high cards and the small pocket pairs.

A badly misplayed hand

In loose-aggressive limit hold'em games, some of the most difficult hands to play are hands that I really *love* in either tight-aggressive or loose-passive games: pocket queens and pocket jacks. In full-ring games where lots of people see the flop even for multiple bets, they are often way too good to get away from, but very hard to defend after the flop if you get what you want: an overpair to the board. Because of the huge pot and the small size of the bets in relation to this pot, people are usually committed to go all the way to the river even with hands as marginal as a gutshot or bottom pair/ace kicker. Now, of course if you flop a set with your Q-Q or J-J under these circumstances, well then this is a *highly* profitable situation (with people putting in a lot of money drawing thin or even dead), but in almost any other case your big pair will be very hard to play.

I like the queens and jacks even less if under the game conditions described here, I am up against an early-position raiser whom I either don't know, or who seems to have very tight raising standards. In a $10-$20 game recently, I was up against someone who had *both* these characteristics. (That is: I had never played with him before, but from what I had seen he needed a hell of a hand to raise up front.) Possibly because of this, I misplayed my pocket queens in a way that would probably not have happened under more 'normal' circumstances – say, in less crazy games than this one and/or against people that I could read more easily.

The situation

While waiting for my regular pot-limit game to start, I happened to bump into a very juicy $10-$20 game. I had two rather inexperienced players to my left who *knew* about my reputation as a rock, but who would still play back at me with some rather marginal holdings. On the seat to their left, there was a man in a wheelchair, who with every flop asked the dealer to call the cards 'because he could not see them'. I had noticed that every time this person had a good hand, he *was* able to see the board cards properly, but still I wasn't convinced if this person was actually a very experienced player who was trying to act weak and ignorant, or if he *genuinely* had problems coping with the speed of the game. What I *did* know was that in over an hour of play he had not made one single preflop raise – but on this hand, he raised from under-the-gun, making it $20 to go. From his general demeanour and the way he acted, I put him on a premium hand.

To tell you the truth, I put him on aces or kings, with a more remote queens, jacks or ace/king maybe, but almost certainly a hand that *he* thought was a monster.

Two relatively loose players called his raise, and on the button I looked down at exactly the hand I did *not* want to see in this situation: pocket queens. While under normal conditions, against people that I know very well, I am usually very good at making the correct pre- and postflop decisions (maximizing when I know I am good, and minimizing my losses when I just *know* my opponent either has a bigger pair or has just out-flopped my queens), in this case I didn't like my hand much. The reason: I didn't know enough of this player to be *absolutely* certain about anything he would say or do – and thus, how I should rate the strength of my own holding. Instead of reraising with my quality hand (what most people would have done in this situation) or folding (which I might have done in a tight/aggressive game against someone that I can confidently put on a monster[13]), I decided to simply flat call. As expected, both blinds called, meaning we had six players for the flop – and I had no clue about what *any* of them held at this stage.

Postflop action: A few bad mistakes and lapses in judgment

With the action flop 10♦-9♣-3♦ and knowing the tendencies of some of my opponents, I wasn't too pleased with my two queens, despite the fact that I had flopped an overpair. This was mostly because of the likelihood of big action when I would not know exactly where I stood, and because I knew that if I was actually behind, I would be drawing very thin. The small blind led into the preflop raiser, the big blind called, the preflop raiser immediately raised again, and the two players in the middle called quickly as well. I took my time to try and analyse this situation. For all the world, it looked like the preflop raiser had an overpair to the board. Now, if he did it would almost certainly be bigger than mine, as I thought it was much more likely

---

13   While folding a premium hand before the flop can sometimes be correct if a) the pot is small, and b) you have an extremely good read on some-one, in this case I knew this would probably be a five- or six-way pot. This meant I would almost be getting the proper odds to call this raise with *any* pocket pair on set value alone! So, in a multiway pot like this, folding seemed out of the question, even more so because of my good position, having most of the action in front of me.

that he had kings or aces than specifically jacks (or, highly unlikely, the other two queens). What's more, if for whatever reason my read on him before the flop had been incorrect, and he *had* a relatively weak hand like nines or tens, then he would now have outflopped me, and I would be drawing to two outs or even less. Also, the small blind led into the preflop raiser, so it was entirely possible that *he* had outflopped me as well! Another problem was the fact that there were almost no cards on the turn that I would really welcome, that would give me a true lock. There was only one 'good' queen in the deck (after all, the Q♦ would complete a flush that, considering the action, was almost certainly out there), and even the 'good' Q♥ would still create two possible straights. I also knew that if I were to call or raise now and small cards or relative blanks were to continue to fall, there was no way I could lay down my hand anymore, having invested this much money already. Also, I knew that if I called now, the flop bettor could easily reraise again, with the danger of the action getting capped – when I *still* would not know where I stood.

Now, while I was contemplating all this, the flop bettor on my left simply called the raise, and then the big blind called as well: they had not even noticed I was still in the hand, trying to figure out what to do. But these out-of-turn actions *did* give me the confirmation that I had the flop bettor beat for sure (I figured he probably held a ten for top pair) and probably all the other callers as well. Now, with all this money in the pot, and the small but distinct possibility that I actually had the current best hand, I decided that folding could very well be an awful mistake. I called, with the intention of letting the turn card and the subsequent action determine my best course of action.

The turn card was the 8♣, completing a possible straight *and* creating a second flush draw. It was checked to the preflop raiser who bet again. One player called, one player folded, and it was up to me.

I thought that it was highly likely now that the man in the wheelchair indeed had aces or kings – but I also knew that both he and other players in the game *did* fear me quite a bit. What's more, the turn card *did* present me with a semi-bluffing opportunity, and even if I wasn't able to get the preflop raiser to fold this overpair against my 'obvious' straight, then at least I could probably get him to slow down. This way, I could probably reach the showdown for just two big bets, which to me seemed like an acceptable price in a pot this big, and if I did actually improve on the river then I would almost certainly gain one or two additional bets. Also, I thought that if I made this move to raise on the turn, I could possibly get the lady in the big blind to check/reraise us and make it three bets, whether or not she had actually made her straight. I knew that it was probably a bit of a longshot, but during the times I had played with her, I had always been pretty good at manipulating her, and at luring her into making decisions that would actually favour me. And with this much action from no less than two opponents, the man in the wheelchair might then reason that his big pair just could not be any good – so I could maybe even win this huge pot with my unimproved queens. After some deliberation, I decided to go for it and use my strong image to represent the current nuts: queen-jack, a hand that I might very well hold in this position, and also a hand that would be consistent with both my preflop and postflop actions. When the small blind folded, I immediately looked for eye contact with the lady in the big blind. And she immediately responded as I hoped she would: by three-betting, something that did not necessarily mean or even indicate that she had my queens beat.

I hoped that the flop bettor would realize that after all this action there was no way that his aces or kings could be good anymore. But alas, after some thought he called the two extra bets – in a manner that indicated that he would reach the showdown, regardless of what the other players did or did not do. I cursed at myself for playing my hand this badly, and for having gotten myself in this situation. Because of the pot odds I had created myself, possibly with a hand that had been second-best to begin with, I was now even forced to call one more bet simply to try and catch a lucky river, knowing that a jack and possibly even a queen could still rescue me. I called, and when after a blank on the river it was bet/call, I knew that with this much money in the middle folding a possible winner would be an absolute disaster. So again I called, only to see all my reads confirmed: the lady having J-9 for a pair + open-ender, and the man in the wheelchair winning a massive pot with pocket kings.

Some final words

When the dealer pushed this massive pot to the opposite site of the table, I replayed this hand once more. I had put a bunch of bets into the pot, knowing from the very first moment that there was a good chance I was behind. And I had tried to make up for that later in the hand by trying to use my tight image to make a move, when I *knew* that the man in the wheelchair would not be a good enough player to lay down the hand that I thought he had.

All in all, I had invested two small bets before the flop, two small bets on the flop, and then three big bets on the turn and one more on the river, with a hand that had been in dire straits to begin with. In fact, I had played this hand like a total amateur, like a sucker who *knew* better but who didn't have the courage to act according to his convictions. The end result: I had lots 12 small bets in just one hand, and all the money went to some-one who at the river suddenly had no problem reading the board anymore. Despite his awful play throughout the hand, he had been rewarded by winning a massive pot, for no other reason than that he had found some-one who had played even worse than him – someone who had very well *known* and *felt* what to do, but was too stubborn to act according to these beliefs.

Compounding errors

When you read some of the works by Mr David Sklansky and Mr Mason Malmuth, you might come across the term 'compounding error'. Even though the authors explain the meaning of this term very well, a lot of people still don't seem to understand it (possibly because they have not read the books). My definition of compounding error would be: 'a mistake that may seem quite harmless at first glance, but may not be so harmless after all' or, better: 'a call early in the hand that may not seem that bad, but that will cause you to make mistakes on the later streets *because of that first call*'. In this article, I'll give an example of such a call, the implications on the later streets, and the thought processes that may, or may not, occur in-side the caller's head.

A compounding error in practice

One of the situations where a compounding error might take place is when you're in the big blind. Let's say you're in the big blind, holding 10-8 off-suit, and you get raised by the button. As there are two limpers as well, you decide not to fold and you call the raise. (For those of you who claim this hand should always be folded 'because it is trash', I refer to an older work by me on blind defence, where I advocate sometimes defending with small, rather than semi-big cards, if of course conditions are right. For more on this, please see my article *Defending the blinds in limit hold'em*). One of the main considerations whether or not do defend would be your esti-mation of your opponents' hands (especially the raiser's). You know that if the raiser has a big pair in the hole, you are in extremely bad shape with your 10-8. If you think the raiser *doesn't* need to have a premium hand, and *especially* if you think he doesn't need to have a big pair (or if you think you can outplay him after the flop; however, we will assume that this is not the case here), you would be more inclined to defend your blind. If you think the raiser and also the limpers are playing big cards rather than big pairs, then your hand has gotten some value in fact (because your hand is live, because you are playing cards opposed to theirs and because you know that when small cards flop you can put pressure on your opponents). This means that if you want to play well, you should defend only if you think that flopping a ten or eight with no bigger cards on the board will give you a reasonable chance to have the best hand.

The implication from all this is that if the flop comes 8-7-3 rainbow for example, and the limpers don't seem very interested in the pot, you are going to assume your hand is best at the moment, until proven otherwise. So you will try to find the best way to a) defend your top pair, b) make as much money as possible when your hand is good, and c) lose as little as possible when it's not. This might mean checking and calling (to give the raiser the chance to bluff off his money with his big or semi-big cards), checkraising (to get the limpers out and play the hand heads-up against the button) or simply betting out on the flop (to put pressure on the limpers and to represent more strength than you actually have). Either way, you are going to put a lot of bets in with your extremely vulnerable top pair/weak kicker, because you judge it unlikely the raiser has a big pair in the hole. Now, if the raiser is the type of player who *only* raises with big pairs (A-A, K-K, Q-Q) but just calls with hands like A-K, A-Q or K-Q, then your defending of the blind before the flop will be an expensive mistake, *because you will get into trouble on the later streets.*

The game: Hold'em $10-20
Your hand: 10-8o (big blind)
The other players: a button-raiser, holding a big pair in the hole, and two limpers, holding big cards
The flop: 8-7-3 rainbow
Pot size: $85

Your reasoning: Hey, I've got top pair, and there's $85 in the pot already. Most people would check to the raiser, but I've read Mr Sklansky's books and therefore I *know automatically checking to the raiser isn't good poker. I'm not sure if my hand is good right now, so I think I'm simply going to bet out to see what happens.* (Other possibilities would have been going for the checkraise, or the weak player's favourite, the check-call.)

The actions: You bet, the limpers call, the button raises.

Your reasoning: I might be beat, but then again the button might still be pushing his overcards here or maybe he's playing his position, going for the free card. However, I've got the limpers beat for sure. I cannot possibly fold. Even if the button has the big pair he's representing, I have five cards (three tens, two eights) that will improve my hand over his; there is $135 in the pot already and it costs me only $10 to call. (A very aggressive player might even reason: hey, I'll re-raise to push the limpers out, get some dead money in the pot and play the hand heads-up. Even when I'm behind, I cannot be *that far* behind.)

The actions: You call, one limper folds, the other calls.
Pot size: $155
The turn: 8-7-3-2 (no flushes possible)

Your reasoning: This deuce certainly hasn't helped my opponents. The button may have raised on the flop with just overcards or some sort of draw and therefore this deuce can be considered a 'good' card for me. The button might have been going for the free card, but I'm not going to let him have that. I'm going to bet into him again, just like Mr Sklansky suggests.

The actions: You bet, the limper folds – and now the button raises again!

Your reasoning: Damn! He must have me beat after all! He cannot be bluffing in this situation, can he? Or can he? How much is in the pot right now, let's see. There's $215 in the middle already, if I call it's $235 and I still have five outs if in fact the button has the hand he's representing. Five cards out of 44 give me an almost certain winner and it's only $20 extra. Hmm, with the pot this big, I simply have to call, I cannot possibly fold.

Pot size: $235
The river: 8-7-3-2-2
The actions: You check, the button bets again.

Your reasoning: I must be beat, it is extremely unlikely he is still betting his overcards here. But then again, he might have raised before the flop with 9-8s or 10-J maybe, and been semi-bluffing all the way. Or, maybe he is still betting his unimproved overcards. Either way, it costs me only $20 and there is $255 in the pot already. I don't have to be right a high percentage of the time to give this call a positive expectation. OK, so maybe it's a crying call, but I cannot risk folding the winner: I cannot possibly pass with the pot this big.

And then, of course, your opponent shows you the big pair he has been representing all along and you knew it, because he *always* has a big pair when he raises. Now, that's the essence of the compounding error. You know you've got the worst hand going in, then you receive a little help – though not enough to beat your opponent – and you convince yourself on every street that folding isn't the right thing to do, that the odds dictate you've got to take off another card, or that you've got to make that call. And maybe you're even right here, maybe it *is* right to make these calls – however, if you had simply folded your hand before the flop, you wouldn't have brought yourself in the situation that you're in right now: chasing with the worst hand.

Some final words

A couple of other situations where compounding errors are likely, are when you're calling a raise with inadequate values, a problem hand, or a hand that is likely to be dominated, or when you're always completing your small blind 'because it's only half a bet anyway'. If you analyse your play very well, you will probably find that you lose the most money in situations you shouldn't even have been in, had you just done the right thing before the flop (folding your hand). Be careful with all 'automatic', 'it's-only-so-and-so-much-more'-calls early in the hand: they will tend to get you into problems on the later streets, when the real money is at stake.

Hold'em:
No-Limit vs. Limit

Part 1: Preflop play and starting hands in no-limit

Not too long ago, if you wanted to become a successful cash game player, your choice was restricted to limit games only. In the US, pot- and no-limit live games were the exception rather than the rule, and if they *were* offered, they would usually be played only a) as side games at big tournaments, and b) for very high stakes. The aspiring young pro would usually have to settle for limit games only, the majority of the games being limit hold'em.

Actually, this was exactly the situation when I started out playing for a living. Even though quite a few Americans think that Europeans play pot- and no-limit poker almost exclusively, in my hometown Amsterdam and my second hometown Vienna almost all of the games were limit – at least for the stakes that I was willing to play at that time.

Now that the World Poker Tour and other televised events have contributed to an unexpected and unparalleled no-limit hold'em explosion, even young and aspiring cash game pros don't automatically have to settle for limit hold'em games anymore. Most American casinos nowadays offer a wide variety of no-limit hold'em games, even for relatively small stakes. And on the Internet, there is actually a whole bunch of young players who play no-limit hold'em almost exclusively. Now, if you come from a limit hold'em background (as is the case with some of the 'old-school' players like myself – and I never thought I would have to include myself in an old-school category of people), then it is far from easy to make the proper adjustments to the different mindset that is required for no-limit. Conversely, those who have started out playing no-limit hold'em may actually be faced with even more problems if they want to make a transition in order to become successful at limit too. They will have to gear down, and will have to learn that one single bet is a lot of money here – now, it should be clear that very few big-bet players are capable of doing this.

In this 14-part series of articles, I will focus on the way that limit and no-limit hold'em relate. To be more concrete, I will discuss some key aspects of limit and no-limit hold'em, the things people should take into account when making a transfer to either one of them. Here, I will begin by analysing things for people who, like me, come from a limit background and who now want to make a successful transition to no-limit. In the final three articles, I will analyse things for those who walk the opposite path. Note that I am specifically talking about cash game strategies, even though a lot of things *will* of course apply to tournaments as well.

All in all, in the first 11 articles on no-limit hold'em, I will analyse a few key aspects of the game, and show you guys how to use the specific characteristics of big-bet play to your advantage. As I said, the focus is on cash game strategies, and while most of it is directed at play in a 'real' casino, lots of things apply to online play as well. In fact, in those cases where online play requires a different approach, I will mention this specifically. One thing to keep in mind is that Internet games often have *shallow money*, whereas brick and mortar games more often have *deep money*. I will discuss this issue in depth later, but please keep in mind that this factor alone makes online play quite different from 'old-school' big-bet games where people could buy in for as much as they wanted.

Anyway, let's begin with one of the first key aspects of no-limit hold'em – one that continues to cause even experienced players some serious problems:

Your hand selection is different

While limit hold'em is considered a big-card game where offsuit big cards like A-K/A-Q/A-J/K-Q are a pro's bread-and-butter hands, in no-limit these hands can get you into an awful lot of trouble, both before and after the flop. In limit hold'em it would be a somewhat rare occurrence for you to lay down a hand as good as ace-queen before the flop, and while I know good limit hold'em players who have *never* folded ace-king in their entire lives, in no-limit hold'em you *will* occasionally have to lay down both these hands. When there is lots of aggressive action before the flop, your big cards may be in very bad shape, especially when the money is deep: When you put in your entire stack before the flop with ace-king and you get any kind of action, you are likely to be anywhere from a slight to a very big dog – despite your excellent holding. In no-limit hold'em, the biggest pots are often won when someone holds a small pair or small suited connectors, and is able to outflop someone who holds top pair/top kicker or an overpair to the board. This is especially true if the person holding the big cards/high pair is someone who cannot lay down a fairly good hand after the flop even when the action suggests that he must be beat. All of this means that:

- ♠ High pairs and suited big cards are very valuable in both limit and no-limit hold'em.

♠ Suited connectors and small pairs may under some circumstances be actually *more* valuable in no-limit than in limit.

♠ Offsuit big cards (A-K) and especially offsuit semi-big cards (A-Q, A-J, K-Q) are not always as good as they seem in no-limit, and actually may get you into a world of trouble a lot more often than you would think. Again, this is especially the case in deep-money games where there's enough room to try to outmanoeuvre your opponents.

On the Internet – where as we said the money is often much more shallow – your no-limit hand selection will be more in line with your normal limit hold'em requirements, meaning that the offsuit big cards are still very valuable, and that small pairs and especially suited connectors should be played under the right circumstances only – circumstances that come up a lot less frequently than in the deep-money play discussed above. This is especially true in the highly popular 6-max games, where especially small pairs can cause even good players a lot of trouble, and where the typical 'problem hands' for full ring games (A-10, K-J, K-Q) can actually be played rather strongly.

Of course, this is not all there is to it. A large part of playing successful no-limit hold'em is taking advantage of specific weaknesses in your opponents. This means that much more than in limit, you may choose to call or even raise with relatively weak hands against some weak players, while throwing away much better hands against people who play at a very high level, people that you know you just can't outplay. This concept of 'outplaying your opponents' is much more of a factor in big-bet play. What logically follows from this, is that accepted opening hand requirements, lists of starting hands that you can play for a profit in certain positions, that these opening requirements just don't apply to the same degree in no-limit. There are just too many factors that may make a situation profitable or unprofitable, apart from the actual strength of the cards. Two of the most important ones are the calibre of the opposition and the depth of the money, but there are many more, and this makes it hard to come up with cut and dried formulas when it comes to no-limit hold'em.

Another very important factor in no-limit hold'em is your position. In big-bet poker it is often correct to enter a pot with a rather marginal hand if you are last to act, and your opponent has to act in front of you on all streets. So, while in limit poker it is accepted and also correct strategy to play very tight, very solid up front, and then loosen up quite a bit the closer you get to the button, this is even truer in no-limit. Especially when the money is deep, you should avoid playing marginal hands out of position, and you should even more avoid playing marginal hands out of position *against strong players*. In part 2 of this series, I will give you a few specific examples of starting hands, and you may be surprised about the number of hands that I consider to be 'marginal' in this respect.

Rolf's Rule No. 1

One of the most expensive mistakes in no-limit hold'em is playing marginal hands out of position. In fact, I consider a lot more hands to be 'marginal' than most players seem to be doing.

Part 2: Preflop play and starting hands in no-limit – some hand examples

The starting hand J♠-10♠: Analysis

In early position:

Is this a playable hand in early position? Well in general, in a full-ring game: no. If you flop top pair with this hand and the pot gets big, then you are almost certainly in trouble. Your aim with this hand is obviously to flop a good draw. But the problem here is that the other players will usually have position on you. This could get you into a lot of trouble when you don't hit your draw on the turn, but to a lesser degree also when you *do* hit your draw. Your best option when flopping a good draw is often to just checkraise all-in for all your money, so that if you get called you will at least have two shots at making your draw. This moves somewhat compensates for your positional disadvantage; however, it is by no means an optimum play. Usually, when making this type of power play, you will win a small pot very often, but when you get called you will probably be facing a good made hand or even a better draw.

In late position:

If the people in front of you have just called, well then obviously you have an easy call as well. In fact, I recommend that in late position you often raise with other hands than just big pairs and premium high cards. Suited connectors like J-10 all the way down to 6-5 or even 5-4 suited are excellent for making this play every once in a while.

However, you should always take a close look at who the limpers are. If there are players who are relatively short-stacked and who in your view may well be planning to limp-reraise all-in, well then of course you should *not* raise, as you may very well be raising yourself out of the pot. Example: Say that with your jack-ten of spades on the button, you have two limpers in front of you. Assuming blinds of $10 and $20, two people have thus called the $20. Now, let's assume that one of these limpers is a top pro with a $360 stack. While normally, you would have made a raise to about $80 or so, in this case you should simply call. Because if you raise, the pro will definitely see that you are on the button, meaning that in his opinion you could very well be raising with a wide range of hands. If he has limped with a big pair, ace-king, ace-queen or even an ace-jack suited, he will almost certainly put you to the test now and move all-in. Your only options then will be to call with a hand that is a clear dog, or to throw away your hand after having invested eighty bucks. Either way, you will have turned a potentially profitable situation into a highly unprofitable one. So, pay attention to who is in the pot before making your 'automatic' position play.

Now, if the pot has been raised in front of you and both you and the raiser have quite a bit of money left, then there is nothing wrong with calling the raise to take a flop. After all, being in position with a decent hand, you could get lucky by catching a good flop, and also you have the possibility to represent a wide range of hands, especially the kinds of hands that the preflop raiser is unlikely to hold. However, you should be aware that you are playing cards that are probably in the same range of those that the raiser holds, with the difference that yours are probably just a little lower. This means that you should proceed with caution when you flop something like top pair and the initial raiser still seems very interested in the pot, as you may very well face something like top pair/top kicker or even an overpair. You should know that your main reason for calling before the flop is *not* just that you have a decent hand. The main reason would be that you have position, and that after the flop you could represent a wide range of hands, possibly causing your opponent to make lots of mistakes. So, you would be more inclined to call the preflop raise if you have labelled the raiser as a weak or predictable player who can easily be outplayed. If you have labelled this person as a top pro, there is nothing wrong with throwing away your cards – despite your decent holding, and despite your good position.

Rolf's Rule No. 2

In big-bet poker, you always take into account who you are up against. Against people who can easily be outplayed after the flop, you should be willing to get involved quite often – even without great or even good hands. This is especially true when the money is deep, and you have position.

The starting hand 8♠-8♣: Analysis

In early position:

Most of the time, this is a clearly playable hand. What you are trying to do with this hand is make middle set. If you can get to the flop for no more than, say, 6 or 7 percent of your stack, then there is nothing wrong with first limping and then paying off a decent raise with this holding. All pocket pairs have a lot of value in no-limit because if you hit your set, the payoff can be enormous. What you are really hoping is to be up against someone who has flopped top pair/top kicker or an overpair to the board. Actually, this is one of the classic 'doubling through' situations in no-limit. Depending on the depth of the money, you would either go for the check-raise on the flop, or if the money is quite deep, it may be best to bet into him, so that he will raise and that you can come over the top – or maybe flat call and then wait for the turn to make your move. You do whatever you can to make him committed in this situation now that your hand is so good that you don't have to worry about protecting yourself against an outdraw. You want to get your opponent into a situation where he thinks: 'I am in too deep now – there is no way back for me anymore.'

Either way, it should be clear that with this type of holding in early position, you want to reach the flop. Your goal is *not* to raise to steal the blinds or to get the others out: Your goal is to reach the flop and break someone who has flopped a good, but second-best hand.

In late position:

If I say that this hand is usually playable in early position, then it should be clear that it is usually playable in late position as well. One word of caution though. You should not become overly aggressive with this type of holding just because you have good position. You should realize that the main strength of these small and medium pocket pairs in no-limit is to flop a set and break someone who has a good, but second-best holding. That is: You want to see a flop with this hand. What you *don't* want is to raise so much that you are opening yourself up for a reraise that you can't call. What's more: You don't want to raise big and then fold what may very well be the current best hand – after all, a big reraise could just as well be from an ace-king or even a total bluff as well as from a higher pair. So, I would basically give the same advice here as with the jack-ten from before. Yeah, sure you can be a bit more aggressive now that you have good position, but beware of the people who (as I often do) will try to make up for their positional disadvantage by trying to limp-reraise people who are a bit too aggressive on the button. And 8-8 is *not* a hand that you want to play against a big reraise. Usually, you will be either a tiny favourite (when you are up against two overcards) or about a 4-to-1 dog (when you are up against a higher pair).

One more thing: When you call a raise with a pair of eights, your main goal is to flop a set. When small cards flop and the preflop raiser continues to bet big, don't value your own overpair too highly. In other words: Don't *automatically* think that he is just pushing overcards. While he *may* be doing this, he may also hold a bigger pair for example. So, pay attention to your opponents betting patterns, so that you can get him to bluff off his money with unimproved overcards, while at the same time avoid losing your entire stack when your opponent *does* have the goods.

Rolf's Rule No. 3:

While it is usually correct to play more hands in late position and to become more aggressive with them, you should avoid raising yourself out of the pot. While this may not be so bad if you were just making a move with a trash hand, it is bad if you have a hand that you would have loved to see a flop with: hands like suited connectors and small or medium pairs.

The starting hand A♠-K♣: Analysis

This hand has been discussed so often that I have nothing much to add to what has already been said. Ace-king is an excellent hand in no-limit of course, but you should be aware that its main strength is its bullying power before the flop. It can actually become a very expensive hand if you allow others to get into the pot cheaply and let them catch a great flop while you get a merely good one. So, this is a hand that you want to play rather aggressively before the flop, in order to clear the field and so that you know who is playing what. And unless you are up against aces and kings (not very likely, considering you've got one of each) you are usually in pretty good shape, even if by chance all the money goes in before the flop – sometimes even in *very* good shape if someone stubbornly holds onto an ace-queen or so. One of the main strengths of moving in with ace-king is the fact that you can put so much pressure on the small and medium pocket pairs, the hands that, hot and cold, are actually a slight favourite over your ace-king. But against a large enough raise, you should usually be able to get them out, because now *they* may fear that you actually have a bigger pair than they do, and thus they are either about even money – or a *very* big dog. All of this means that your ace-king is a very strong holding when you can play the hand aggressively, and the money is not too deep. It is even stronger when there are people in the game who call huge raises with hands that are clearly dominated. However, when playing a very deep stack, the ace-king is not nearly as strong, and can actually get you into a whole lot of trouble. This is especially true if you are up against good players who are actively trying to snap you off with speculative holdings. Against these players, you are likely to win many small pots, but when the pots grow big they are usually favoured to take your entire stack. So, if your preflop play is too predictable and people can easily label you with an ace-king type of holding, then the ace-king with deep money may actually be a mixed blessing for you. You will have to make sure that you are going to mix up your play a lot, both before and after the flop – or else the good players will take advantage of your predictability, bluffing you out when they know you have missed, and making you pay off when *they* have actually hit.

Rolf's Rule No. 4:

Ace-king is an excellent move-in hand in no-limit when the money is relatively shallow. With very deep money, this is a hand that may actually put you into a lot of trouble, especially after the flop, and especially if your overall play is rather predictable. When you have

flopped top pair/top kicker and very large stacks go in after the flop,
you could very well be in awful shape, putting your entire stack in
danger. On the other hand, if you are capable of releasing hands
this strong under certain circumstances, then good players will al-
most certainly try and take advantage of this. As a result, they may
occasionally bluff or semi-bluff you out of the pot, causing you to
fold the current best hand – an absolute catastrophe.

Please note that all comments above relate to full-ring games. But many
games nowadays are not full-ring; they are 6-max. In these games, all
hands mentioned in this article become raising, yes even reraising hands.
Especially when the money is deep and when I have good position, I will
happily reraise an open raiser with a J♠-10♠, and as the first one in, I will
also happily open-raise with this hand. Of course, the same goes for 8-8,
and it *definitely* goes for A-K. However, keep in mind the following:

♠ In 6-max games, relatively small pocket pairs can get you
   into a lot of trouble postflop, especially if there are one or two
   overcards to your pair and an opponent shows strength. But
   because people play very aggressively in 6-max games, you
   cannot always fold these hands even if your opponent shows
   a lot of interest in the pot, for the simple reason that there's
   an awful lot of bluffing and semi-bluffing going on in short
   games. However, if you are wrong and your opponent *does*
   have you beat, you may be playing for just two outs, meaning that you may make an awful mistake if you decide to go
   with your hand.

♠ A hand like J♠-10♠, even though I *will* often play it aggressively in 6-max games, can still cause you a bit of problems
   postflop – especially if you flop top pair. While in full-ring
   games, a preflop raise with a J-10 is usually enough to get rid
   of the 'problem hands' A-J, A-10, K-J, K-10 and Q-10, in 6-
   max games people will *not* lay down these hands easily to a
   raise. This means that if you flop a jack or ten, you could very
   well be in kicker trouble, and lose a big pot – especially because in aggressive, shorthanded games, it is awfully hard to
   lay down a hand as good as top pair/decent kicker.

Part 3: Preflop play and starting hands in no-limit – the size of your raise

The size of your raise can make a tremendous difference.

A lot of poker authorities recommend that in big-bet poker, your raises should usually be about the same size. Say, if the big blind is $20, you would usually raise to about $60 to $80 or so, and with one or two limpers in the middle, to about $100 or $120. All of this would be like pot-sized raises. The reasoning: You show your opponents that you are serious about trying to win this pot and you make it expensive for them to come in, yet you don't invest so much that you cannot get away from your hand anymore once someone comes over the top. And by always making the same size raises, you avoid giving away information about your hand, and it will be hard for your opponents to get a read on you, to see if you have a 'real' hand like K♠-K♣ or are simply making a play with the 10♥-9♥.

While this advice is good in itself, one should know that it is usually directed at tournament play. In cash games, I actually violate these rules habitually. I will often make raises that according to some people are totally useless. I will make minimum bets from time to time that for those who don't look carefully seem to serve no purpose whatsoever, and before the flop I will sometimes just double the blinds instead of making a serious play for the pot. And I also adjust the size of my raise to the atmosphere at the table, the size of my opponents' stacks, on the read that my opponents will have on me, and the hands they figure me for when I choose to make either a very small or a very large raise. In other words: I will use these strange bets and raises to get inside their heads, to gain a lot of information at minimal cost, and to lure them into making exactly those decisions that I want them to make.

An example. In a deep-money game, I will not hesitate to make three or four consecutive minimum raises with speculative hands like A♥-4♥, J♠-9♠ and 4♣-4♦. Now, of course when I get re-popped, I am out, as I am not going to stand a reraise with hands this weak, and certainly not out of position. But what it does, is to show my opponents that I am trying to run over the table. In fact, I am actually trying to irritate them a little with my small raises. Invariably, someone will find an ace-queen type of holding and come over the top, because they are 'fed up' with my raises. And when I have a big pair/ace-king type of holding *then*, all of my money will go in as a huge favourite, and there is no way back for them anymore. So, what I am trying to do with these small bets and raises, is setting up the situation where I can get all the money in as a huge favourite. Now, people always call this lucky when I get myself in these kinds of positions, but it has nothing to do with luck. It has to do with setting up a situation, and with working towards a climax. Now, this is extremely important in big-bet play. Yet, the people who consistently follow the 'book' advice of standards bets and raises fail to see that in cash games you don't just have to play your own hand well. Just as importantly, you have to play in such a manner that you give your opponents maximum room for making mistakes. You want them to fall into the traps you have set, because that is exactly what big-bet cash games are about: trapping your opponents into making the wrong decisions – especially when the real money is at stake.

So, what is this strategy of mine all about – what is it exactly that I am doing? Well, what I often do is come in for a small raise as the first one in. In fact, I almost *always* come in for a small raise as the first one in; I hardly ever come in flat. This is especially true when I am playing a medium-sized stack, say anywhere from 40 to 50 times the big blind. With a small stack, say less than 20 times the big blind, I often go for the limp-reraise with my good hands, while folding all the mediocre ones. And with a big stack, say over 80 times the big blind, I usually come in for a decent raise whenever I choose to play. The reasoning behind this is almost always the same. In big-bet poker, you usually want to play for your entire stack. So, you should base your preflop raise for a large part on the size of your stack, so that after the flop you will be in good position to get things all-in in two or three betting increments (say, by betting out, getting raised and then moving all-in, or by checkraising all-in if the money is not that deep). Either way, what you do with your preflop raises is to make sure that either you have lots of opponents for little money, or very few opponents for lots of money. What you *don't* want is being up against two or three opponents for, say, 10 or 15% of your stack when they actually have a very good clue about the type of hand you are holding. That's why you want to keep them guessing – and making lots of small, seemingly random raises is an excellent way to keep them off-balance. This way, you willingly take the worst of it in a few small pots, in order to put your opponents in the state of mind where they will make mistakes when the real money is at stake. By the way, this has not all that much to do with the 'wild image' that Mike Caro introduced long time ago. For me, it is about creating a dangerous and somewhat erratic image, so that just when your opponents think they got you labelled, you surprise them by taking their entire stack because of this trap that you have been preparing all along.

So, while I often employ a small bets and raises type of strategy, it is usually unwise to make these small raises when you are in position (say on the button) or in the big blind. This is because you are reopening the betting, and you may actually invite one of your opponents to take a shot at you and try to raise you out of the pot. Again, this is not so bad when you are just making a positional play or are simply setting a trap for future hands, but it *is* bad when you have a hand that you would like to see the flop with. If you make a little raise in that situation and one of the initial limpers comes over the top, you will have wasted a potentially profitable situation.

Anyway, what I have described here is how *I* usually play. I have created an overall balanced strategy that suits both my image and my personality well, and that allows me to take control over the table. But it is by no means the *only* successful style in no-limit. What I would recommend is that you experiment a little with what you think you can get away with. In general, there is nothing wrong with starting out with the decent, ABC, 'uniform raises' type of approach, and of course I recommend having fairly tight starting requirements in *any* game. However, always be aware that no-limit hold'em is a game where you want to keep your opponents off-balance. If you think you can accomplish this by the standard-raises strategy, because you can sometimes play a bad hand like a great one, and a good one like a merely decent one, then there is nothing wrong with that. Just make sure you don't allow your opponents to get a good read on you. Because if you do, the edge that you used to have will be gone *immediately*. And even if you usually play the correct hands, and play them in the correct manner, you simply won't stand a chance against any kind of thinking players – they will take advantage of your predictability, and will truly *devastate* you.

Rolf's Rule No. 5

In big-bet poker, it is often best to adjust both the size of your raises and your actual plays to the atmosphere at the table and, most importantly, the tendencies of your opponents. It isn't 'one size fits all'. Quite the contrary: It is those specific adjustments that you make to lure your opponents into making mistakes that will help you crush the games.

Part 4: Differences and adjustments – the danger of 'automatic' calls in no-limit

In the first three articles in this series, I provided you with some concrete and sometimes controversial advice on preflop play in no-limit. I talked about specific starting hands, and analysed their strengths and weaknesses with regards to their position in the betting. I also took a closer look at proper betting and raising strategy, and the reasoning behind this.

Here, I will focus on some more key aspects of no-limit hold'em that may cause serious trouble for those of you who, like me, come from a limit hold'em background. So, without further ado, I will simply start my analysis here, discussing the different calling requirements for big-bet play.

Learn to avoid the calls that are sometimes 'automatic' in limit

If in limit hold'em you call one small bet before the flop and it gets raised behind you, it is almost always correct to call that one more bet, even if you hold what is considered to be a 'problem hand', two semi-big offsuit cards that *look* good, but that may actually be dominated by the preflop raiser's hand. There are two main reasons why you should avoid making these calls in no-limit:

Reason 1 to avoid 'automatic' calls

You are probably getting much worse odds to call that raise in no-limit than in limit. While in limit, you would probably have to call one more small bet in a total pot that contains six, eight or even ten small bets, in no-limit you may have to call an additional four or five small bets in an only slightly bigger pot. Because in limit you are often getting such a good price, calling the raise is usually the proper strategy, but in no-limit you may not be getting the correct price to call. This is especially true because you will be out of position for the rest of the hand, which means that a) you may not be maximizing your profits in case you flop a good hand because your opponent always has the advantage of acting after you, and b) you may now lose a lot more money with a second-best hand than your opponent would lose if he were to end up with a second-best hand. In fact, in no-limit someone may actually outplay you because of his position alone, because he is able to use the information that you have given to his advantage in order to make the best possible decision – for instance, to bluff you out when your body language and/or your betting decisions in the hand suggest that you may be weak. All in all, big-bet poker puts an even bigger premium on position than limit does, which means you should at all times try to avoid being out of position with only a marginal hand – especially when you are up against a good or experienced player who knows how to take advantage of his position and the information you have given him.

Rolf's Rule No. 6

Playing a good hand out of position against a mediocre player is usually a dicey proposition at best. Playing a mediocre hand out of position against a good player is plain suicide.

Reason 2 to avoid 'automatic' calls

The cost of being wrong is much more expensive in no-limit than in limit. Let's say that in limit hold'em you do the obvious, calling that one more bet with your problem hand, and now you flop top pair. If your opponent indeed has top pair with a better kicker or even an overpair to the board, then you are probably going to lose some six to eight small bets if you cannot release your hand at any stage. But the final pot will probably be anywhere from 18 to 30 small bets, meaning your loss is actually not that huge in relation to the total size of the pot. What's more, you may get lucky at one stage in the hand (for example, by hitting your kicker on the turn or on the river), so that you may actually win the pot or split it – despite having started with the worse hand. In no-limit, you may well lose your entire stack in the process. This means that the cost of being wrong is much more serious, much more severe than in limit – and conversely, the premium on being right is also much higher. This is especially true if you are playing in a 'deep-money' game, where people have fairly large stacks in relation to the blinds. Online, games are often played with relatively shallow money, where after just one or two raises people will be all-in, meaning that the implied odds/negative implied odds thing discussed above is a bit less of an issue here than in brick and mortar casinos. In B&M casinos, the maximum buy-in is often a little higher than on the Internet, and quite a few B&M casinos don't have a cap on the buy-in at all. Now, in cases like this, the things discussed above are of paramount importance, and those who do not take them into account, will probably find that not only will they have trouble beating the games – but rather that, in all but the very softest games, they will get creamed.

I will illustrate this with an example. Let's take the following match-up: A♠-A♣ versus K♥-J♥ on a flop K♦-8♣-4♦ – in other words, top pair versus an overpair. *CardPlayer's* 'Texas Hold'em Calculator' shows that the aces as a very clear favourite to win: 81.6%-18.4%. Now, when in limit poker you go all the way to the river with your top pair, and will have to invest something like three more big bets in a total pot of about ten big bets to reach the showdown, then you just lose just a little bit of money on average, simply because the pot odds you are getting are only slightly worse than your actual drawing odds. But in no-limit poker, it may well cost you something like 45 more big bets to reach the river – in a total pot of about 100 big bets. Now, knowing that your expected return of this 100 big bet pot is just 18.4 big bets, you are actually losing no less than 26.6 big bets on this hand!

So again, if in no-limit you are wrong, you are often very wrong, and if you are right, you are often very right. This is even more so because in no-limit hold'em big pots are often contested heads-up, unlike limit hold'em that has quite a few three- or four-way pots. Now, in combination with the limited size of the bet in limit compared to the total size of the pot, this means that even with hands that are clearly trailing, the odds are often there to call in limit – but not in no-limit. In no-limit, a decent hand like top pair can easily bust you for all your money, while in limit you may actually get the proper odds to take this hand to the river. It is important to take this into account. Those who come from a limit background and make the automatic play of going all the way to the river with top pair even when one or two opponents have shown tremendous strength, these players will have to adjust and change their mindsets very quickly if they want to become successful in no-limit.

Rolf's Rule No. 7

No-limit hold'em puts a premium on being right, and will punish you severely for every time that you are wrong. Because the odds are not there as in limit, the people who often take a bit the worst of it, will now take way *the worst of it.*

Part 5: Differences and adjustments – premium on aggression and deception

Know that big-bet play puts a premium on aggression and deception – much more than limit play.

While in limit hold'em a somewhat unimaginative, but tight and disciplined player is often able to beat the games for a decent amount (especially if he pays considerable attention to things like table selection and game selection, in order to play with the best possible edge), this is much harder in no-limit hold'em, especially in no-limit hold'em games with deep money. In games like this, aggression and deception are often the key to winning – especially *selective* aggression and deception. Those who play in predictable patterns and who may have a somewhat weak/tight style of poker may not be real *big* winners in limit, but they will still be able to make at least *some* money. In no-limit hold'em, they won't stand a chance – unless of course they are smart enough to be playing against truly weak opposition only, against people who don't recognize or simply don't pay attention to their obvious betting patterns, and who let them get away with it.

I will analyse this with an example. If in *limit* hold'em an unimaginative player only raises with big pairs and ace-king, his results will suffer – more than anything because reasonably good players will simply stop giving him action once he raises. But now let's say that this player has one specific weakness: he can't get rid of these good hands on the later streets, even when it is clear that his hand just cannot be good anymore. Will this one specific weakness that this player has make it correct for the others to sometimes call with some speculative hands, in order to take advantage of this? Well, the answer is: in limit no, in limit it is usually *not* worth it, for the following reasons:

- ♠ The cost of entering the pot is fairly high. While it is sometimes correct to call a raise with a 7♦-5♦ from the big blind against this type of player (because it is just one more small bet), calling the raise cold with this hand is usually just too expensive.

- ♠ The odds make it sometimes correct to call more bets once the flop gives you a pair or a gutshot, even when you know or suspect that the raiser has a big hand. Thus, you will usually lose some additional money even when it seems likely that you are trailing.

♠ You will miss the flop too often. If you are playing a longshot hand, you want the initial costs to be low, with a very high potential reward. But here, the initial costs are high, and the potential reward is only moderate.

Now, compare this to *no-limit*. Here, the rewards can actually be enormous: you could take the predictable player's entire stack! Also, if this player does what a lot of weak no-limit players do (make one more bet on the flop with an unimproved ace-king, to then shut down on the turn), then calling this preflop raise of his will actually be a highly profitable situation for you. All in all, in no-limit calling a raise in position with a speculative holding is correct, even when you know you are up against a very good hand, under the following circumstances:

♠ The money is relatively deep.

♠ Either the raiser is someone who can easily be bet off an unimproved ace-king, as we saw most likely on the turn, or…

♠ The raiser is someone who just can't lay down his good starting hand after the flop – even when it is clear that his hand just cannot be good.

So, what you are doing in this case is not playing according the strength of your own hand, but rather you are *playing the player*. Let's take our example hand 7♠-5♥, and see how playing this hand works in practice against the predictable player described above. (By the way please don't ever make these kinds of plays against either very good, very aggressive or very tricky players!) Anyway, with blinds of $10 and $20 this player makes it $60 to go from middle position. Since you and the preflop raiser both have a $1500 stack, you decide to call the raise, knowing that almost certainly you are up against a big pair or two high cards. The flop now comes 10♥-8♠-2♦, giving you absolutely nothing: no pair and no draw. The raiser comes out betting for a normal-sized bet, something in the range $90-$120.

So, now you fold, because you have absolutely nothing – right? Well, not really. Against this player, it may well be worth it to call a pot-sized bet on the flop, *if you know that because of his predictable play on the turn you will al-*

most always have an easy decision here. Let's say the 9♠ comes on the turn and now your opponent checks. Now, if your read on this player is good enough to label him with an unimproved ace-king, and if you know that he is the type of player who will *not* stubbornly hold onto this ace-king, then you know that you can easily take the pot away from him with a standard bet. You know that this player will reason: 'Hey, he called my bet on the flop, so he either has me beat already with a pair, or he has a straight draw. In all cases, my ace-king has been outdrawn now, and it is extremely unlikely that I can make him fold his hand if I make an aggressive move. So, now is the time to simply throw away my ace-king.' And when he does, you have succeeded in taking yet another pot, almost irrespective of the actual cards that you had.

One thing, though. Remember that I said 'Never make this type of play against either very good, very aggressive or very tricky players'? Well, in all cases the reasons are the same: With these players, a check does *not* automatically mean 'I have nothing, I am prepared to give up.' Aggressive players may actively have been trying for a checkraise in this situation with something like J-J or Q-Q for an overpair + straight draw, hands that they are willing to play for their entire stack. And with a deceptive player, a check can actually be more dangerous than a bet, simply because these people just love to be tricky. Also, with players of this kind, a preflop raise does not automatically mean 'big pair or high cards', as they will often raise with a very wide range of hands – and this makes it much harder for you to get a good read on them. So, against these players you should not actively search for trapping situations with marginal hands – because in the end, *you* may be the one who gets trapped.

Anyway, what these examples show is that both aggression and deception are of major importance in no-limit. And at the same time, being predictable is probably the biggest no-no of all. Unless they are playing against extremely weak players, or in games with very shallow money, then predictable players simply stand no chance in no-limit.

Rolf's Rule No. 8

In big-bet poker, even more than in limit play, you should always try to keep your opponents off-balance. If you play in predictable patterns, your opponents will certainly start taking advantage of this. This means you can never be more than just a marginal winner in the relatively weak games, and you will never be able to beat the really tough ones.

Part 6: Differences and adjustments – about bluffing

Know that the bluff has a much higher chance of success in no-limit than in limit, but keep in mind that the costs of failure are also much higher.

When people talk about no-limit hold'em as opposed to limit, you will always hear them say the same things: 'It is much easier to protect your hand here.' 'You cannot bluff in limit, but you *can* in no-limit.' Both of these statements are only partially true in my opinion. Yes, it *is* easier to protect your hand when you can choose to bet any amount that you wish, but you should be aware that protecting your hand is not always your main objective in poker. Often, your goal should be to maximize your wins on a hand and at the same time try to minimize your losses. Now, those who focus on this 'protect your hand' thing too much, forget that rather frequently it is actually *great* to have four or five people calling you – especially when you either have a very strong made hand, or when you have a premium draw where you've got lots of nut outs. The same holds true for this other adage, that you cannot bluff in limit poker, but you can in no-limit. Again, this is only a small part of the truth. Yes, it is much harder to bluff in limit, but one should never forget that in the few cases where you actually succeed in making the better hands fold, the reward will be enormous. If you are able to steal an entire pot while putting just one flat bet at risk for it, then it should be clear that from a risk/reward point of view your bluff does not have to succeed very often to still make a significant overall profit. And yes, in no-limit you may indeed be able to bet your opponents off even fairly decent hands simply because of the size of your bet (an option you don't have in limit), but the downside is that when for whatever reason this bluff of yours fails, you may have lost a whole lot of money this way.

What's important is that you should correctly analyse (in *both* betting structures) the chances of getting away with a bluff as opposed to the costs. In addition to this, you should try to find the optimum betting strategy when going for a bluff in no-limit, taking into account the texture of the board, the tendencies of your opponents, and also your own image. In some cases, against certain boards, and against certain types of opponents, a small bet in no-limit may have just as much chance of successfully stealing a pot as a large bet does. You will have to find the situations where this may be the case, in order to minimize your losses because of your failed (semi-) bluff attempts, and to maximize your long-term expectation in the game because of these bluffs of yours that *have* been successful.

Let's analyse a few examples. Let's say you have raised preflop, and now the flop comes Q-Q-A. If you are heads-up, a bet of about half the pot, and probably a bit less, may be just as successful and just as scary as a full pot bet. So, when trying to pull off a bluff, it may actually be better to come out betting with a bet that seems to imply 'please call me' than a big bet that shows a lot of fear – a bet that good players may find 'suspicious'.

Another example. You have called a decent raise before the flop against what very much looks like a big pair. I will leave your exact hand for what it is, because it is not exactly relevant in this example. Let's say the flop comes J♥-9♥-3♠, your opponent has bet the pot and you have called. The turn comes a very scary-looking 10♥ and your opponent now makes a fairly small bet that you have analysed as a *feeler bet* but could also be the ace-high flush, for example. In this case, just doubling his bet may be your best option rather than making a large raise – assuming that you don't have much, really. If your opponent's bet *was* indeed a feeler bet, you know he is not going to call you, especially because you are making a bet that seems to be *wanting* a call, a bet that shows a whole lot of strength. At the same time, if you raise big, you will probably just get called when you are beat. So, this is a situation where you can go for a 'cheap' bluff or semi-bluff, because the texture of the board makes these kinds of bets look very *strong* rather than weak. If you raise big, you will now get called only when you are beat, and the likelihood of pulling off that bluff has not increased a lot because of this much bigger bet of yours.

Now please note that this is the kind of play that will often work against *good* players, against *thinking* players. With all the experience they have, they usually expect people who hold monster hands to try to 'sell' their hand. They have a tendency to give you credit for what you are representing when it seems you are 'milking' them. At the same time, they tend to become deeply suspicious when someone comes out with a huge overbet in an either/or situation, where either you have the hand you represent or you don't – and if you do, you almost hold a certain winner. The boards that present these kinds of either/or situations are paired boards (especially paired boards with two aces on it), boards that scream for a slowplay, or boards with three or four of a suit, where if you really got what you are representing, your opponents won't have a chance.

But these plays *won't* work well against weak players. Weak players often fail to see the strength that these minimum bets and raises represent in the situation here. Or, maybe they just don't have the guts to fold a decent hand now that calling seems so 'cheap' to them. Against these kinds of players, you will have to do the obvious: bet or raise big when you want them out, and bet or raise small when you want to keep them in. But against good players, you often use reverse psychology. You can some-times pull off a bluff against good players by making a *small* bet, and at the same time you can often get them to pay you off when you have the nuts, just because your massive overbet looked suspicious to them.

So, always know who you are up against. Try to figure out how *they* are thinking, and then use this knowledge to your advantage by luring them into making mistakes – either by making them pay off when they should have folded, or by making them fold when they should have called.

Rolf's Rule No. 9

A lot of poker authorities say that it is easier to bluff a good player than it is to bluff a weak player. They are only partially right. The best players to bluff are the ones who think *their reads are good, but who instead don't think on a deep enough level about the im-plications of the board, and about how you* would *have played the hand if you really had what you are representing.*

Part 7: Differences and adjustments – positional considerations

Positional considerations are much more important in no-limit than in limit – not just your position relative to the button, but also your position on the pre-flop raiser.

We have talked about the importance of position before, meaning that I will keep this analysis fairly short. There is one *very* important thing though that I have not mentioned yet – something that is actually ne-glected quite often when it comes to proper analysis. When people talk about position, they almost always think in terms of their position relative to the button. In big-bet play, there is another factor that is sometimes even *more* important than this one though. It is *your position on the preflop raiser*. I will give two examples that clearly show how this factor alone can make some rather weak hands profitable, and some fairly decent hands unprofitable. The keys are of course, as so often in big-bet play, implied odds and reverse implied odds.

Example No. 1

Your hand:

9♣-8♣ on the button

The situation:

One UTG limper for $20. Now the cutoff makes it $70 to go. We will assume everyone is playing a $900 stack. What do you do?

The play:

Well, you are on the button, what is conceived to be the best possible position – yes that's true. You have a decent no-limit hold'em hand, and yes, you may even have a good snap-off hand against the big cards that the raiser probably holds, meaning that your cards are probably very live. And there is also quite a bit of money left to be bet, and taking into account your position your implied odds seem to be quite good. Right?

Wrong! This is one of the clearest folds you will ever see in no-limit. While your position *seems* to be good, it is actually quite horrible. In the first place, your call doesn't close the betting. If either one of the blinds wakes up with a real hand, or if the initial limper decides to come over the top, you will have wasted almost 8% of your stack without even getting to see a flop. What's more: Even if the 'normal' thing happens (both blinds folding and the initial limper calling the raise), then your position is still not as good as it seems. Knowing that in three-handed no-limit pots preflop raisers will almost without exception bet the flop, whether they have hit or not, the limper will almost certainly check to the raiser on the flop to let him do the betting. Now, this means that the limper's check on the flop will give you no information whatsoever. Because he may very well be bagging a good hand, he now has you caught in the middle. You will be sandwiched between a bettor who may or may not have a good hand, and a third player who may very well be lying in the bushes with a monster. This means that the preflop raiser is now *betting through you*. And because you cannot be sure about the price you are getting on a call and the relative strength of your hand in this three-way situation, you are in an extremely bad spot. The way to avoid this predicament is by simply folding your decent hand before the flop, rather than call and get yourself into a whole lot of trouble.

Example No. 2

Your hand:

The same hand, this time unsuited: 9♠-8♣. This time you are in the $20 big blind.

The situation:

The UTG player makes it $70 to go. The cutoff calls, and it is up to you. As before, everyone is playing a $900 stack. What do you do?

The play:

Well, it seems you are in even worse shape than in the previous situation. After all, being first to speak on all streets, you have the worst possible position. Also, your hand is not even suited now, and the raise comes from under-the-gun, and this is usually a sign of considerable strength. So, if the first situation is a clear fold, then this will *definitely* be one – right?

Wrong! Your position *seems* to be bad, but it is actually quite good. You are now the one who is in the good position to simply check every flop, to let the preflop raiser do the betting for you, and thereby putting the cutoff in the middle. You are now in an excellent position to both minimize your losses when the flop is bad or the action behind you suggests that bigger hands are out there, and also to maximize your wins for the times that you have actually caught something. With $830 left, if you check, the preflop raiser will probably bet anywhere in the range from $100 to $300. Now, if he gets checkraised by you, knowing that the bet is 'just' $530 to $730 more, he may very well feel committed even with unimproved overcards. And if you are *really* strong, you may actually make a smaller raise to give him a 'discount' if you think that he is the type of player to fall for this trap.

Also note that with the $20 big blind in already, you will have to call just

$50 more, not $70 like in the first example. Now, calling $50 or $70 when you have a stack of $900 is a substantial difference – even when this difference *seems* to be small. Coupled with the fact that in contrast to the previous example your call will actually close the betting here, this means the situation is like this: In these two examples, you would fold the better hand in seemingly excellent position, while calling with the worse hand in what seems to be a very bad position. A strange situation, but undoubtedly correct – and most of all because of this one simple factor: your position *relative to the raiser*.

Rolf's Rule No. 10

In big-bet play, one of the worst possible situations is to have someone *bet through you. Good players know that very few hands are worth calling a raise when the raiser is seated to your immediate right, even when you are on the button. If after the flop there are other players still in the hand who act before the pre-flop raiser, this puts you in the middle – a situation with clear reverse implied odds.*

Part 8: Differences and adjustments – giving away information

Know that while you can bet as much as you want to in no-limit (a good thing), these bets of yours can give away considerable information to your opponents as to the strength of your hand (a bad thing).

In general, you should usually try to select your betting amounts in such a manner that if your opponents call your bet, they will be making a slight mistake. You want to give them slightly short odds if they choose to call and try to outdraw you. At the same time, you want to choose a betting size that will help you pick up pots at a relatively cheap price, even when you don't hold that much, actually. (These goals are slightly conflicting, and for that reason the optimum betting size is not the same in both cases. When you are protecting your hand, you would usually like to bet close to the pot, and sometimes even overbet the pot slightly – especially if there are many draws available. But when you are just trying to pick up the pot with a weak hand, a half-pot bet or even slightly less than that would seem more than sufficient – especially against non-descript boards like K-7-3 rainbow. Of course, as you would be giving away so much information about the strength of your hand through betting patterns like this, you should try to bet in a more 'uniform' way, and if you vary your bets, it should be based more on the texture of the board or the number/characteristics of your opponents than on the strength of your hand. More on this in the remainder of this article.) What you don't want to do is bet so much with a medium-strength or even strong holding that you will only get called when you are beaten – that is: that you will never get the chance to make money off a hand worse than yours.

The problem is, of course, that this size of your bet *does* give away some information about the strength of your hand, making it easier for your opponents to read you. So, what you are trying to do is make your bets around the same size to avoid this problem. Usually, you don't want to bet too small, as you will be giving your opponents the correct odds to try and outdraw you – even with very weak hands. But you should also be aware that many players in no-limit will actually make small bets when they hold a powerhouse and are hoping to get called. And for players who fit this description, fairly big bets may actually be an indication of fear – not necessarily the sign of a big hand. All in all, this means that in no-limit a lot of bets are in the range of one-third of the pot to slightly more than the pot, with the occasional all-in bet or raise. In games with deep money, where there is room enough for betting on all streets, the betting often goes like this:

Flop:

Full pot bet

Turn:

Full pot bet (especially when there are still many drawing possibilities)

River:

A much less than full pot bet (usually in order to 'sell' a hand, or to try for a relatively cheap bluff)

This last concept is very important. On the river, the lead bettor will often slow down considerably, knowing that he no longer has to charge his opponents for trying to outdraw him. This means that on the river he will often make a much smaller bet when he has a decent hand, hoping to get a call from his opponents who may have as little as a small pair or even ace-high. If there were many drawing possibilities on both the flop and the turn and then the river is a total brick, you should pay attention to the bet size of the lead bettor at this stage. If he has been betting big all the time and now makes a relatively small bet on the river, he may very well be trying to sell his hand. After all, he knows that since his opponents have just called him on both the flop and the turn, they may not have enough of a hand to call a very big bet by him. What this means is that if in this exact situation this player bets *big* on the river, that it is actually quite likely that he has a busted draw himself. After all, he knows that his opponents probably don't hold much, and with a hand that he figured to be best it would seem normal to make it much easier for them to call him. But as he has not done that, it is actually quite likely that he does *not* want to be called! Anyway, you should pay attention to specific betting patterns like this. Many players, even very good ones, have clear giveaways in some specific situations – now, if you look carefully, you may be able to use them to your advantage.

Rolf's Rule No. 11

If on the river a good player comes out betting big when the draws don't seem to have gotten there, then there is usually a good chance that this player is on a stone-cold bluff. This is especially true if this player has a tendency to 'sell' his decent hands on the river.

Now, to close off, I will give you six important recommendations when it comes to betting in no-limit. These are simple rules of thumb that I actually don't *always* hold onto – but that in general are clearly correct.

♠ If you choose to bet out at all, you should usually bet big against a board with many drawing opportunities, say something like K-10-6 with two of a suit. This will help clear the field and will make it easier for you to make the correct decisions on the later streets.

♠ If the board doesn't offer many drawing opportunities (ill-coordinated boards) or if there is a pair on the board, then you are usually better off by making smaller bets. Most of these bets will be 'probing bets' – bets designed to see who is interested in this pot, under the assumption that (since there are no draws) you will only get called if people actually *have* something. This way, you can often pick up some decent pots with fairly small bets even when you don't hold much yourself.

♠ If you are in the big blind and there are quite a few callers but you don't smell much strength, then you may sometimes be inclined to raise even with relatively marginal hands. However, if you decide to raise in this situation, it should usually be a very large bet, almost always more than the size of the pot. The goal of your raise should be to shut out the field and to negate for your bad position. You don't want to give your opponents the chance to see a relatively cheap flop when they a) have position on you, and b) because of your raise, have a good feel on the type of hand you probably hold.

♠ If you have a stack of, say, just 10 big bets and a 'normal-sized' pot bet would account to about five big bets, then if you choose to bet at all, it may be best to commit fully and go all-in. There is no way back for you anyway, so unless you hold an absolute monster that is looking for action, you should just stick it in and get the hand over with.

♠ Always be aware when it is the right time to collect. Let's say you have been lucky enough to flop a set and you think you are probably up against a hand like top pair/top kicker, then you should know that the flop is the time to get the money in. Don't think you should automatically slowplay because your hand is so strong. Your opponent having just one pair may get scared when the turn card presents possibilities for completed straights or flushes – and you will have lost your market.

♠ If your stack is not too big and you have a combination of a decent made hand and a decent draw, then it is often best to make what I call a 'no headache' bet. If your stack is not too big, it is often correct to just go all-in, even when it's a slight overbet of the pot. Because you don't know if your made hand is good right now, and you also cannot be 100% certain if your draw is good when you hit it, then betting all-in is often the proper play. Unless you get called by a better made hand *and* a better draw, you are usually in good shape.

Some final words

That's about it for now with regards to the differences and adjustments. In the next couple of articles, I will focus on some important postflop aspects in no-limit that may cause people who come from a limit background quite a bit of trouble.

Part 9: Play on the later streets – the depth of the money

The amount of chips you have in front of you is a major factor in choosing the optimum strategy.

As I said before, the money in no-limit hold'em cash games is usually a bit deeper than in tournaments, especially in brick and mortar casinos (as opposed to online). Of course, there are exceptions like large buy-in tournaments where the structure will allow you lots of play, but in general the size of the blinds in relation to the average stack is much higher in tournaments than in live games. This means that stealing the blinds may be a viable goal in tournaments in order to stay alive, in cash games stealing the blinds is usually not much of an issue. And as a result, *defending* your blinds is also not much of an issue. Let me put it another way: If in your full-ring no-limit hold'em cash game stealing and defending blinds are major concerns, then I suggest you find yourself another game. However, they do become a bit more important in online no-limit hold'em games. Because here some people buy-in for the minimum, and just as importantly because there is a maximum amount you can buy in for, the size of the blinds will sometimes account for quite a significant percentage of your stack, and thus will have to be factored in when making your decision.

When looking for the optimum play, it is not just the size of your own stack that is important. It is also important to look at your *opponent's* stack.

If he is about to go all-in, you can often use this to your advantage by us-ing his all-in bet to maximize the size of the pot for instance, by using his all-in bet as a way to get the other players in the middle so that you can checkraise, etc. But it is also important to know whether someone is play-ing a very *large* stack in relation to yours. If you are a short stack, waiting patiently for the right hand or situation to move all-in, then this big stack may actually call you rather loosely, because to him this all-in bet of yours accounts to just a small percentage of his stack. In fact, if there are also other big stacks in the hand when you are already all-in, you may even get protection from one of them, especially from those who have a rather loose/aggressive style of play – as is often the case with big stacks in this game. To make things clear for those who don't know: Protection means that one of these big stacks will bet another big stack out of the pot who in the end very well might have won the pot.

Now, if you are the shortest stack at the table, your major concern should be to try and maximize your expectation for the few hands that you do play. In fact, because one single bet accounts to a rather significant per-centage of your stack, you should often employ the simple system 'play for my entire stack, or don't play at all'. An excellent way to do this is by checkraising or limp-reraising overly aggressive players on your left. Now, as we shall see later, this is why I recommend sitting to the immediate *right* of maniacs once you have a fairly small stack, and especially if *they* are playing a big stack. Now, I know this is contrary to the common wis-dom that says you should always try to sit to the immediate *left* of maniacs, so that they will always act before you and so that you can choose to iso-late him on your good hands. But as we shall see later in this series, in big-bet poker when playing a small stack, I recommend the exact opposite. Anyway, by using the big stacks to your advantage in some of the ways I have suggested here, you could win monster pots even when playing very shallow money, and you can create situations where you have a clear over-lay.

Rolf's Rule No. 12

Playing a short stack doesn't always have to imply weakness.
There are lots of players, myself included, who have made tremen-
dous amounts of money by using a short-stack/checkraise/move-
in-early type of strategy.

Of course, most people would argue that if you are the best player in your game, you should have the largest stack of all, so that you can break them on any single hand – and obviously there is a lot of truth to that. Not only will you take every penny off your opponent once the two of you get into a major clash and you win, but there is also something else to consider. With a lot of chips in play, you will have the opportunity to do two things:

♠ Outplay the opposition, regardless of your cards.
♠ Use your chips as a weapon.

The first point should be easy to see. When both you and your opponent are playing very deep money, then not too many pots between the two of you will go to a showdown. Or, better: not too many *big* pots between the two of you will go to a showdown. This means that you should often be able to make your opponent throw away his cards because of the hand you are *representing*, whether you in fact hold these cards or not. You will be using the texture of the board, the tendencies and specific weaknesses of your opponents to your advantage to, in combination with your big stack, lure him into making the wrong decisions. One principle is very important here, and it is this:

Rolf's Rule No. 13

When playing very deep money, the threat is usually more important than the execution.

What does that mean exactly, you may ask. Well, it means this: In big-bet poker, if you bet $100 all-in on the flop, your opponent will have to make a decision whether he thinks it is worth it to call you for this amount or not. He knows the cost: $100. So, if he thinks that his hand may be best, or has a decent chance to improve to the best hand, and the odds seem favourable, then he may call you – or else he may fold.

But when you bet that same $100 on the flop but this time you still have $1200 behind, then your opponent knows that seeing the hand through to the river may well cost him $1300 – which could well be his entire stack. So, while betting a mere hundred bucks, you basically threaten your opponents that if they call you now, the rest of your stack may follow later. And if this threat is credible to your opponents, they may very well fold some fairly decent hands, hands that may even be better than the one you are betting with – simply because they don't want to risk their entire stack for it. If your image is strong, you should be able to win quite a few pots without a fight in the manner described here. So, while *you* are just betting $100, *they* may feel that if they call now, they could be committed to call for the remainder of the money as well. So, you are betting $100, but they feel like they have to call $1300. This is an *extremely* important concept in big-bet poker, one that does not exist to even remotely the same degree in limit.

Rolf's Rule No. 14

Playing a big stack profitably in no-limit hold'em requires excellent postflop abilities. It requires you to use your stack as an intimidating factor in order to pick up small pots, it requires making plays at your opponents, and taking advantage of their specific weaknesses. If you are not great at reading people, at playing the players, and at both bluffing and snapping off bluffs, well then you should probably just stick to playing a short stack.

Part 10: Play on the later streets – following through

It is imperative to know when to follow through, and when to simply give it up.

You may have heard this quote somewhere: 'You should know when to fire again and when to retreat.' This is one of the keys to successful big-bet play. If your flop bet gets called, quite often the deciding factor whether or not to bet again on the turn will be your read on this specific player. Quite a few no-limit hold'em players will flat call a bet on the flop with a good made hand, waiting for you to bet again on the turn so that they can make their move *then*. You should first know who these players are that like to make these plays, because some players are afraid to just call with a good made hand, and will almost always make their move on the flop. Also, the players who like to wait until the later streets to make a move often have tip-offs, little tells they give away about whether they are drawing or not.

One of the most reliable tip-offs for me is one that good players exhibit. When good players are drawing, they will often call a bet fairly quickly, possibly to show strength, hoping that on the turn you may back down because of their quick call. But when they are actually slowplaying a big hand, they usually take just a little more time – as if they are not so certain whether they should call that flop bet of yours. Of course, the reason is simple: They want you to fire one more bet with your second-best hand, hoping that by that time you will be committed. Now, online this tell is not very reliable of course, but in real life this little give-away that *many* good players exhibit has made (and *saved*) me tremendous amounts of money.

Anyway, let's make this all a bit more concrete. Holding Q♠-J♠, you have made a pot-sized bet on the flop Q♥-10♥-5♠, and one late-position player has called your bet. Based upon your read on this player, you judge it quite likely that this player is drawing, and that thus your top pair/marginal kicker is good. Assuming that you don't know much about this player other than that he does not seem to be out of line very often, how would you play the turn in each of the following four situations. Will you follow through, and if so – in what manner, and why?

Situation No. 1 – Turn card: 3♠

Well yes, obviously you should fire once more here. Your hand is quite likely to be best and if it's not, well then at least you have just picked up a flush draw. (Note that it is impossible for your opponent to both hold the best hand *and* have a higher flush draw in your suit – spades.) Depending on the exact amounts of money here, a pot-sized bet would seem OK. Had your hand been K♠-Q♠ instead of Q♠-J♠, then you could have considered betting a bit less than the pot to lure your opponent into calling if you figure him for a straight draw rather than a hearts flush draw. Let's say your opponent has a king-jack here, well then his king overcard is not an out anymore. He will now be drawing to just six outs, as two of his straight cards will actually give you a flush. In that case, because he is drawing so thin here, you could afford to give him slightly better odds by betting a bit less than the pot.

Situation No. 2 – Turn card: 10♦

Not the prettiest of turn cards for you, this ten of diamonds. If your opponent has a third ten, then it is now *you* who is drawing extremely thin. On the other hand, if your opponent *doesn't* have the ten and is still drawing, then this card will look extremely dangerous to him as well. After all, it *could* mean that he is now drawing dead! And frankly, it is not all that likely that your opponent has actually called your flop bet with a ten in his hand, as that was just second pair on the flop. And besides that, there is no way he can have a ten in his hand as part of a draw, so this means that his call on the flop should be made thinking that this second pair could have been good against your big bet. As I said, not all that likely – even though it *is* possible.

Now, assuming the money is relatively deep, you should usually start making some minor adjustments to the size of your bets once the board pairs. I almost never make very large bets once the board has paired. But on the other hand, making a very small bet is not recommended either if this means that your opponent may use this small bet of yours to get tricky and *represent* the three tens. After all, with your hand (top two pair/marginal kicker) you absolutely *don't* want to face a big raise that could very well be a big semi-bluff. So, what you should do in almost all cases when the board pairs is to make a decent-sized bet, about half the pot. That way, you will probably get a reliable response from your opponent, and this makes it more likely that you will be able to make the correct decisions later in the hand. What's more, this bet will probably help you pick up the pot the majority of the time – and this would of course be the best result of all with your vulnerable hand, and all the draws out there.

Situation No. 3 – Turn card: J♥

This card is a mixed blessing. It has improved your hand to top two, but it has also completed many straight and flush draws. At first glance, I would be terrified of this card. But then again, there is some good news as well. We are up against someone who has just called our flop bet. Being in position, if he had a big flush draw, or a flush- and straight-draw, he may well have become more aggressive with his hand. So, while it is possible that we are up against a completed flush now, it is almost certainly not the ace-high flush, meaning that our opponent cannot play his hand carefree either. And it is almost certainly not a straight flush either, as then our opponent would need to have flopped both a flush draw *and* a straight flush draw. Now, being in position, most people would have played a hand like that a bit more aggressively on the flop than by just calling.

And there is some more good news: All the straight draws that have been completed now were actually gutshot straights, and people with gutshot straight draws usually don't call pot-sized bets on the flop – even though A-K would be a gutshot + two overcards for a quite reasonable call. Open-ended straight draws like K-J and J-9 have *not* drawn out on you. In fact, if your opponent *did* have you beat on the flop with something like A-Q, K-Q or even Q-10, then you have now outdrawn *him*!

All in all, when the board gets as scary as here with a completed draw, then again I usually like to make moderate sized bets rather than very big ones. But frankly, in this situation you are likely to make mistakes no matter what. The board is full of semi-bluffing opportunities for your opponent, so even if you bet half pot and then get raised, it is far from certain that you are actually beat: Your opponent may have something like K♥-J♣ or A♥-J♦ and use the scary board to try and bet you off the current best hand. So when the money is not *too* deep, this may well be one of those situations where I could get broke with top two pair against someone who has 'obviously' completed his draw. With very deep money, this may be one of the cases where you may be better off to just give it up, to either check-and-fold or bet small and then fold to a raise. This is one of these situations where you may very well be forced to throw away the best hand, especially if the person who has position on you is either very good or very tricky. But then again, you have no one else to blame for this apart from yourself. With a hand as weak as Q♠-J♠, you should *never* have gotten to the point where you are out of position against a good player with lots of money still to be played.

Situation No. 4 – Turn card: A♥

Now, here you almost always have an obvious check-and-fold. The ultimate scare card has popped out of the deck, and there is hardly a hand you can still beat. If your opponent is incredibly weak or predictable, then you may get away with making some very small bets, 'feeler' bets if you will, so that his response will tell you if there is some chance that you are actually still ahead. Against anyone who can be considered a *player*, you will simply have to surrender here. Yes, a few times you will actually be folding the winning hand, but since the pot is still fairly small, you don't really worry about that. What you *do* worry about is the rest of your stack, and if against this board you are willing to put in a lot of additional chips, well then usually you will be making a very big mistake.

'But hey,' you may ask, 'Why shouldn't *I* use this ace of hearts to represent the straight or flush myself? Wouldn't that work?' Well yes, that would be a good play sometimes – but probably not in this situation. The flop betting has suggested that it is *your opponent* who is drawing. Now, if he has made a small flush or a straight, it will be *very* hard for him to lay that down in the heads-up situation that we have here. Very few players are capable of first calling a big bet to complete their draw, to then fold it once they have made it. So, I would recommend saving your bluffs and your moves for another time – more specifically, for the times when it looks like the opposition may be weak.

Rolf's Rule No. 15

Knowing when to follow through depends on three things mostly. First of all, the texture of the board, then the tendencies of your opponents, and finally the strength of your own hand of course. It should be easier for you to make the correct decisions here in a 'real' cardroom, because good players can often 'feel' when their hand is not good anymore – a luxury they don't have online.

Part 11: Play on the later streets – stack-size based strategies

You should be able to make significant changes to your overall strategy based upon the size of your stack.

While we have already established that good players should *usually* try to have the biggest stack at the table, in lots of no-limit games nowadays you cannot buy-in for as much as you want. Often, there will be a cap on the buy-in. So, this means that even if you buy in for the maximum, most of the time you will *not* be able to cover everyone. If this is the case, there is something to be said for an interesting alternative: buying in for the *minimum*. This way, you can play multiple tables using a very simple system based on two things mostly: moving in with the best hand, and taking advantage of the fact that your opponents will not take your bets seriously, as your stack is so small in relation to others.

In fact, this is a strategy that I often recommend to people who come from a limit background. In general, limit players are not very comfortable with playing a big stack in no-limit, because this requires abilities that they have never trained in limit. Now, this strategy of playing a small stack and then moving in early with their good hands is actually a strategy that is not that far from the way they have always played their limit games. And thus, this is an excellent way for them to get used to the flow of no-limit play while still making money, because especially in the smaller and the softer games this strategy *can* be very profitable. Actually, this is exactly how I did things when I moved into big-bet play, and it has paid off well for me – so I guess it might work for you too. And in fact, I still use this strategy very often, especially when there are very experienced players in my game who have one exploitable weakness: playing their weak hands in a very loose-aggressive manner. By taking advantage of this fact through keeping a small stack and moving in early, I will make a lot of money off them – despite the fact that *they* may be world-class players, and I may just be better than average.

Anyway, let's make a short list of these strategy changes based on how much money you are playing. In general, things look like this:

Short stack play (say, less than 25 times the big blind)

- ♠ Play for all your money, or don't play at all. (An exception may be calling on the button in a multiway pot.)
- ♠ Try to move in early in order to maximize your wins.
- ♠ Take advantage of the overaggression of some players by sitting to their immediate *right*. This way, you will get excellent opportunities to checkraise or limp-reraise them. You will usually be all-in either before or on the flop with the current best hand – a very profitable situation.
- ♠ You may get *protection* from the big stacks, making you an even bigger favourite than you already were. Being all-in, you would obviously welcome the fact that other, potentially winning, hands will be bet out of the pot. In the end, you could win three or even four times the amount of money that you have put in, and you may have to beat just one player to get it.

Medium stack play (say, about 40-50 times the big blind)

♠ You can play a few more speculative hands like small pairs and suited connectors now, especially in position.

♠ You focus a bit more on postflop play, rather than the simple 'move-in' approach from your short-stack play.

♠ You will usually want to come in for a limp or a minimum raise, but *not* for a big raise, not even with A-K. You don't want to invest 10 to 20% of your stack before the flop, making clear to your opponents the type of hand you probably hold. With a hand like A-K, you want to play either for a very small percentage of your stack, or a very large one – say more than 40% of your stack. This way, you know you are commit- ted and the rest of the money will go in anyway – regardless of the flop. By the way, in online games you can often make the strange play of making a big overbet with your A-K after a couple of limpers. In these games, even your huge raises of- ten get called by hands like ace-rag, and thus this can be a rather unorthodox, but very profitable play. Just make sure that this big raise amounts to a significant enough percentage of your stack.

♠ If you flop well in early position in an unraised pot, the size of your stack means that you are in perfect position for a checkraise. This is especially true when there are one or two very aggressive players sitting behind you.

Big stack play (say, more than 80 times the big blind)

♠ You are playing 'real' poker now, and you can start to use the size of your stack as a weapon.

♠ Bluffs have a much higher chance of success, now that you can fire on *all* streets rather than just one or two.

♠ If you flop well in an unraised pot, the best play may now be to bet out, hoping that one of your opponents will play back at you, so that you can then move in. Don't use the checkraise too often when playing a big stack, because you are likely to win lots of fairly small pots, while *losing* the really big ones.

♠ Position is now of paramount importance. Again, not just your position relative to the button, but just as importantly your position on the preflop raiser.

OK guys, that was a *lot* of information I guess – information that applies to full-ring play, not the 6-max games that have become so popular nowadays. (In 6-max, shortstacking is a bit less effective, even though it can still be done.)

To close things off, I will pick one starting hand, and analyse how one can or should play that hand under the circumstances described – that is, when holding either a short, medium or big stack. Again, we are assuming a full-ring game. The hand: two red deuces, 2♥-2♦.

2♥-2♦ with a short stack

With a short stack, two deuces is an easy fold, especially in early position. (On the button in an unraised pot, you could call though.) You don't want to invest a significant percentage of your stack calling and hoping to hit the flop, and your hand is not strong enough for an all-in coup either. What you would really hate is first limping with this hand, and then having to give up the hand when the pot gets raised behind you. While in some cases it may be correct to *go* all-in with a small pair, you should almost never *call* all-in. Note that heads-up, two deuces are *never* a clear favourite, except in the unlikely case when your opponent holds a deuce as well, but they may actually be a very big dog when you are up against another (bigger) pair. And while a very small pair has at least some value all-in in a heads-up situation, in a three- or four-way pot the hand is absolutely horrible.

2♥-2♦ with a medium stack

Now here, you have a pretty good situation for your two deuces. You are hoping to get into the pot cheaply, and then if you flop a deuce the rewards can be enormous. Say the flop comes something like Q♥-8♠-2♣, now this is a perfect situation to break someone with top pair. If you are in early position, this may be a good time to go for the checkraise, because once he has bet the flop he is probably committed. And if you are in late position and the top pair bets out, then an excellent strategy may be to just double his bet. He will then usually look at the size of your stack, say something like 'How much do you have left? Not much, huh. OK, let's just stick it all-in', and you will be a *very* large favourite to win the pot. Again, don't wait until the turn to make a move, because if either an overcard to the queen falls, or else a jack, ten or a nine, your opponent could get scared and you may have lost your market.

So, why do I think it is OK to call the first bet with this hand with a medium stack and not with a short stack – the money I will lose when the pot gets raised behind me is the same, right? Well yes, obviously the money is the same. But in big-bet play you always think in terms of percentage of your stack. You know that the odds of flopping a set are about 7.5 to 1. So, you know that you will have wasted that call before the flop about 7 times out of 8. And when you can win a really large pot, then it is worth it to take a chance, even at the risk of having to fold when the pot get raised behind you. So, the two reasons why you *can* limp with deuces with a medium stack but usually not with a small stack are quite simple, actually:

♠ The costs are lower. The initial call amounts to a much smaller percentage of your stack now.

♠ The upside is bigger. If you do reach the flop cheaply and flop a deuce, you could now win a very large pot instead of just a good one.

2♥-2♦ with a large stack

You could now even call a raise with your deuces, and in fact when you do this you are *hoping* that the raiser actually has aces – so that you can break him when you manage to flop that deuce. With the same Q♥-8♠-2♣ flop, it may now be best to bet into him though, so that he can raise and you can then reraise. This is usually a better way to get him committed than by going for the obvious checkraise. And when you are in position, just make a decent raise on the flop. In a heads-up situation, with you being on or near the button, it will be hard for your opponent to give you credit for a set here – so play it fast. And if your opponent by chance has Q-Q for top set or 8-8 for middle set, well then hey good luck to him. You were going to lose your entire stack anyway, regardless of whether you played the hand fast or slow.

One final thing: With *very* deep money, pairs like sevens and eights are actually much better than deuces, most of all because they build middle set instead of bottom set. And if you happen to run into a set over set when the money is very deep, then this can be very expensive obviously. So beware of this, and in borderline situations call preflop with the sevens or eights but fold the deuces. This is especially true if there has been quite a bit of action, and the hand seems to develop into a four- or five-way situation. If just two of your opponents have higher pocket pairs than yours, then set over set is suddenly not so remote anymore. So, take this into account before making that preflop call, because when you have a losing set-over-set it will almost always cost you your entire stack.

Rolf's Rule No. 16

Make sure that at all times you make the necessary strategic adjustments based upon the size of your stack. Deep money play requires an entirely different approach than shallow money play, both with regards to hand selection, seat selection and the postflop decisions.

Part 12: From no-limit to limit – considering the size of the bet

In previous articles in this series, I have analysed many key aspects that one should take into account when making the transfer from limit hold'em to no-limit hold'em, the two most popular poker games nowadays. Please note that this list is far from exhaustive, as there are many more differences between the two. Here, I will start discussing the difficulties that someone who is used to playing no-limit hold'em may face when taking on limit hold'em. I will mention only things that I have not talked about before, as it should be clear that a lot of problems and difficulties that occur when moving from limit to no-limit are the exact opposite when moving into the opposite direction. All in all, here are some things that you should be aware of when moving into the 'wrong' direction, from big-bet play to limit, or more specifically, from no-limit hold'em to the limit version of the game. A lot of players nowadays actually start their poker experience by playing no-limit hold'em, and if they then decide to take on limit hold'em as well, they will usually find that this is far from easy. In fact, it is generally accepted that moving from limit to no-limit is much easier and much more 'natural' than the path that so many young people make nowadays, starting with big-bet play and taking on limit much later. As before, I will be discussing cash games only, not tournaments, and most comments are aimed at brick and mortar play – even though quite a bit may apply to Internet games as well.

Learn to appreciate the fact that one bet is a significant part of both the total pot size and the amount of money that you stand to win, and that your goals in limit are simply not the same as in no-limit.

While in no-limit hold'em one would often be looking for opportunities to double up, or try to get yourselves into situations where you could take your opponent's entire stack, limit hold'em is a different breed. At the middle limits, making one big bet per hour is considered quite an accomplishment, and this would translate into $40 per hour for a $20-40 game. (Note that very few players at these players are actually capable of making this much; most good players would be very happy to make $20 or $25, and some of them don't even make this much.) What this means is that your total earn is rather limited compared to the amounts of money put at risk. In other words: Even good players in limit hold'em are ahead by a much slighter margin than no-limit hold'em players would be, given the same type of game circumstances. All of this means that gaining and saving bets is a very important aspect of limit hold'em, because saving a small bet here and making a little extra there really adds up in the long run. But no-limit players who are used to calling, say, five percent of their stack with hands like suited or even offsuit connectors in order to break the opponent who is marked with a big pair, these no-limit players will have to learn to accept that in limit hold'em these kinds of situations don't come up very often, simply because the implied odds are not the same as in no-limit. Those who habitually call a raise in a heads-up situation with a six-five suited, which may be correct in some no-limit games (of course, only against certain types of opponents, and of course only when the money is deep, having position over the raiser), may be burning their chips in limit.

An example

I'll explain this with an example. Let's say that in limit you call a raise from the button with the 6♥-5♥ in order to break an early-position raiser who you know has a real hand, and who you have actually read for a big pocket pair – as he only raises preflop with the very best hands. As we have seen in earlier articles in this series, this is a very reasonable play in no-limit, provided that the money is deep, and especially if your opponent plays rather weakly or predictably after the flop. But, is it reasonable in limit too? Let's take a closer look at this.

One thing that is perfectly clear is that if the two of you are heads-up and you flop a pair, you will at least reach the turn. This is especially true when there are no aces and kings on the board, because of the distinct possibility that your opponent has nothing more than an unimproved ace-king, and that thus your mere pair of fives or sixes is actually good now. Either way, you know that if no aces and kings are on the board and you have flopped a pair, your read on this opponent has to be *very* reliable to even consider laying your pair down. What this means is that you will often take your small pair to the river and when your opponent does have overcards that don't improve on the turn or river, you win a decent-sized pot, and when he does have the overpair you read him for and you are unable to outdraw him, he will usually win a good-sized pot.

A negative way to look at your small cards in this situation would be this:

- ♠ You are playing a longshot hand, hoping that if you get lucky against a premium hand, you could win a very big pot.

- ♠ Even if you do hit, it may turn out that your opponent doesn't hold much after all, and you will win just a marginal pot.

- ♠ There is too much danger of leaking chips because of second-best hands that you may make. This is not just the case when things get down to just you and one opponent, also in a multiway pot this is a distinct possibility. Why, you ask? Well, because other players may now be in the pot who are playing cards in the same playing range as you. If you are up against three players who are all holding high cards, then you would not mind that at all, because your cards are very live, because you have 'maximum stretch' and because you are getting good odds. But if people are in there with hands like 8♥-7♥ or even just a 7-6 offsuit, it is actually quite possible that even if you improve over the preflop raiser, your hand will still be second-best – because a third player will have improved more than you.

Of course, there is some good news as well. The good news is that you have called the raise with the exact type of holding that fares the best against big pairs and high cards. It is *much* better to call an early-position raiser with a 6-5 suited than with a king-jack offsuit. Because you know the range of cards that the preflop raiser can be holding, and your cards are in the opposite range, then you obviously have some edge postflop. There is also some possibility of outplaying your opponent after the flop when you know the flop must have been bad for him, while *he* cannot be certain about your hand. So, my guess is that for a good postflop player, calling this raise on the button is not such a bad play. But it is not nearly as profitable as in no-limit, and the former no-limit players who make these calls habitually rather than just under special circumstances – these players are making a clear mistake. What they tend to forget is that in limit hold'em they miss that specific no-limit tool that they cannot use here: the possibility to apply pressure after the flop, to put someone to the test with a large bet or raise when you know that the board looks scary to them. In limit, lots of players who raise before the flop will take their unimproved ace-king to the river, no matter what. And while this may be good for you when you have caught a good flop, it clearly limits your possibility to bluff and bully them out of the hand.

In limit, most pots are won by those who start with the best hand. While this does not mean that there is no room for creativity or that you cannot make moves on specific players, if you take too much the worst of it before the flop, it will usually be hard to regain that edge after the flop. In other words: If in limit you give your opponents too much of a head start, they will beat you in the long run – even if in fact you are by far the better player.

Lots of big-bet players feel that limit hold'em is too boring, because they incorrectly think in terms of working towards a climax/creating situations/setting up plays/breaking players on one hand. They should realize that limit hold'em is a long-term grind where lots of small profits really add up in the end, and that it is *not* a game where one or two big scores can make up for a rather large number of speculative plays. In other words: While in no-limit you can afford to be wrong on one or two occasions if you make sure you are correct in the all-important pot later, in limit you simply have to be right all the time, because there *is* no all-important pot that can make up for things here.

Rolf's Rule No. 17

Limit hold'em is a game where you should try to play according to the odds, and where you cannot get out of line too often. Whereas in no-limit it is perfectly acceptable strategy to play u couple of crappy hands in order tu pave the way for a massive pot later, in limit poker it will be impossible to recoup these initial losses later – simply because of the way this game is structured. In limit, you should learn to appreciate that every hand is a struggle where you may be playing for one small bet profit, and sometimes even less than that. Little things that add up in the long run, and quite dif- ferent from the 'working towards the climax' that is so common of no-limit play.

Part 13: From no-limit to limit – protecting your hand

Learn that the odds are different, and that the concept of protecting your hand is not the same as in no-limit.

While in no-limit hold'em it is possible to bet so much that your opponents won't be getting the proper price to call you, in limit you don't have this luxury. This means that in some situations you should not focus on nar- rowing the field in order to protect your hand, but rather to try to get yourself in a situation of 'the more, the merrier', knowing that all legiti- mate hands will call you anyway. Of course, there are lots of situations where you should take an aggressive approach to win pots immediately, to protect a rather vulnerable holding, to gain information, or to simply put your opponents to the test right now – but please be aware that things are not always about thinning the field in limit. Let's say that you are lucky enough to flop a great hand like a set when there is also a straight- and a flush-draw on the board. Now, of course you would almost always raise with your set here. However, your goal should not be what most players think it is (narrowing the field to give your hand the best possible chance to hold up); your goal is to get as much money as possible into the pot now that you clearly have the best of it. In this case, the best possible situation for you would be to be up against as many opponents as possible, for as many bets as possible. After all, if after raising things come down to just you and two other players, you may well have narrowed down the field to just you and the only two players who are drawing very live, for instance you and both the nut-flush draw and an open-ended straight draw. The hands that you have gotten out are probably the ones who would have been drawing dead or drawing thin considering what they are up against: hands like bottom pair/good kicker or even just a backdoor flush draw, holdings that you would have truly *welcomed* into the pot. Now, of course this does not mean that you should *not* raise with your set, because of course you *should* raise now that you have the best of it. But what you should try to accomplish with your raise is keeping as many opponents in the pot for as many bets as possible, *not* trying to get them all out without having invested a thing.

Also, it is important to realize at all times the odds your opponents are getting, and how this should influence the proper way for you to play your hand. That is: to try and find the best way to give your opponents *improper* odds to continue (meaning that they will be making a mathematical mistake if they do call). Things like waiting to raise until a safe turn comes off with what looks like the best hand but with many draws on the board, or going for the checkraise instead of betting out to face the opposition with having to call two bets cold instead of just one, things like this are important tools for the limit hold'em player to manipulate the odds into his favour – and very few players who come from a no-limit background are capable of doing this correctly.

Let's give two examples from the things I just mentioned.

Example No. 1: Waiting for a safe turn card to make a raise

My hand:
A♠-Q♠

Preflop play:
On the button, I have raised two limpers. The big blind has called, as have the limpers.

The flop:
Q♥-9♥-7♣

Flop action:

The big blind has come out betting, and both initial limpers have called.

My play:

While I think I have the best hand right now with my top pair/top kicker, it may be better to wait until a safe turn card to make a move. If the turn card is as third heart and there is a whole lot of action, I know that I am beat. By waiting to raise I now save one or two small bets in the case of a bad turn, and if the turn is a blank I will have the chance to defend my hand on the expensive street. So, by waiting to raise I may lose a bit less in case my hand turns sour, and I will probably still get the same or even a bit more money in the pot if the turn card turns out to be good.

Analysis:

Losing a bit less, and winning a bit more – the exact characteristics of what limit hold'em is about. By the way, lots of people who come from a no-limit hold'em background will make this play automatically, as they are used to making these delayed raises in no-limit. But in limit, these plays should clearly be the exception rather than the rule. The reason why this delayed raise is the proper play here is the way the betting has gone: bet/call/call, and then it is up to you. If you raise now when in fact your TPTK is good, you will get called by a wide range of holdings and will not lose any players. In fact, you will make it much harder for yourself to defend your vulnerable hand on the turn if you choose to make the flop raise. But had the flop bet come from someone to your immediate right, then you would have had an automatic raise, as you could have put pressure on all others by facing them with a double bet that they will have to call cold, rather than being in for one bet already and having to call one more.

Example No. 2: Going for the checkraise instead of betting out

My hand:

A♥-9♠

Preflop play:

I have completed from the small blind. Four limpers, six players total. On the button, there is a very aggressive player who will almost always bet when checked to.

The flop:

9♥-7♣-4♦

My play:

While I have a decent chance of having the current best hand with my top pair, I know that if I bet out into a field of six players, I will get called by hands as weak as a gutshot straight draw, a backdoor flush or even two live overcards. Holding just a pair of nines this is not what I want: I want all these players out. If I check and behind me the action goes crazy, something like bet/raise/reraise, then I know that I am out and I will have saved myself a bet. But more importantly, if no one really holds much and it gets checked to the button, I have an excellent opportunity to go for the check-raise here. I will probably be able to get everyone out and play the hand heads-up against someone who does not figure to hold much, making me a clear favourite. What I have done here is *manipulate the odds in my favour*. Had I taken the obvious path of betting out, my opponents would have been correct to call me. By facing them with a double bet now, they would be making a mistake by calling.

Analysis:

This is the type of play you will have to make fairly often in limit. Because the size of the bet is fairly small in relation to the total pot, you sometimes have to make an unusual play in order to give your opponents insufficient odds to call you. People who come from a no-limit background will have to get used to these types of plays, as they will be strange to them. After all, in no-limit hold'em, these kinds of plays are usually not necessary, as you can always bet as much as you want – and then manipulate your opponent's odds without the help of others.

Rolf's Rule No. 18

In limit hold'em, the odds are all-important. Those who fail to adjust their decisions not just to the odds they themselves are getting, but also the odds their opponents *are receiving, these players will not stand a chance in limit.*

Part 14: From no-limit to limit – playing the blinds

Learn that in limit, it is not just your initial hand selection that is the key. Just as importantly is playing the blinds correctly – in fact, I consider this the cornerstone of anyone's game.

One of the largest series of poker articles I have ever written was a five-or six-part series on blind defence for *CardPlayer*. (Not as large as this 14-part series obviously, but still the third-largest series ever.) From this alone, it should be clear to see that I consider this an extremely important area of play. And at the same time, you will read more rubbish on playing the blinds than on anything else in poker. For instance, over the years I have read and heard things like 'Don't think about the money you already have in as the big blind. Play your hand as if you have nothing invested yet,' and lots of similar crap. While a lot of excellent material is available on which hands you can and should play out of free will, there is a lot of bad information out there when it comes to playing the blinds correctly. Basically, things are quite simple though. The following three things should *always* be taken into account before deciding whether or not to defend your blind.

♠ Beware of dominated hands. They can cost you an awful lot of money after the flop – especially once you have hit.

♠ Take into account the fact that you are in the pot already, and that thus you are getting a good price on a call (a 'discount' if you will).

♠ Beware of the positional aspects. Does your call close the betting, and where does the raise come from? Is there a danger of someone betting through you? For instance, if you are the big blind and the small blind raises with at least one limper in the pot already, then you will need a *very* strong hand to continue playing now that you may get sandwiched. In general, you will have to act first on all streets if you call a raise from one of the blind positions, and this is obviously not the best position to be in – so factor this in when deciding whether to call or not.

Rather than talk about blind play in a very abstract and analytical manner, I will analyse things for you with three simple examples. The thought processes here should obviously be very helpful to those who are used to playing no-limit, where the blind play is just not that important – simply because the blinds usually account to a very small percentage of both the player's stacks and the total pot size.

Example No. 1

You are in the $20 big blind with 7♥-5♠. The under-the-gun makes it $40 to go. The cutoff and the button call, all others fold, and now it's up to you. What do you do?

Well, despite the fact that your hand is not exactly a monster, you do have a fairly easy call in my opinion – for three reasons mostly:

- ♠ You are getting a great price on a call. You have to put in just $20 more for a total pot of $170, odds of about 7.5 to 1.

- ♠ You are probably playing cards that are opposed to the raiser, meaning that your hand may very well be live. While this is not as important as it is in no-limit, it is still important. So, your hand would be especially strong if the callers in the middle are playing paint cards as well, because you will be the only one with the small cards here.

- ♠ You've got good position on the raiser. Basically, this is the same thing we talked about in no-limit, that you are in good position to go for the checkraise after the flop. But in limit, this relative position of yours may have one additional bene-fit: It may allow you to see fourth street cheaply with rela-tively marginal hands. Let's say that you flop either a gutshot or bottom pair/weak kicker. Had someone been betting into you, or betting *through* you, then you would almost always have to fold, most of all because of the possibility of a raise behind you. But in the position you have now, you can sim-ply check to the raiser. If he bets, quite often the people in the middle will just call or even fold, rather than raise, meaning that you can close the betting calling for one small bet. Now, *many* hands are worth this call here, and usually with hands like this gutshot or this bottom pair you would happily pay one small bet on the flop to catch a lucky turn. Your good relative position will often allow you that here. And just as importantly, if you now catch the card you want on the turn, you will be in perfect position to bag the field and go for a checkraise. All in all, two clear benefits of your position here: You could reach the turn cheaply with marginal holdings or even longshots, and if by chance you get lucky on the turn you will be in perfect position to maximize your profits.

Rolf's Rule No. 19

Just as in no-limit is it important to realize how your relative position will affect postflop play. Knowing in advance where profitable and unprofitable situations may occur, will allow you to sometimes make a profitable call with hands that seem very marginal, and that in the eyes of people who don't look close enough are clear folds.

Example No. 2

You are in the $20 big blind with A♥-9♠. The UTG makes it $40 to go and everybody folds. What do you do?

Well, even though you seem to be holding a much better hand than in the previous example, in my view you have a rather clear fold here. Your hand is likely to be dominated, because the preflop raiser most likely has a high pair or a big ace. This means that even if you receive help from the board, you may now actually *lose* a whole lot more, because your hand is *still* second-best. And if in fact you do have the best hand after the flop, then the pot you win will be significantly smaller that the pot you will lose if in fact your hand is just second-best. After all, if your opponent has J-J and an ace flops, then it will not be hard for him to see that you may have made a pair of aces now. This does not mean that he will automatically fold his hand, but it *does* mean that he will not give you excessive action. Possibly he will be trying to get a free card somewhere, and actually he is quite likely to succeed here for the simple reason that *you* fear that your kicker may not be good. Coupled with the fact that you will be out of position during the entire hand, this is a typical example of a hand/situation with *reverse implied odds*. By the way: Note that many decent players would have folded the 7-5 from the first example without much thought, whereas a lot of them would have thought the A-9 was a fairly easy call. As you can see from this analysis, I think that the almost exact opposite is true.

Rolf's Rule No. 20

For most decent but not great limit hold'em players, a large part of their winning strategy consists of the concept of staying out of trouble. For these players, in situations where it is not clear exactly where they are at, or being out of position in a very small pot with a possibly dominated hand, it is almost always correct to simply fold there and then and take a small loss. As these players are likely to make compounding errors, it is usually best for them to take a small loss rather than to battle things out in tough spots that require good reads, good judgment and lots of 'feel'.

Example No. 3

Again you are in the $20 big blind, and again you hold the 7♥-5♠. A pro has called under-the-gun, and a loose-aggressive player now makes it $40 to go on the button. What do you do?

Well, at first glance this situation would not seem that much different from example no. 1. In fact, one might argue that this situation may actually be *better* than the first one, because in the first one you were almost certainly up against a big hand, and in this case it is clear that the raiser does not need to hold much. So, this would be even more reason to call – right?

Wrong! While it is true that indeed the button could very well hold a rather weak hand and may simply be playing his position, I would fold my 7-5 here – for the following reasons:

♠ You don't know where you're at. In example 1, you knew you were probably playing cards that were opposed to the raiser, but here the raiser may well have a hand like K♠-7♠, A♥-5♠ or even 8♠-7♠ – meaning that even if you flop the cards that you want, you could still be in trouble.

♠ Assuming that both you and the under-the-gun player call

this raise, you are in danger of being sandwiched after the flop. If both you and the under-the-gun check to the raiser, you will be put in the middle. After all, if the button bets, he will be betting through you, and it is the pro who can close the betting – not you. In fact, he may very well be planning a checkraise to use the loose-aggressive style of the button to his advantage. Because you know that on the flop you are probably going to have to fold many marginal hands, it is better to recognize this problem in advance – and fold *before* the flop.

♠ A pro calling under-the-gun is usually a sign of strength. If he sees that behind him the only action comes from a loose-aggressive player raising on the button, and the big blind defending against this loose-aggressive player's raise, then the pro may actually decide to three-bet with a very wide range of hands – knowing that even fairly marginal hands for him to hold like A♥-10♥ or K♠-Q♠ are probably best on this given deal and can be raised for value. Because your call does not close the betting and you are in danger of getting *squeezed* both before and on the flop, your hand will have lost a lot of its potential value.

Rolf's Rule No. 21

In limit hold'em, it is very important to try and anticipate your opponents' actions. Don't make a call in borderline situations when you know that this call will a) look weak, and b) put you in the middle. The third player may use your apparent weakness to his advantage by pumping up the pot – costing you a lot of money in the process.

Pot-Limit Omaha

Pot-limit Omaha and table image

In 1998 I started playing poker for a living. In the first 18 months, I played mostly limit hold'em (my main game at that time), but I also tried to improve my game at stud, Omaha and high/low-games. Then I started to focus almost entirely on improving my pot-limit game, since in Holland, France and Austria pot-limit poker was becoming increasingly popular (even in the US pot-limit was starting to gain some more attention). The game that is best suited for playing pot-limit is Omaha high. It offers much more action to the gambling types of players than pot-limit hold'em, yet it is an extremely skilful game, so the top players figure to make a lot of money. Because of its pot-limit structure, a large percentage of pots are won without a showdown. In this game, it is impossible (that is, it is very unwise) to chase all the way to the river or to call someone down with a weak hand. What becomes important when deciding whether or not to play your hand is who you are up against: do you think your opponent has the goods he's representing or not? Table image comes into play.

At the beginning of my poker career I did everything I could to create the image of a tight, unimaginative rock who is never involved in a hand without having the goods (in Vienna people called me 'The Ace', because they claimed that I would never play a hand that did *not* contain at least one ace). I tried to achieve that image by playing only a few hands, showing a winner every time I played a hand, and assuring my opponents that they did the right thing whenever they folded their hands against me on the turn or river. At the same time, I tried to profit from that image by stealing some pots and getting away with bluffs that no other player would have been able to get away with.

In pot-limit Omaha (PLO), how others perceive you is of paramount importance. If you sit and wait for the nuts, you'll grow old doing so, but more important, this strategy is – by itself – not good enough for two reasons:

♠ You've got to invest a lot of money before you can *get* the nuts. If you haven't invested a lot of money into the pot already whenever you get the nuts, you will rarely win a big pot. In this game, you have to *build* the pot to win a lot.

♠ Even when you have the nuts early, most of the time there are so many draws out against you (remember, this is Omaha where the draw can be the favourite on the flop even over the temporary nuts), that you might still lose.

What then is the correct strategy for playing this game? Here are a few suggestions:

♠ **Play aggressively.** You must show your opponents that you're willing to put your entire stack in whenever you're involved in a hand. Lots of times, your aggression will make others give up (unless they flop a great hand like a set or a premium draw) and you will win the pot uncontested. However, make sure that you have more money than any other player on the table (that is, any player you figure to make money from in the long run). If you buy in for the minimum, people will fear you less and you will have to show the winning hand every time.

♠ **Call only when you're setting someone up.** Sometimes in PLO, you're last to act on the flop, there has been a small bet and, let's say, two callers. You have a good draw so you call because you have the proper odds, and folding would be too tight. Sometimes this call is logical; sometimes it is right. Always consider your alternatives, though; always consider whom and what you're up against. If you think that there are no great hands out against you, this might be the time to make a big raise and blast your opponents off their hands. If you have a big stack and show the other players that you're willing to put all your money in the middle, the pot might end right there. In PLO, you have to bet or raise at some point in the hand, unless you're setting someone up to bluff off all his money. However, when making a call, always consider implied odds (how much extra money will I probably make if I hit my hand?) and bluffing rights (can I bluff my opponent out of the pot if a scare card comes?).

♠ **Play very tight before the flop.** A great starting hand can, with a favourable flop, become a huge moneymaker. With an average hand and the same great flop, the pot won't be nearly as big most of the time. Quality starting hands might also give you some escape hatches, some additional backdoor outs to get lucky and win.

♠ **Play your position.** Position in PLO is much more important than it is in most other games. In PLO, you can pick up quite a few pots just because of your position and/or the weakness that is shown by players who've acted before you. Plus, if you have a good hand in position, you'll make a lot more money than when out of position.

♠ **Always aim at the opposition's entire stack.** Don't worry too much about trying to win small (unraised) pots. Instead, do everything you can to build a big pot when you have a hand that has the potential to flop something good, so that when this does happen, you might break your opponent(s).

♠ **Put your chips in before your opponent puts his in.** In Omaha you often flop decent-but-not-great hands like the bare nut-flush draw or a small wraparound straight draw, hands that you may not be willing to pay off a pot-sized bet with. Note the intimidation factor here. When you bet $200 into a $200 pot, and both you and your opponent have a $2600 stack, you're basically betting your entire stack. When he calls your bet on the flop, you might very well bet the turn ($600) and the river ($1800). He may re-evaluate his hand, thinking, 'Is this hand worth my entire stack?' and then decide to pass. Unless someone has the temporary nuts or a monster draw, you might win the pot uncontested. But when you check, someone else will certainly bet and you may have to fold. Of course, don't be aggressive *every* time you flop some kind of draw, but when you do get involved, play aggressively and, most of all, make people fear you. Intimidating your opponents, coupled with utilizing the hand-reading and psychology skills that I hope you've developed when moving up the ranks, will pave the way for you to become a successful PLO player.

♠ **Play the people *and* the cards.** A favourite quote by action players, whenever they win a pot uncontested, is: 'Rocks play their cards. I play the players.' In PLO, you've got to play the cards *and* the players. Can your opponents stand the heat? Can they fold a good draw? Do they call with two pair? When you check, will they bluff? It may be correct to play exactly the same hand in a totally different way depending on whom you are up against.

This is, in short, what I consider to be a basic, winning pot-limit Omaha strategy. When you're new to PLO, it might be good to gain some experience in tournaments or small cash games, or to buy in for a smaller amount than I have advised here to get used to the flow of the game – and to avoid some of the huge swings that are part of it.

A hard day at the office

In the previous article, the first I ever wrote in a poker magazine ('About pot-limit Omaha and table image') I gave a short game plan, some sort of optimum strategy to approach most PLO games. I recommended playing tight but also very aggressive, and I explained the importance of making people fear you and of having more chips on the table than anybody else. The result: winning lots of pots uncontested, I argued.

It was not long after my article had been published, that I was shown the downside of this strategy: when you lose, you might lose big. However, this was mostly because I was unable to apply these strategies in a correct manner. Here's what happened:

The game

Pot-limit Omaha high/Texas Hold'em (button chooses), buy-in $500, blinds $5-$5-$10 (so, three blinds instead of two), nine-handed.

The players

Five Dutch players without much pot-limit experience, two Danish players I hadn't played with before, a tight Dutch player and me.

The play

I bought in for $1000, as did the tight Dutch player, all the others bought in for $500. During the first hour of play nothing much happened. I used this time to watch how my Danish opponents played. There was one I had seen in Vienna a couple of times, who didn't play many hands and who seemed quite comfortable with the pot-limit structure. His friend, who was seated to my right, seemed a better hold'em than Omaha player (he lost a pot in Omaha against a Dutch player who had been betting the pot all the way after the flop came K-K-J and who, sure enough, showed K-J and won). In my opinion he didn't have much PLO experience, but he played pretty tight and seemed like a serious player to me. I used this first hour to establish my image as super-rock and folded every hand. I didn't make a single call during this time, nor did I complete any (small) blind.

Then I picked up A♠-Q♣-J♥-4♥ and completed the – first – small blind. Seven players took the flop, which came A♥-K♥-4♣. Even though this was a pretty fair flop to my hand, I decided to check rather than bet into the field. Everybody checked to the button (the young Dane), who bet the pot, $70. I figured that I had a fair chance of having the best hand, and if not I probably had quite a few straight or flush outs. I figured that the button was unlikely to hold aces or kings (considering the way he played, he would probably have raised preflop), so I decided to try to end the pot right there and raised to $250. A Dutch player in middle position called my checkraise (he now had about $150 left) as did, after some hesitation, the Dane. I didn't like this. My hand was in danger of being second best in two ways. I figured the Dane for 4-4, A-4 with something extra (like my hand), but most likely A-K with nothing else (by the way he called, it seemed to me like he had some kind of made hand and wasn't drawing). Now there was suddenly a big pot, with most likely the nut-flush draw out there (what else could the Dutch guy have?) and I was out of position with a hand that I don't like playing against two opponents.

The turn was the 6♦. I decided to try to use my tight image to blast the Dane out of the pot (surely he couldn't call all his money on a small set or two pair, could he?) and to play the probable drawing hand heads-up: I figured that he would only have seven flush outs – I also had two hearts – and maybe two or three outs for a gutshot straight. This decision turned out to be a huge mistake. I bet $700, the Dutch guy (with indeed the nut-flush draw) called all-in $150, but the Danish guy also called for his last $650, showing A-K-4-x, which left me drawing to just my flush, the gut-shot straight and a split pot four). The river was a blank though, and I lost a lot of money, having only myself to blame. I cursed myself for playing my hand this badly. I thought that the guy to my right would have been able to lay down his hand. I imagined that he was more observant about who he was up against than he really was, so my bet on the turn was al-most certainly a mistake, given that even if I had made my hand on the river, I would still probably just have won the side pot. But hey, I figured, my chance will come, and so I bought in for $1750 more, enough to cover everybody at the table.

Some more mistakes

Then I got involved with Smile, the Dutch player who had won that pot against the Dane with K-K-J, and whom I have a pretty good read on. This time I was in the big blind with A-J-6-5 in an unraised pot. We took the flop seven-handed, flop 6♠-6♦-4♠. Because the players on my left would some-times draw for flushes even with a pair on the board, and also to make pos-sible overpairs pay to draw out on me, I decided to bet out ($70). Everybody folded except for the button (Smile), who called. For sure he had a six, pos-sibly 4-4 or 6-4 (however, he would probably have raised with them, but maybe he wanted to wait until the turn). The turn was the 4♣, making two pair on the board. I bet the pot[14] (figuring my ace kicker might be good if he had a six), trying to make him pay as much as possible for his (maximum) nine kicker-outs. He raised me $400 more however, acting very strong. Most of the time when he acts like this he has a good, but vulnerable hand which prefers to take down the hand without a call. I thought for a long time over what course of action I should take. I chose to reraise him all-in ($250 more), because if I called now I would almost be forced to call on the river as well, even if I didn't improve. In other words: If he had me beat I would lose the same either way, but I would win more by reraising all-in in case he could *not* beat my ace kicker. Now *he* had to think for a long time (it turned out that he feared I might have quad fours or a made full) but he finally called, showing A-6 also. A three came on the river, which made him a full house, so he won the pot. Though I was unlucky in this hand, I also played it badly. Knowing my opponent, he would have bet the pot on the turn even with a hand like 9-8-7-6 or J-10-8-6 (that I could beat). I should have checkraised him *then*, putting him under as much pressure as possible. The end result might have been the same, but by betting the pot on the turn myself (con-sidering the money was pretty deep) I made it easy for him to call me if he didn't have me beat, yet have some betting leverage left in case he improved on the river – and if he had me beat already, I would have lost exactly the same in both cases. Bad play, Rolf!

---

[14]   This hand was played at the beginning of my poker career, when I still played according to the common belief that if you bet out, you should almost always bet out the size of the pot in order not to give away any information about your holding. Nowadays, I don't follow this rule any-more, meaning that I probably wouldn't have made a pot-sized bet on the flop into the field, and I almost certainly also wouldn't have fol-lowed through with another pot-sized bet on the turn.

No milk today?

The following three hours nothing much happened. I played four small pots, won three and was feeling pleased with my game again. The Danish guys who had been pretty lucky during the first couple of hours had lost back most of the money they had won before, and I was still losing a little but playing well – and feeling confident that my chance would come. Then, the following hand came up. I was in the big blind with A♣-8♣-J♥-4♥. There had been a small raise by the (other) tight Dutch player, who made it $20 on the button and I called, as did five others. The flop came J♦-5♥-2♥. I had a pair, a gutshot straight and a (non-nut) flush draw – not a big hand by any means, but still a hand with quite a few possibilities. Thinking that I might be able to pick up the pot, I bet out $140, the size of the pot. The three guys in the middle folded, the button then raised to $450 and when the small blinds folded it was up to me.

What could the button have? Was he making a play at me? He might have a set of jacks (if he has three jacks my flush draw will most likely be good since both his jacks must be non-hearts); however, I also had a jack. A smaller set was very unlikely; he wouldn't raise preflop having fives or deuces and even if he had them he wouldn't necessarily raise with them now, fearing top set which would leave him almost drawing dead. (Re-member, I bet into four players *and* into his raise, so he must give me credit for something good.) He may well have suited (hearts) aces or kings for an overpair + flush draw, trying to win the pot right away, yet still having outs if called by a better made hand.

Given that I had reasonable doubt regarding the validity of his holding and the multiway nature of my holding, I decided to call, and when the turn came the 8♠, I bet the pot into my opponent, $1040. I now had top two pair, a flush draw and a gutshot straight draw. I figured that he would have to pass suited aces or kings now (calling would leave him as a rather big dog with just one card to come), so he could only call with top set (not too likely, since I also had a jack) or if he just didn't believe me. He raised me all-in to $1150 total, which of course I called. He showed J-J-10-10, the top set that I had feared all along. Since he held no hearts, I still had eleven cards that would give me a winner (eight hearts and three treys), but un-fortunately, I received no help.

Some final words

Pot-limit Omaha can be like this. Most of the time you only get to play two or three big pots a night, and if you get outdrawn, don't get lucky or simply play badly, the money will be gone. The main thing, when moving up the ranks (like I've done), is to stay focused on some very important things: Try to always play your A-game, don't fall victim to the Fancy Play Syndrome that lots of otherwise good players suffer from, focus on good and solid poker without getting too predictable, play only when the conditions are right, and most importantly: don't *ever* think that you can stop learning.

On this particular day (which ended up as the biggest loss I had ever experienced) I was unlucky for sure, but I also made a few mistakes that I shouldn't have. I have tried to learn from them and can honestly say that since that day, I have not been guilty of making these types of mistakes as often, and as pronounced, as on that particular night.

An unusual play

People who know me or have played with me always tell me the same things: 'You are a very lucky player.' 'Man, you hardly ever play a hand, but when you do you always win.' 'When *I* play ace-king, the board comes with rags, but when *you* do, there's always an ace or king on the flop.' I've been hearing this stuff for years, and I usually agree with the people who make these claims. I say: you're right, man, it's true, I *am* a lucky player.' Of course, it is *not* true – I'm no luckier or unluckier than any other player. The truth is: I play extremely tight and *very* solid, and I still think that my discipline is more important to my edge than my knowledge of all kinds of different plays and strategies. Most of the time, I play right out of the book, with an occasional exception. In this article, I'll discuss one of these exceptions.

The game
Pot-limit Omaha, buy-in $400, two blinds ($8-$8), nine-handed.

The situation
You are under-the-gun with Q-J-J-10 (no suits) and have called before the flop, playing a $360 stack. Six people call the initial bet, no raises. The flop comes to your liking: J♠-8♥-4♠, giving you top set and a gutshot straight draw. You bet the pot ($48) and get one caller, an aggressive and tricky player who has you covered. The turn comes 5♥ and you are first to act. What do you do?

The play

There is no way for you to know whether the five has made your opponent a straight or not. Your opponent might be in there with 7-6-5-x,
Q-10-9-x, the ace-high flush draw or some kind of combination hand that
might, or might not, contain a seven and a six. If you bet the pot ($144) and
get raised, you will almost certainly have to call, because even if you think
you are beat, you can improve with a nine (for a straight) or any pair (for a
full house or quads) and it will cost you only $160 more for a total pot of
$740. However, if your opponent calls rather than raises, you will still have
the same $160 left in front of you, when almost every river card will scare
the hell out of you. Any spade, heart, six, seven, ten or queen may improve
your opponent's hand over yours, even an ace or king may be bad for you
(if your opponent is in there with an overpair + flush draw, for example)
and also a blank may not necessarily be good (if your opponent *does* have
the 7-6 but for whatever reason chose not to raise). This means that you
might very well be bluffed out on the river if a scare card comes that was
in fact of no help to your opponent – whereas if you decide to pay off, you
might lose a lot if your opponent *does* have the goods. On top of that, *you*
probably won't get any action if your hand stays good (i.e. if a deuce or
three comes or the board pairs) and if your opponent happens to have
missed his draw.

By now it should be clear that betting pot on the turn is not as automatic as
it would seem to many players who are not very familiar with pot-limit
Omaha. How about betting small 'to see where you're at'? (Meaning that if
you get raised, you can safely fold 'since your opponent won't be bluffing
in this spot'.) This is almost always a very weak play, in my opinion. Anyone who can be considered a 'player' and even tight, solid players like me
are going to semi-bluff raise you off your hand here, because by making
this kind of bet you are *asking* your opponent to take the pot away from
you. If your opponent is not that savvy and just calls here, you've still got
the same dilemma as before: almost every river card looks dangerous and
might have improved your opponent. That is: you are vulnerable to being
bluffed out on the river, especially since your opponent is aggressive and
tricky, as stated. Now, it's these two characteristics that are the key to the
unusual play that I would recommend here.

I would simply check the turn, rather than bet the pot or bet small. My opponent knows that I don't have the nuts: the most likely hands for me to
have are J-J, 8-8, nut-flush draw + pair or the big Q-10-9 wrap. It is almost
impossible for me to have the 7-6 after having bet the pot against a two-

suited J-8-4 flop with four people behind me still to act, but even if I did have it I wouldn't check on the turn, would I? On top of that, he knows that I fear that *he* might have made the nuts, because *he* might very well be in there with a seven and a six. Since he's tricky and aggressive, he will almost certainly bet here to take the pot away from me, *whether he has made his hand or not*.

So, I'm going to fold, because he might have made a straight and I only have a set, right? Or better still: I'm going to call him because he might be bluffing, and even if he's not I might still improve on the river, right? Wrong: I'm going to checkraise him all-in! Because he is more likely to still be betting his draw than to be betting the nuts, I'm going to charge him the maximum for trying to make his draw. By doing so, I take away his implied odds on the hand. I don't have to worry about a possible bluff on the river and if he calls and my hand stands up, I will have made extra money that I would not have otherwise made. If he has a good draw, he will probably call me (in which case my hand will be the favourite over his) but he might even fold, which would be best of all.

The problem here is if my opponent *does* have the straight he has represented, of course, but even then I am not dead. Any pair or nine might still give me a winner, which will be (depending on the exact hand of my opponent) anywhere from 10 to 14 outs. I have won quite a few massive pots by making this unusual play, and I always got the same reactions from my opponents: 'Man, you are certainly lucky!' 'How could you make a play like this?' 'Didn't you see the straight?' (It didn't matter if I had to improve to win or not; even when my set was in fact best I would still get these kinds of comments.) Well, I agree that you should be careful in using this play, and avoid getting carried away with it too much. However, under the right circumstances, against the right opponent and with the right stack size, this play can make (or save) you a lot of money, and it will add tremendously to your image of a fearless, merciless and lucky player. Plus, after people have seen you making this play, they will think twice about trying to bully you out of the pot in the future.

Starting hands for pot-limit Omaha: part 1

A lot of hold'em players who are new to Omaha, have trouble adjusting to the game. This is partly because playing Omaha requires a different mindset than playing hold'em (because Omaha is a drawing game, and because therefore there isn't necessarily such a thing as 'best hand' on the flop, like there is in hold'em), and partly because it's not as easy to know what to look for in a starting hand. (For those interested, Mr Bob Ciaffone had an excellent chapter on this exact topic in his book *Omaha Hold'em Poker*.) In the two articles on pot-limit Omaha in this series, I will discuss some of these starting hands – if, when and how they can be played for profit. Please note that the game here is pot-limit Omaha, high only. For PLO/8 (hi-lo, eight or better) totally different comments would apply.

Hand #1: A♥-K♣-Q♦-J♠

Analysis

A lot of hold'em players think that this is a super hand, and treat it like it's the Holy Nuts. Even though it is a good Omaha hand, I am not too fond of it, actually. For a big part this is because the hand has no suits, which weakens it considerably, especially its potential to flop a big hand/big draw when lesser hands and weaker draws will pay you off. Even though you hold four connected cards, it's not that easy to flop a big wrap (if the flop comes 10-9-x for example, you just play the K-Q-J, and your ace is practically worthless). What you want to flop with this hand is top two pair (giving you a gutshot straight as well, for example K-J-6 rainbow), and face an opponent with the same two pair, but nothing extra. You will be freerolling with the ace, queen or ten: you are practically certain to get half the pot, but have a lot of outs to improve over your opponent to take the entire pot, free of risk. Some other excellent flops are J-10-x (top pair + wraparound straight draw), Q-J-x, J-J-x when you're up against the other jack/weaker kicker(s), or Q-Q-J. The quality of your hand lies in the fact that if you're up against someone holding Q-J as well, all the money is likely to go in on the flop and you've got six outs twice (three aces, three kings) to improve over your opponent – and again, free of risk (as you can never lose). Hold'em players might think that the best flop would be A-A-K, but how are you ever going to make money with your hand here? Pot-limit Omaha players know better than to keep calling with A-x-x-x to try and make a full house. You might get some action if your opponent is in there with K-K-x-x, but any reasonable player holding those kings will be deeply suspicious if there's a lot of action after he has bet, called or raised with his kings – and therefore may not be all that likely to take his hand all the way to the river.

Early position (EP)

Of course you are going to play this hand, but keep in mind that it's not as strong as it seems at first glance.

Late position (LP)

You've got a nice hand and a pot-building raise (note: this is not the same as a pot-*sized* raise) is OK. Just beware that even if the flop comes the way you like (you flop top two pair with no made straight or flush possible) and there's been a bet and a raise when the action comes to you, your hand has become *very* marginal.

Against a raise

Against one raise this hand is usually playable; however, against two it is usually not. A lot depends upon stack sizes and the psychology of the situation, but in most cases a second raise before the flop means aces, or kings with high cards. Whenever that's the case, your hand is a big dog, and it should be mucked without a shred of doubt. There are other hands in Omaha that you might want to play when up against aces, but this one (big cards/no suits) is not one of them.

Hand #2: J♠-10♥-9♠-8♥

Analysis

Now, there's a real Omaha hand! Any good pot-limit player will know that this is a premium hand, and in some cases might be worth your entire stack, even before the flop. You will hit a lot of excellent flops with these type of hands: straight + redraws, a big wrap, pair + wrap, two pair + open-ender, all possibly with a flush draw to go with it, creating the possibility of a huge draw. Still, it's important to emphasize that if you only flop a flush draw, with no other outs, then your hand should usually be mucked against significant action. It is only in *combination* with the big straight draw or the made straight that the flush cards become important. They may give you added redraw/freeroll possibilities, or may give you such a powerful draw that you have become a mathematical favourite over almost any made hand – and therefore, you might choose to play the draw aggressively, rather than passively.

EP

In PLO, I almost always come in for a baby raise[15] whenever I'm the first one in; I hardly ever come in flat. You want to build a nice pot with this hand, which is very strong, even in early position. When you raise with these type of hands occasionally, your opponents might figure you for bigger cards than you have, and you might get a lot of action when you flop a monster like 7-6-5. Depending on stack size, the aggressiveness of your opponents and the exact type of flop, you might make a lot of money by going for the checkraise when the flop is favourable (say, when medium cards flop).

LP

You have a big hand, which is even stronger in late position. What you want is to create a big pot, and you don't mind having a lot of opponents in (in fact, the more, the merrier). Don't even *think* about just calling here. You have a raising hand – now treat it as such.

Against a raise

Against one raise your hand is definitely playable. In fact, I would sometimes reraise rather than call simply to disguise my hand. If my opponents are figuring me for aces when I hold this type of hand, then I might make a lot of money if I hit the flop, and bluff them out when I miss – a pretty favourable situation, to say the least. Against two raises (indicating aces) this hand is still playable, especially when there's enough money left to bet after the flop (implied odds). You don't mind being up against aces here,

---

[15]   Assuming full-ring games and medium-sized stacks, like in online games where you buy in for 100 big blinds. This is the maximum on almost all sites and considered 'deep' by many players, yet in live games with no cap on the buy-in, starting stacks of 300 or 400 times, sometimes much more, are common. When I have a stack in the range of 60-100 big blinds, I will often come in for a min-raise, in contrast to how I usually play with either a short stack or with very deep money. These exact strategies based on stack size, and the reasons for them, are described into detail in *Secrets of Professional Pot-Limit Omaha*. Similar strategies for 6-max games will be described in my forthcoming book *Secrets of Professional Pot-Limit Omaha II*, to be released in the spring of 2009.

because your cards are live and opposed to the reraiser's hand. You *do* mind being up against someone holding the same type of hand you do, but just a little bit bigger (Q♠-J♥-10♠-9♥) – your premium hand is in *very* bad shape here.

Hand #3: J♠-J♣-6♦-2♥

Analysis

A lot of hold'em players think this is a good hand, almost as good as a pair of jacks in hold'em. It is not. You've got no suits, no straight draws, nothing – the only thing you have is a pair of jacks. You *have* to flop a jack to continue playing, but that's not the main problem here. The problem is that even when a jack flops (with no overcards – you don't want to flop middle set in an unraised pot only to get excessive action), there will be many draws out against you: when you're up against a premium draw you might not be in as good a shape as you think you are. Take the flop J-10-2 rainbow – just about as good as it gets for your hand, right? Well, if your opponent is holding K-Q-9-8, he's got four aces, four sevens, and three kings, queens, nines and eights – 20 outs twice! If the flop comes with two of a suit, then it's even more power to the draw. Of course, you can still improve to a full yourself and sure, if you can get all your money in on the flop with the temporary nuts (top set), by all means do so. The thing with this hand is: a) you've only got two cards; the best Omaha hands have four cards that coordinate with each other, and b) you need to flop a jack, but this jack will almost certainly create serious straight opportunities, and you don't have any straight blockers in your hand (even the, still weak, J-J-8-7 holding would be a lot better from this perspective).[16]

---

16   In fact, this J-J-6-2 hand is not just very weak in a full-ring game – even in today's highly popular 6-max games the hand should not be played very often. Of course, in position and with deep money, against no one who has shown any strength yet, there are many hands you can play aggressively. And yes, this hand is probably one of them. But please note that you would not be playing this hand in the first place because of the strength of this holding, but more because of your good position and the fact that – because of the depth of the money – many pots will be decided without a showdown. Of course, in these highly aggressive games, this weak, no-suits J-J-6-2 has one advantage. If on the button, in a raised pot, you happen to flop top set with it, you may get excessive

EP

No way are you going to play this hand, not ever!

LP

On the button, you might want to call in an unraised pot, especially in a game with some relatively new and/or extremely loose players, who might pay off generously in case you flop a jack. Against tougher opposition, there's nothing to think about – you have an easy fold.

In the second part of this article on pot-limit Omaha, I will discuss four more starting hands, and the considerations if, when and how to play them.

Starting hands for pot-limit Omaha: part 2

In the first part of this article, I discussed three starting hands in my favourite game, pot-limit Omaha high (PLO), the big money game. Almost all of the top professionals in Europe prefer this game over any other, because it offers an almost perfect combination of luck and skill, and the danger of the game dying out is therefore not as strong as in pot-limit hold'em, for example. Even though the long-term expectation for the pro in PLO is huge, on any single night *everything* can happen. It is entirely possible for a weak player to clean out the entire table, and big losses for even the most successful pros are commonplace. For a hold'em player wishing to step up to this beautiful game, it isn't always clear what to look for in a starting hand, and this series might be of assistance here.

---

action from someone with top two or a lower set who is simply unwilling to give you credit for the current nuts – who thinks you may just be playing your position or pushing a draw, for instance. So, in this case you *could* get your money in with maybe even 90% pot equity (usually less because of additional or backdoor draws for the opponent, but against top two/no back up you could even have more than 90%!), and this would be a situation where, despite the fact that you have just top set/no back-up or blocker cards to possible straight draws, you could be in a *very* +EV situation.

Hand #4: 9♥-8♠-7♥-6♦

Analysis

According to most point count systems, this hand is trash and should just about always be mucked before the flop. Actually, this is a very nice moneymaking hand *when played under the right conditions*. Even though it seems that this hand would fare best in an unraised, multiway pot (because of the straightening possibilities), I prefer to play the hand in raised pots against one or two players only who are marked with big cards/high pairs. This way, I know when the flop hasn't hit my opponents – and I can put pressure on them, even when I have flopped a relatively weak hand myself.

EP

This type of hand performs better in late position than in early position. If I play the hand in EP, I would almost always come in for a raise to disguise my hand.

LP

Depending on the game, the players, stack size and circumstantial factors, you would either call or raise with this hand. If people are short-stacked and therefore willing to go all-in with all kinds of hands, then simply calling might be best, hoping to catch a good flop.

Against a raise

Contrary to the big cards/high pair hands, a rundown hand like this gets *more* value when the pot's been raised – if the raiser is marked with big cards, that is. In fact, you hold an ideal hand to snap off somebody's aces, because your hand has maximum stretch, you know what you're up against *and* because you might only need two pair to win.[17]

Hand #5: J♦-9♥-8♠-7♥

---

[17]   For more discussion on this subject, and also for some words of caution with regards to this strategy, see the classic article 'Snapping off aces' in *Secrets of Professional Pot-Limit Omaha*.

Analysis

Many hold'em players might think that this is a better hand than the hand above, but it's not. The gap makes it almost impossible to flop the nuts with the jack, and you've lost the six that made your hand strong from a flop hitting/moneymaking perspective. That said, in late position the hand is usually still worth a call, but not against a raise. The Omaha hand that we have here, J-9-8-7, may to some hold'em players seem to be about the same as J-10-9-7, but the latter hand is very good (the one gap being at the bottom, meaning that the key card eight plus one other flop card between a six and queen could give you a very strong draw, having lots of outs that would all give you the nuts), while in the J-9-8-7 hand the gap is at the wrong place. Any ten would not thrill you nearly as much now, as if the flop also has a jack, nine or eight (*seemingly* good cards for you as you would now have a big straight draw), you are in danger of drawing to a non-nut hand that could actually *cost* you a lot of money if you make it. Or, even if you *do* make the nut straight on the turn, someone could have the same nut straight + redraw, still putting you in fairly bad shape.

Hand #6: K♠-K♥-8♠-6♦

Analysis

Kings single-suited is a fine hand. However, it's not nearly as strong as a pair of kings in hold'em. The fact is, you will usually need to flop a king (for top set), two spades (for a flush draw + overpair) or 7-5-x (for an open-ender + overpair) to be a serious contender for the pot, and even with the last two flops your hand is not necessarily worth your entire stack. What's more, you cannot be *too* aggressive with your hand before the flop. Whenever you make a big raise and someone comes over the top, you are almost certainly up against aces. Then – depending on stack sizes, the type of opponent and possibilities to bluff after the flop – you might have to give up the hand, and you will have raised yourself out of the pot. That said, this hand is playable in any position and for any reasonable amount – even though it's not necessarily good enough to reraise with.

Hand #7: A♥-A♦-10♥-8♠

Analysis

Aces are strong in any game, pot-limit Omaha being no exception. However, aces are strong mostly if you are able to go all-in with them before the flop. When you cannot do this, your aces will – just like any other hand in Omaha – simply need help from the board to continue playing. In a multiway pot, this means hitting the ace or flopping two hearts, maybe with some straight draw as well. Against only one opponent, your aces may be good enough by itself, especially when you think your opponent holds a big pair himself and/or is unlikely to have received help from the board. There are a lot of players who don't know how to play the aces in PLO, especially those coming from a limit hold'em background, and the strategy of simply raising the pot every time you get them (which a lot of players do) is a guaranteed recipe for disaster.[18]

EP

If you are playing a small stack, you can limp to try and reraise a raiser, or, if you have more chips in front of you, you might come in for a small raise. However, make sure that you are not giving away your hand by doing this, and that you also raise with other types of hands in EP.

LP

You are in good position to build a big pot, and raising here will not mark you with aces by any means – if you are a good PLO player, you will raise in LP with a wide range of hands.

Against a raise

If you are able to put a large percentage of your stack in, then reraising pot is obviously your best option. If this is not possible, you have the options of flat calling or reraising small (to reopen the betting), if you think the texture of the game, your table image, the quality of your opponents or other

---

18   For more on this, see another classic article ('A few pot-limit Omaha starting hands') in the same book.

situational factors dictate that this may be best. Don't reraise pot when there's still a lot of money left to bet, as you will give your opponents implied odds on the hand: because *they* know *your* hand, but you don't know theirs, you are more likely to lose money to them after the flop, than they are to lose money to you.

Some final words

Choosing the right hands to play in PLO and then playing them well is far from easy. It will take new players quite a while to become proficient in making the right decisions in this game, and I hope this part of the series might have been of assistance in speeding up this process a little.

Playing the player

Most poker literature is aimed at limit play, how to play a specific hand in a specific situation. In pot-limit, it is not so much the hand you play that is important – it is much more *how you play the hand from the flop onwards* (note the difference). Because in limit a large percentage of the pots ends in a showdown, you will simply need a good starting hand to have a decent chance to win. In pot-limit, this is not necessarily the case. For a lot of good pot-limit players it is often more important who they are up against than the hand they are holding. To be more specific: in pot-limit, good players can often win against weak, predictable players almost irrespective of their own hand, and they try to do everything they can to get involved with these players as often as possible. (That said, I am considered to be one of the tightest 'good' pot-limit players around, and I hardly ever enter a pot without a good starting hand, even against relatively weak opposition. Still, this doesn't take away the importance of the strategies I'm going to share with you here.) In this article, I will discuss a situation where a top professional is not playing according to the strength of his own hand, but where he is *playing the player*. He is making his decisions based on the cards his opponent probably holds, or better: on the cards his opponent *does not* hold. I will share with you some of the thought processes that may guide the pro's decisions at the different stages in the hand.

The situation/plays/actions

A pot-limit Omaha game, buy-in $500, blinds $10-10, no rake (you are pay-ing time collection). You (the pro) are on the button with a very weak Omaha hand, A♥-6♠-5♠-4♦, and have the biggest stack on the table. A weak player in middle position, playing a $800 stack, has called. What makes him weak is not that he plays bad starting hands (quite the contrary in fact, since this player needs a fairly good hand to enter a pot), but that he doesn't play well after the flop: he plays in predictable patterns and is easy to read, as his betting actions almost always represent the exact hand he holds. All other players fold, and it's up to you. What do you do?

Professional player's thoughts

Gee, this hand is really horrible, and it can never be played on the basis of hand strength alone. The player in mid-position almost certainly holds a better hand than I do, most likely some sort of high cards/big pair type of holding. Normally I would throw away a hand like this almost every time, even on the button. However, if I raise and I can get the pot heads-up between me and the caller, then I might be in a profitable situation even with the poor hand I hold. I will be in position, heads-up against a predictable player who is easy to read and also easy to bluff – which means that I almost certainly have a positive expectation here.

You decide to raise to $30, your standard raise in this game, the blinds fold and you're heads-up against the caller in mid position (just as planned). The flop comes Q♥-9♦-3♥. Your opponent bets into you for the size of the pot, $80. What do you do?

Professional player's thoughts

I can never win this pot on the basis of the strength of my hand. My opponent almost certainly holds a good made hand like Q-9, 9-9 or Q-Q, maybe 3-3 or even A-A-K-J. After all, he almost always has a good made hand when he comes out betting; he doesn't like to bet his draws as a semi-bluff, for example, and certainly not into a preflop raiser. In the past I have always won the big pots against him, and there's no doubt he fears and respects my play – which has caused him to play even more predictably against me. Therefore, the most likely scenario is that he simply wants to win this pot right away with a hand that he thinks is probably good now. He doesn't want to fight, he just wants me out, as he fears that I might outdraw him on the turn or river. Even though it is possible that he has a flush draw in addition to his made hand, I hold the ace of hearts, the nut-flush blocker. It is unlikely that he will want to risk his entire stack calling me down if a third heart comes on the turn. Plus, from his perspective: if I call his flop bet, taking into account my preflop raise, he will figure me for precisely the nut-flush draw (or, less likely, a straight draw). This means that if a third heart comes, I will almost certainly be able to bluff him out of the pot. If a straight card (king, jack, ten, eight) comes, I will let my opponent's betting actions dictate my own course of action: if he checks or bets small – and therefore doesn't have the straight – I just *know* that I can bet him off his hand, either on the turn or river.

You call the $80. The turn is the deuce of spades, as much a blank as your opponent could have hoped for. Once again, he bets the pot ($240). What do you do?

Professional player's thoughts

Even though this is not the card I had initially hoped for, it is still a great help for my hand. I have created quite a few nut outs with this deuce, and I will have my opponent in deep trouble on the last betting round. My opponent still has $470 left and will almost certainly make the wrong decision on the river if I call now. From his perspective, I am in there with the nut-flush draw or a straight draw if I call his turn bet – possibly even a combination of the two. This means that if a club, a king, a jack, a ten or an eight comes up he will almost certainly check, and he will have a hard time calling me on the river for all his money, when I put him to the test. What's more, the cards that look like blanks to him, actually give me the nuts. With a four, five or six he will most likely bet all-in (so I can simply call with the nuts), and with an ace he will most likely check-and-call (when I bet the nuts). Either way, I will probably get his entire stack when I improve and make him lay down the best hand when I don't – now, in pot-limit things don't get better than this. There are only three river cards that don't change anything (the three sevens), in addition to the cards that pair the board of course (in which case I will simply give it up). There are over 30 river cards left in the deck that can force him to make a bad decision – either by folding the best hand or by calling with the worst hand. Therefore, folding or raising are not options here. Folding is not an option because the situation is just too favourable, and raising is also not possible because I cannot make my opponent lay down his hand (because it's pretty obvious that I would be semi-bluffing) and because I will give away my good prospects for the river. In this case, calling is clearly best.

Some final words

The thought processes described here are the way that excellent players, the top professionals, think when playing pot-limit: they play *your* cards, rather than their own. (These thought processes also show that top players always think at least one or two steps ahead. They know exactly what the possibilities for the next card are and how they can, or should, adjust to each and every one of these possibilities. This should be second nature for any serious player, even in limit poker.) Please keep in mind that I don't consider myself to be in this category of really excellent players, playing on an incredibly high level. I still think that playing from a solid basis – good starting hands – is the way to go in almost all poker games, PLO being no exception. (Also, it should be clear that for people who have just stepped up to pot-limit poker, that trying to use the strategies I have described here is not something I would recommend.) That said, playing ABC tight in pot-limit will make you easy to read, and if you're playing regularly against good or even excellent players, they will easily take your money by representing hands that you cannot hold (based on your starting requirements and/or the way the betting went), on the assumption that you cannot call. And if you try to counter their strategy by simply check-calling all the time, they will pick up on this faster than you can imagine, and you are going to lose a lot of money; in pot-limit, there is just no place for people who check-call on a regular basis.

The advanced plays I have touched upon here need to be understood very well in order to be a successful pot-limit player. Without at least a basic understanding of the thought processes I have discussed here, you will stand no chance playing pot-limit.

Choosing the best seat versus a maniac

A lot has been written about some of the difficult situations you will encounter when there's an extremely aggressive player, a maniac, at your table. Most poker writers have claimed that you should try to sit to his immediate left, so that you will be in position to isolate him. That is: when he raises before the flop, you can reraise with your good hands to shut out the entire field and play heads-up, in position with a hand that figures to be best. In my opinion, choosing this seat is not necessarily the best way to neutralize the maniac's power. In fact, I think that for quite a few games the advice given might even be dead wrong; I would contend that in some cases the seat to the maniac's immediate left might be the *absolute worst seat at the table*. (Note that I said in *some* cases, not in *all* cases.) In this article, I will take a closer look at some of the problems you might face, seated to the maniac's immediate left.

The best seat in pot-limit Omaha

In pot-limit Omaha, one of the most important considerations in choosing your seat is the size of your, and your opponents', stack. If you are playing a small stack, then the best seat is almost always the one on the maniac's immediate *right*. You will be able to create some monster pots by either limp/reraising before the flop or by checkraising after the flop. Because you can almost always count on him to do the betting for you, you have basically given yourself last position. You can let the actions from not just the maniac, but from the other players in the middle as well, dictate your best course of action (fold/call/raise).

Had you been seated at the seat that is recommended by a lot of writers (to the immediate *left* of the maniac), you would indeed have been able to isolate him on a few occasions.

By reraising pot you would have been able to shut out the others and have the maniac all to yourself, while having position on him. There are a few problems with this strategy, however:

♠ By reraising, you will usually be able to get only 20 to 40 percent of your stack in before the flop (depending on the size of the blinds, the size of his preflop raise and your exact stack size). Therefore, the maniac can put a lot of pressure on you later in the hand, when it looks like the flop hasn't helped you but might have helped him. He may semi-bluff you out when in fact your hand was still good, or he may make you pay off when he *does* have the goods.

♠ The advantage of a good hand over an average hand is not as big in Omaha as in hold'em, for example. It's pretty easy for someone to beat aces or kings when holding a random hand, especially a no-pair random hand – and this is exactly the type of hand that the maniac is likely to be holding.

♠ If you reraise the maniac with an excellent hand like K-K-Q-J (you would definitely reraise with this hand, wouldn't you?) and someone behind you comes over the top, you are almost certainly facing aces. If the maniac chooses to fold, you will have to call an extra 60 to 80 percent of your stack with a hand that is very good, but a big dog heads-up against aces.[19] Had you been on the maniac's right, you would have been able to let go off your kings without it costing you too much, or you would have been able to see the flop rather cheaply in a multiway pot (which is desirable in the situation described here, because if you hit the flop you figure to have a nut hand, and you don't mind being up against a lot of opponents).

♠ The hands you do win by isolating the maniac will not be that big – you will either double up your small stack (sometimes not even that if the maniac folds to your reraise or simply check-folds on the flop) or lose. In pot-limit Omaha, it is

---

[19] For the exact match-ups of aces vs. either kings, high cards or medium rundowns, see 'Defending against aces', one of the 'Classic Articles' from *Secrets of Professional Pot-Limit Omaha*.

possible to do a lot better than that. You can easily turn your $200 minimum buy-in into $700 or $800 if you try to maximize your winnings by sitting on the maniac's immediate *right*.[20] (Of course, after you have tripled your initial buy-in you have to change seats *immediately* – you don't want to play a medium or big stack with the maniac having position on you.) But had you been playing this same short stack seated to his left, and your strategy had worked (i.e. you isolate the maniac and double up through him) then your stack is *still* relatively small – and you still face the same problems you had before you doubled up. So, it is rather obvious that the only time when the seat to the maniac's left is good, is when you are playing at least a medium stack. Still, even then I think this seat is far from perfect – and not nearly as good as the seat two, three or even four players to his left. Especially if you have a few loose and/or weak players in the middle, this seat a few more places away from the maniac is much better than to his immediate left.

Some final words

What all these points illustrate, is that the seat to the maniac's immediate left isn't necessarily the best or most profitable one. I know that equally valid points can be made *in favour of this seat*, and I think that in some cases (especially when your opponents respect your reraises and fold all but the very best hands) choosing this seat *will* be profitable for you. However, in quite a few of the games I have played in, the problems associated with this specific seat outweigh its benefits by far, and I guess that in your game they might too. Therefore, I suggest you take a closer look at the exact type of game you're in, at the tendencies of your opponents, at the atmosphere at the table, and in pot-limit games also at the stack sizes of the various players, including the maniac. You should take all these factors into consideration when choosing your seat and then use this seat as a starting point to a) neutralize the power of the maniac and b) to exploit his weaknesses.

---

[20]   For more on the exact strategies required when playing a short or medium stack, see my classic article 'Adjusting your basic strategy to game conditions', part of the same book. In fact, the cornerstone of this entire book is based on stack-size PLO.

24 vices in pot-limit Omaha

In one of my other articles, I discussed 24 vices in limit hold'em, or how much your overall results will be harmed if you lack in any one of these 24 areas in poker. As I see it, four of the main vices in limit hold'em are: lacking in discipline, patience, being vulnerable to tilt/steaming and having bad starting hand selection. Here, I will discuss these same vices for pot-limit Omaha (PLO) live games. That is: I will not be discussing play on the Internet (where there's often a cap on the buy-in, and you cannot see your opponents, meaning that you have less information to rely on when making your decisions), and I'm not talking about tournament play either. Because PLO tournaments have a totally different flow than live games, there's often much tighter play since losing only one pot may mean busting out. Also, in tournaments the average stack size in relation to the blinds is often much smaller than in live games, where some of the best players like to play large stacks. Once again, I will rate every one of these vices on a scale from 0 (makes no difference at all to your results if you lack in this area) to 100 (lacking here will harm your results terribly). I will also show you the ratings I gave for limit hold'em (LHE) in the article mentioned, so that you can see the differences in importance for both games.

24 vices in pot-limit Omaha (in alphabetical order)

1) Not *adjusting* enough to changed or changing circumstances

Points – LHE: 75/PLO: 75

Has the game become a bit tighter than a few moments ago? Is the player on your left on tilt, and if he is what adjustments to your play should you make? Is the atmosphere at the table likely to change now that an obnoxious player has entered the game and if so, what does this mean for your pre- and postflop strategy? The ability to adjust your game is important, and something top players seem to be able to do automatically, almost without needing to think about it.

2) Not *aggressive* enough/not maximizing wins

Points – LHE: 72.5/PLO: 77.5

Pot-limit Omaha puts a premium on aggressive play, not only for made hands, but just as importantly, for playing the big draws. Playing good starting hands only, but then playing them in a weak/tight manner will not even make you a break-even player in this game: you will get creamed.

3) Playing with insufficient *chips*/buying in for an insufficient amount

Points – LHE: 42.5/PLO: 77.5

In PLO, the stack size is an important consideration. In some cases, buying in for the minimum might be good strategy, but especially when there are a few weaker players in your game playing big money, you should have a big stack in front of you – so that you can break them on one single hand.

4) Not *disciplined* enough (in the broadest sense of the word)

Points – LHE: 90/PLO: 85

See my comments on patience below.

5) Not capable of *folding* when a hand turns sour

Points – LHE: 77.5/PLO: 82.5

If you are not capable of folding your nut straight when the dreaded flush card shows up, or if you are unable to fold your unimproved aces against significant action, you have no business playing pot-limit.

6) Not capable of creating a healthy *gambling atmosphere*

Points – LHE: 70/PLO: 77.5

In big-bet poker, it would be nice if you have a little hustle in you, so that you can help creating a pleasant, and also profitable, situation. PLO attracts quite a few gambling types of players. Now, if they like to play with you because they see you as 'one of the guys', you will do a *lot* better than the serious professional who says nothing, gets no action from them, and who might in fact be a main reason for these gamblers to pass on the game (and instead go to the roulette, or play craps or so).

7) Not enough *heart*/courage/determination

Points – LHE: 80/PLO: 80

Pot-limit Omaha is no game for the meek. Even though it's hard to decide how much your overall results will be harmed if you don't have enough heart, courage and determination, I have no doubt they are very important. With the big swings that are part of PLO, you will need all of these factors to keep your faith, your motivation, and to stay on top of your game.

8) *Knowing* the right play, but not always making the right play

Points – LHE: 75/PLO: 77.5

Because one mistake can easily cost you your entire stack in PLO, this is an important, though somewhat intangible, factor. Those of you who have been around for some time have undoubtedly encountered players who usually know what to do, yet don't always do it. In pot-limit (also because of the added pressure) you will see this even more frequently.

9) Not *loving* and/or enjoying the game enough

Points – LHE: 72.5/PLO: 65

If you don't love or enjoy this type of highly fluctuating, action-packed games where, if lucky, you can book a mammoth win, then which type of games *do* you enjoy? While playing limit hold'em on a daily basis can easily become a bore once you've become at least fairly good, this will not be the case for PLO live games – however, be prepared for a rather bumpy ride.

10) Having poor *money management*

Points – LHE: 62.5/PLO: 70

Because of the huge swings in PLO, you will need a *lot* of money to play comfortably, and to avoid getting broke. A $50,000 bankroll may seem like a solid basis to play poker, but when playing regularly in $500 or $1000 buy-in games, you are quite likely to go broke, no matter how well you play. Then, if you can't get staked, your recklessness (being negligent in this area) might have crippled an entire poker career – despite the many abilities and qualities you may well have.

11) Not knowing the exact *odds*/percentages

Points – LHE: 67.5/PLO: 87.5

It takes quite a bit of study and practice to know the exact odds and percentages for every situation. Knowing exactly how many outs you may have, and comparing this with the (implied) odds you are getting, and also the bluffing rights (will I be able to bluff my opponent out if a certain card shows up and if so, what amount of money will I have to risk?) – all of this is far from easy. Lacking in this area alone will prevent you from winning even marginally in the long run.

12) Not enough *patience* in waiting for the right hand/situation

Points – LHE: 87.5/PLO: 82.5

Still important, of course. However, in PLO the dynamics are not the same as in limit hold'em. Because one big pot can make up for quite a few minor mistakes, the penalty for being a little impatient isn't necessarily as severe as it is in full-ring limit hold'em (where you can *never* be a long-term winner without enough patience).

13) Playing your own cards only, lacking in *playing the players*

Points – LHE: 70/PLO: 87.5

A hand that may be worth your entire stack against one player may not even be worth a call against another. Also, knowing if someone is capable of making a big bluff on the end, knowing if he *can be bluffed*, knowing how he usually plays certain type of hands, which tells he may or may not have, and then basing your decisions on this exact information – all of this is invaluable in big-bet play.

14) Lacking in *preparation*

Points – LHE: 67.5/PLO: 62.5

Even though this is not as important as in limit hold'em (especially since in most places there will be only one or two PLO games anyway, and if you are a reasonably good player this game will almost always be the most profitable in the house), I still like to come prepared and in the right frame of mind before entering *any* game.

15) Not performing well under *pressure*

Points – LHE: 70/PLO: 82.5

If you snap under pressure and are vulnerable to making the wrong decisions, especially when the pots grow big, PLO might not be the game for you, and you should stick to limit poker.

16) Not good enough at *reading hands*

Points – LHE: 80/PLO: 85

If you are able to deduce the hand your opponent is holding, you will know whether you still belong in the hand and if so, which strategy is best (push or pull). Especially with drawing hands, it is important to know which type of hands your opponents might be playing, and if you figure to win the entire pot if you make your hand. (Are all the outs you are counting for real, or is your draw contaminated?) Because you are playing pot-limit, one bad read per session may cost you your entire stack, so it pays to be proficient in this area.

17) Lacking in *seat selection*

Points – LHE: 77.5/PLO: 82.5

Extremely important. Being in one chair, compared to another, may make a highly profitable situation unprofitable – and the other way around. When playing a big stack, it is very important to avoid the seat to the immediate right of good, or very aggressive players who also have a big stack. Because you may lose your entire stack on one single hand, you cannot afford to be out of position in this type of situation.

18) Lacking in the selection of *starting hands*

Points – LHE: 85/PLO: 82.5

Very important, and still one of my biggest edges over my opponents, who are often less strict in their starting requirements. (It also involves playing the right type of hand for a specific situation, for example when you decide to play a less than premium hand like four low or medium cards, and you know that your opponent is playing a high pair/big card type of hand. Now, if he is the type of player that can either be bluffed out after the flop, or can be induced to pay you off even if it's clear you have him beat, then calling before the flop with this type of hand might be a profitable play.)

19) Lacking in *table/game selection*

Points – LHE: 80/PLO: 82.5

Even though pot-limit Omaha games are almost always good, if you're a less than expert player you will have to be selective, and avoid either very tight games, or games with quite a few people who play significantly better than you.

20) Bad *table image*

Points – LHE: 47.5/PLO: 65

In big-bet poker, your image becomes an important factor, and you should be able to profit from the way other people view you. For instance, if you have a tight image, you might be able to get away with bluffs more often than most other players, especially on the river. However, pot-limit Omaha being a value-driven game, the specific image you may or may not have is a bit less important than in pot-limit hold'em, for example.

21) Lacking in *talent*/natural ability

Points – LHE: 55/PLO: 62.5

Even though raw talent and having a natural ability for cards are more important here than in limit hold'em, they are of less importance than in no-limit hold'em or five-card stud, for example. Because in PLO a relatively large percentage of pots ends up in a showdown (compared to other big-bet games), there is often a 'right' way to play a hand, based upon the strength of your hand. (If you hold a wrap plus flush draw on the flop, it doesn't always matter who you are, and how much ability you may or may not have, as all experienced players will do the same thing here: they will go and take their hand to the river no matter what, and probably they will try to get their entire stack into the middle by doing most of the betting and raising themselves.) In my opinion, by reading the right stuff and learning the right way, almost everybody can become a decent Omaha player, regardless of talent or natural ability.

22) Vulnerable to *tilt* and steaming

Points – LHE: 87.5/PLO: 85

Extremely dangerous in big-bet play. However, because of the nature of pot-limit Omaha (with such big, and often multiway, action, where you almost never that far behind – even when you are up against an extremely strong hand), habitual steamers are often able to steam their way out of a big loss, simply by pumping up the pots and then getting lucky once or twice. Pot-limit Omaha both 'protects' steamers (because in this game they *can* recoup a few early losses easily even without playing well), but it also punishes them (because on the occasions where they don't get lucky, they are likely to experience a *very* big loss).

23) Not *tricky* and/or creative enough

Points – LHE: 55/PLO: 60

You don't want to become too predictable in big-bet play, as predictable players are often the natural prey for expert players. On the other hand, PLO – like I said – is a value-driven game, where quite often there is an obvious best way to play a hand. Often, this is an aggressive approach, also without holding a big *made* hand, for example when you have flopped a big draw and decide to do the betting yourself. If this type of action is considered tricky or creative (in my opinion it is nothing more than fairly standard, a common and integral part of every decent player's weapons arsenal), then the rating should be higher than 60, at about the same level as the second vice, 'not aggressive enough'.

24) Being plain *unlucky*

Points – LHE: 35/PLO: 42.5

Of course, there *is* no such thing as long-term luck. But in pot-limit Omaha, with the possibility of massive pots every once in a while, winning only one or two of these huge pots more than you are actually entitled to may make a *huge* difference to your weekly, monthly and even yearly results. Also, by having been nothing more than just lucky on these occasions, you may start to become more confident about your abilities, and other players may respect and fear you more, making it possible your future results will indeed be better than they would have been had you lost those pots.

Some final words

Some of the most important differences between limit hold'em and pot-limit Omaha, regarding the vices discussed here, are these. Patience and discipline alone, combined with good hand selection, may be enough to be a slight winner in limit hold'em, but not in PLO. Because of the big-bet factor, things like maximizing your edge, folding when you're beat, creating a good gambling atmosphere, your image, playing the players and knowing the *exact* odds and percentages become imperative in order to be a winning player.[21] Because any wrong decision may cost you your entire stack, you will have to stay on top of your game at all times. On the other hand, a few mistakes early in the session can be made up for later by creating, and winning, just a single big pot. In fact, winning only one or two big pots a session may be good enough for a *huge* win in this game.

Making the transition from limit to pot-limit Omaha

Rolf,

I am a successful limit Omaha player, trying to make the transition to pot-limit. I had a terrible outing in Tunica a couple of weeks ago, and I decided to e-mail you for advice. I dropped about $2300 in side-action games, most of it on one hand. And I dropped $1800 in the rebuy pot-limit Omaha tournament. It's not that I can't play poker. I did take second in the no-limit hold'em championship event, and won $20,000.

I thought I would start by asking some specific questions, and maybe engage you in a dialogue about my play, if you have time.

Question #1

Could my losses reflect an intolerance for the normal volatility in pot-limit Omaha, i.e. do I just need to bring more money to the game?

> *Rolf: Well, while it's true that pot-limit Omaha is a highly fluctuating game, it is also a highly skilful game. I would say that if you're still down after 150 hours of play, you should be a little bit worried if you are in fact a winning player, and if you're still down after 300 hours of play you should be very worried. While I'm glad to hear you are doing well in limit Omaha, in my opinion the pot-limit aspect (vs. limit) is much more important than the kind of game you are playing. To be more specific: while*

---

[21] Also highly important, one factor that for whatever reason hasn't made it into this list of 24: playing your position. Especially when the money is deep, this is one of *the* major factors that will dictate the quality of your play.

*there's a big difference between limit hold'em and limit Omaha,
there's an even bigger difference between limit Omaha and pot-
limit Omaha. Your (poor) results may possibly be a result of in-
experience with big-bet play.*

Question #2

Here's a typical scenario. I flop a set, bet aggressively and someone draws
out on the turn or river with a straight or flush and I lose the hand. Am I
misplaying these hands?

*Rolf: Pot-limit Omaha is a great game. It is also a drawing game.
Sometimes draws can be the favourite over made hands on the flop,
even when the hand to beat is as strong as top set or even the nut
straight. Draws can and should often be played aggressively.
Don't think that if you hold Q-9-x-x on a Q♠-9♠-3♦ flop and your
opponent, holding K♠-J♠-10♦-8♦, wins the pot, you were unlucky:
his hand was a favourite over yours on the flop, even though you
had top two pair and he had nothing.[22] That is: don't overestimate
the power of draws, but don't underestimate it either!*

Question #3

I am avoiding tricky plays that I normally do in tournaments and limit
games, because I am trying to avoid people drawing out on me. Do you
rely on tricky plays more?

*Rolf: Well, it depends upon your definition of tricky plays. In this
game you should be willing to back a good hand with all your
money, but good hand doesn't necessarily mean good made hand.
If I have a big draw and I think the nuts (most likely top set) is
not out there, I might very well try to make my opponents lay
down their hands, even though I have nothing yet. In fact, I might*

---

[22] Matching this K♠-J♠-10♦-8♦ hand against Q♣-9♣ plus two random cards
shows that the draw is actually no less than a 60.43%-39.57% favourite
over the top two pair. Calculations were done using the Omaha Hi
Simulator on www.propokertools.com.

even bet a super draw aggressively even if it is quite likely that the nuts is out there.

One more thing: in big-bet games it's very important not to be too predictable. A lot of players, coming from a limit hold'em background, try to play ABC tight, raising with the big cards and the high pairs, and fold everything else (like they are used to in limit hold'em). Pot-limit Omaha is a lot different because it's a game of implied odds, and of playing the players. Knowing who will pay you off, and who can be bluffed out if a certain card comes, is often much more important than the cards you are holding. Deception, reading hands, heart and courage are the name of this game, in addition to knowing how to handle your stack. The weakest players in this game are the predictable and timid players, who play their own hand (rather than their opponent's).

Some final words

As most of the readers of my works will know, I have devoted a lot of time, and quite some effort into making pot-limit Omaha as popular in the US as it is in Europe. It is not a game to be feared by the casinos, nor by the players. When I discuss poker strategy with even the best money players in the US, some of them still seem reluctant to take on the game, fearing its swings. In my opinion, professional players should not fear these swings. They should simply pick the game where the most money can be made in the long run – and there should be no doubt whatsoever that pot-limit Omaha is *the* biggest moneymaking game for top professionals at the moment. Nor should casinos fear the game. OK, in pot-limit Omaha it *is* entirely possible for players to lose big time and yes, it sometimes happens that one player cleans out the entire table, taking away almost everybody's stacks. But the beauty of this game is that the next day almost certainly someone else will be the big winner, and on the next day yet another person will have the chips.

More than this, the game tends to attract new players to the cardroom, most of whom are gamblers who can afford to lose big time once in a while. It is exactly these characteristics of the game that will ensure that the game will still be there tomorrow, next week, next month. Even though pot-limit Omaha games are highly fluctuating, the danger of the game dying out is not nearly as big as in pot-limit hold'em games – especially if the size of the blinds and the amount of the buy-in are not too high.

Plugging some leaks

In this article, I will give a short overview of some common poker leaks, an analysis of mistakes that are quite common and that can easily be solved. I will try to come up with some quick solutions to problems that especially somewhat inexperienced players may sometimes encounter. This discussion will involve small stakes as well as large stakes, cash games as well as tournaments.

Leak No. 1: Playing A-A-A-x

I get lots of questions from people who in Omaha high want to know about the strength of their starting hand when they have a big pair, but also hold a third card of that same rank, also known as 'trips in your hand'. (Remember that in Omaha high and also in Omaha/8, you have to use exactly two cards from your hand and three from the board, making the third ace in your hand worthless.) It should be fairly easy to see that having a third card of the same rank diminishes the strength of your hand, but quite a few people don't know exactly by how much, and in what way.

The problem with a hand like this is that in Omaha you will often need to receive help from the board to have your aces stand up; unlike in hold'em it is very hard to win with them unimproved. (This is especially true in multiway pots. Against one player only, the big pair *does* hold up a large percentage of the time, especially if your opponent is playing also big cards.) So, you would like to hit a set on the flop, but because there is only one card left in the deck that can help you instead of two, it has become much harder to get what you want here. What's more, even if you flop top set, you've still got that third useless ace in your hand, meaning that one of the good turn or river cards that can give you a lock is now in your hand. (Instead of the usual maximum number of seven and ten outs on turn and river to improve to a full house or better, you may now only have six and nine outs.) Also, you've got one 'blocker' card less against the straight and flush draws that your opponents are probably pursuing. Say that the flop is A-10-3. With A-A-A-6, you've got top set with no back-up. If your hand is something like A-A-Q-Q or even just A-A-Q-4, you make it much harder for your opponents to outdraw you by making a straight – heck, you make it even harder for them to have a good *draw* to a straight. Even if they hold the K-Q-J-x inside wrap, if you've got two blocker cards in your hand, your opponent will now have only seven outs to outdraw you, instead of nine. Now, with two cards to come this is a significant difference, and, depending on the depth of the money, this might be the difference for your opponent between making a *profitable* or an *unprofitable* call. Pot-limit Omaha players know that there is a *huge* difference in being up against someone with nine outs twice, as opposed to someone with 'only' seven outs twice. It is the quality of your own starting hand that may give you this extra edge, an edge that a hand containing three cards of the same rank could not give.

By the way, this A-A-A-x is a rather funny hand. Quite often, I will not even call the initial bet with it because of the drawbacks mentioned above. But in tournament play, this hand can actually be quite profitable. Because in PLO tournaments, play is often much tighter than in cash games, and because the money is usually not very deep in tournaments, big pairs become not just more valuable, it is also much more likely that if you raise, no one will have enough of a hand to call you, or to try to snap you off. And a second exception of where the A-A-A-x is actually pretty strong, is when you can go all-in before the flop against someone who is marked with big cards as well. As an example, let's say you have a $500 stack in a $10-$10 game. An early-position player raises to $40, and then gets reraised to $140. In this case, reraising all-in is undoubtedly the proper play, because the first raiser is likely to fold, and then the second raiser might choose to fold as well (winning you the pot without a fight), or call you with a hand that is a dog to yours. With the most likely hands for him to hold (K-K-x-x, or something like A-K-Q-J), you will be a pretty large favourite over your opponent – despite the fact that you hold a bad and uncoordinated hand.

Leak No. 2: Failure to move in preflop with aces, playing a short stack

Let's say that you are playing a $400 stack in a $10-$10 blinds pot-limit Omaha game. You are in the big blind with A-A-J-7 single-suited. There is a raise to $30, one caller, and now the button raises to $120. Quite a few players would be scared to move in with their aces here, figuring that someone may easily make two pair or better, fearing that they may not be the only one holding aces, or thinking that it may be better to just flat call and then move in after the flop, in order to protect their probably vulnerable hand. They are wrong. It is almost always correct to simply move in with the aces, for the following reasons:

♠ You've got the best hand preflop. By moving in now, you will reach the river regardless of the cards on the board. You are maximizing your wins because if you catch a good flop (say, an ace flops or three cards to your suited ace) you might not have gotten much action, while the money is in the pot already now. Also, you cannot get (semi-)bluffed out of the pot if the flop comes something scary like 6-5-4 of one suit that you don't have.

♠ There's no reason whatsoever to assume that one of your opponents must have aces as well – in fact, you will almost certainly be the only one holding them. The button may simply be playing his position, or raising with something like K-K-x-x or A-K-Q-10. If by moving in you can get the pot heads-up between you and the button, you will be in very good shape, especially if by chance he was playing big cards or high pairs, rather than something like 8-7-5-4 or 10-9-7-6.

♠ You will get some dead money into the pot by moving in. If the people who have invested $30 will fold to your reraise, then you don't even have to win the pot 50% of the time to still have a positive expectation.

♠ If you get called in more than one place, you may well get some protection after the flop. The hand that would have won on the end may actually get bet out of the pot on the flop because of a big bet by the third player who wants to see the turn and river card for free, hoping to get lucky against the announced pair of aces of the all-in player (you).

♠ Even if your opponent indeed has the two remaining aces, then folding is still not an option, especially with your relatively small stack and the $10 blind money you've already put in. (Remember, even if your total expectation of the pot was just $391, then moving in would still be better than folding. After all, you will put in $390 more with an expected return of $391, or a profit of $1. This despite the fact that you would lose $9 on the hand on average.) If you just call, you will almost always have to call after the flop as well because of the tremendous odds you are getting, so you shouldn't make things more difficult than they are, and simply move in now. You get maximum value, you get it all-in with the current best hand, you will reach the river regardless of the cards on the board *and* you avoid giving your opponents any kind of implied odds. The only time when flat calling might have been better is when you are 100% certain that your opponent also has aces, and you want to try to make him lay down the same hand that you have after the flop by representing whatever dangerous cards come on the board. But for this to be successful, you will have to know for a fact your opponent has aces also (which is not the case here), *and* the money has to be deep enough that folding after the flop will be a serious option for your opponent – and once again, in this situation this will probably not be the case.

Some players claim that under certain circumstances it might not be worth it to move all-in before the flop with A-A-x-x. Well, I am not one of them. I would say: Don't try to outthink yourself. By simply always moving in with aces whenever the possibility presents itself, you will be slightly wrong a very small percentage of the time, and you will be very right a large percentage of the time. Unless you've reached expert status already, you should simply do the obvious: move in with the current best hand, and hope to have it stand up. This is what I would do – so I guess it might work for you too.

Leak No. 3: Underestimating the value of rundown hands

People who are new to Omaha often have trouble analysing their starting hands correctly. Coming from a limit hold'em background, they know how to appreciate the high cards and the big pairs, but they fail to see the potential strength of hands like 10-9-8-6 and 7-6-5-4. When the circumstances are right, these hands can make you a tremendous amount of money. This is especially true if you are up against someone who is known to overplay his big pairs, and who is simply unable to release them even when the texture of the board and/or the significance of the action indicates that this may be necessary. (If you are up against someone who cannot release his bare aces against a board 10-8-5 with two of a suit, then playing the small and medium rundown hands may be very profitable for you – especially when you are in position and the money is deep.)

Hold'em players who are giving Omaha a try habitually overestimate the strength of high pairs, especially after the flop. They also fail to see the need to play coordinated cards, and thus they habitually *underestimate* the small and medium rundowns. If you want to become truly successful at the high-stakes pot-limit Omaha games, you shouldn't be one of them.

Leak No. 4: Making the wrong decisions when a scare card comes up

A common scenario for players who are relatively inexperienced in pot-limit Omaha (high only) would be something like this. They call in early position with Q-Q-8-7 and get a flop 6-5-4 with two of a suit that they don't have. Then, reasoning that they have the current nuts and thus have to charge their opponents to draw out, they bet the pot, a bet that is about 15 or 20 percent of their total stack. They get called in two places, and then on the turn the board pairs. What should they do?

Well, while a *good* player will usually be able to make the correct decision here and thus doesn't have many problems, someone who is *not* that good or who doesn't read people well should probably have tried to avoid this scenario in the first place. For him, it might have been better to simply check on the flop and then go for the checkraise, and if everybody checks the flop and a blank comes on the turn, simply go for the checkraise again. This way, the player will minimize his losses in case he gets outdrawn on the turn, and he will avoid tough and tricky decisions later in the hand. After all, with a scare card on the turn, a not very experienced player is likely to make one of the following mistakes:

- ♠ Losing more money with a hand that has already been out-drawn, and that has zero percent chance of winning.
- ♠ Getting bluffed out by a good player who knows his opponent has a straight and also knows that he can make him lay it down – when in fact this good player doesn't have him beat at all. (He might have a flush draw that hasn't gotten there yet, or have the same straight.)

To avoid these delicate situations, the player who is not very experienced in this game should often base his decisions more on the size of his stack and actively look for move-in situations, meaning that he will either try to play for a very small pot or a very large pot, but almost never for a medium-sized pot. This is especially true if this player is relatively short-stacked and has just enough money for one raise when someone else has bet the pot. If this is the case, he should almost never make the first bet, but should usually wait for someone else to do the betting for him, and then either release or move in for all his money. This is especially true when there are still cards to come, meaning that he should try to make his move on the flop or turn. He might even try to move in before the flop, in order to a) maximize his wins, b) to avoid the tricky decisions that come with a scary flop, and also c) to take advantage of the fact that he is all-in and thus can reach the river for free while his opponents might bet each other out of the hand.

Leak No. 5: Putting your entire stack at risk in big-bet poker, in order to win a little

A big mistake that quite a few not-so-good, and even quite a few fairly good players often make, is this. You are playing in a big pot-limit Omaha game (I could have picked an example from no-limit hold'em as well, because the principle is the same), and on the river you have the nut straight but there is also a flush possible, as three hearts are on the board. Both remaining opponents check to you, and you think it is entirely possible that your straight is good, because both on the turn (when the third heart came) and on the river, both players have done nothing but check. There's $800 in the pot and you are playing a $1400 stack. Now, some people would actually choose to bet the nut straight here, thinking that it is unlikely someone actually has a flush, and thinking they might very well 'milk' their opponents for some additional money. After all, their opponents might be tempted to pay off this small, somewhat suspicious bet with something like a smaller straight, a set or even two pair. So, quite a few players would choose to bet $150 or $200 in this situation, a relatively small bet compared to the size of the pot.

Now, in last position when everybody has checked to you, this is almost always a horrible bet! First of all, the person who is most likely to call you is someone with a small flush – yes, in PLO quite a few players will check a small flush twice and then pay off any bet that someone might make as some sort of bluff-catcher. But perhaps even more importantly than the fact that you might get called only by better hands quite often, is the fact that you are reopening the betting with a bet that basically says 'I think I might be best, but I don't have the nuts by any means'. One of your remaining opponents may actually have been bagging with this nut flush or even the second-nut flush and decide to go for a massive checkraise, and perhaps even worse someone may also take the opportunity to *represent* the nut flush, knowing that from the way the hand was played, *you* cannot hold it. This means that with this little bet of yours, you have put your entire stack at risk to win a little. In order to milk your opponents for a mere $200, you are now in danger of losing your entire stack if you decide to pay off a pot-sized checkraise (only to get shown a flush), or of losing the pot when in fact you had the best hand (when you fold your straight against what proved to be a checkraise bluff).

In this situation, holding the probable best hand when everybody has checked to you, but also a hand that is nowhere near the nuts, it is often better to simply check it back, even when you think you may have a 65% or 70% chance of having the best hand. Even making a very *large* bet could have some merit in this situation. This way, you may get paid off for a large amount by a worse hand from someone who thinks this is a highly suspicious bet (in late position, having been checked to twice, you suddenly come out firing for an unusually large bet – now *I* might actually become deeply suspicious about a bet like this myself), while at the same time there is actually some – but not much – chance that someone with a small flush may actually fold because the bet is so big. But this small bet is probably the worst possible option in the situation described here – yet it is a bet that numerous players would make without a moment's hesitation.

Leak No. 6: Not being aggressive enough at the final stages of a tournament

People who are familiar with my works know that I'm a big fan of pot-limit Omaha: I guess it has become my main game for money play now. Even though I love pot-limit Omaha when played for money, I am not that fond of the game in tournaments, actually. One of the main reasons for this is that in this game hand values run fairly close, meaning that whenever there's a clash there is always a high chance of busting out, even when you hold the current nuts when the money goes in. (Because of this high chance of busting out, or this large short-term luck factor if you will, pot-limit Omaha tournaments almost always have one or two rebuys, even the big tournaments that have a very large buy-in.)

Because you are almost never a *very* large favourite in this game, your best strategy at the final stages of a PLO event is probably to do a lot of betting and raising, but to avoid calling for your entire stack, even when you hold a fairly good hand. Your opponent will almost always have a 35% or 40% chance of beating you, and thus a good chance of busting you out (assuming that he has a bigger stack than you). But if you play an aggressive game yourself, coming over the top of your opponents by moving in yourself, then *they* will face this same problem of having to call and then having to come up with the best hand at the end. In PLO tournaments, there is quite a bit of luck involved at the final stages of the event, especially if two players have put in their entire stacks early in the hand. By playing a highly aggressive game, you may be able to pick up a lot of pots uncontested, and if you get lucky on the pots where your opponent makes a stand (and remember, in this game your opponent is almost never more than a 2-to-1 favourite over you, not even when he holds a premium hand and you hold some random garbage) then you may well acquire a freight load of chips, and you can continue to bully your opponents. And with a large stack, this strategy is usually *very* effective, simply because in this game there are very few hands your opponents can comfortably make a stand with. And even if your opponent comes over the top of you while holding a pair of aces or kings, then you are not that far behind if you have been raising with some random double-suited hand – in fact, depending on the exact cards you hold, you may actually be close to even money.

All in all, there is nothing wrong with a risk-averse strategy in the early stages of a PLO event, especially if the tournament has just one rebuy. But make sure that from the middle stages on, and especially at the final stages of the event, *you* are the one doing the betting and raising. You want to be the one who is in control, putting pressure on your opponents and presenting them with difficult decisions, knowing that one bad decision on their part or just a little bit of bad luck may be enough to bust them out. Of course, a bullying type of strategy like this will be much more effective when the money is relatively shallow, when just two or three raises are enough to put someone all-in. With deeper money, an aggressive approach like this is much more dangerous, because your opponents will have more opportunities to try and trap you, in order to let you hang yourself.

A few Omaha simulations: part 1

Professional poker players work hard to maintain – or increase – their edge in the game. There are hardly any serious professionals who *don't* use any kind of computer software to improve their game. I have used Wilson's software for Hold'em and Omaha for quite some time, have used AceSpade's software for hold'em tournaments and hi-lo games and have special (non-commercial) programs that focus on big-bet play. Software programs like Wilson's *Turbo Texas Hold'em for Windows* are not just good for relatively inexperienced players; they are also excellent for professional players wanting to improve on specific things, for example their shorthanded skills. There are quite a few professionals who don't get to play shorthanded poker a lot[23], since there will almost always be full ring games available to them, games that they may view as more profitable and/or less risky than tables with five or less players. Now, by using this software and analysing situations for these types of games, they may suddenly find that shorthanded play might be just as, or even more, profitable to them than the full games that they usually play in. Also, playing on the computer against tough opponents (in full ring games) might be a good practice for serious players wanting to move up to the higher limit games. Most software programs have an advisor option, where you can ask the computer the best course of action (raise/call/fold) for the specific situation. Especially in the most recent – updated – versions, where semi-bluffing and even checkraise (semi-)bluffing are part of the advice, this is a very useful tool.

The game where I think software programs might be of most help is Omaha – either straight high or hi-lo. Wilson's *Turbo Omaha for Windows* software is excellent for players wanting to become proficient in this game, since they can decide whether or not to play their hands by using one of the point count systems the program offers, and because they can easily see the proper decisions on either street. There are many additional options (zip the hand, peek at cards, replay the hand) that make the software consumer-friendly and the statistics section of the hands played is truly impressive. In Omaha, things are not always as clear-cut as in hold'em. After a night's session of Omaha you'll often wonder: did I make the right decisions in playing my hand the way I did, or did I make any kind of mistake? The automatic test capability the program offers will enable you to analyse your decisions and to simulate 100,000 or more hands in just a few minutes.[24] In this article, I will take a look at a few interesting Omaha hands I've played over the past few years and the sometimes surprising statistical data I found, using this computer software.

---

[23] Of course, nowadays most (online) games *are* shorthanded, as 6-max games have taken over from full-ring as the dominant game – also, and especially, at the higher limits.

[24] Nowadays www.propokertools.com is better for this purpose.

Hand No. 1: 10♦-9♥-8♥-5♦ all-in on flop 7♥-6♦-2♥ against A♣-J♠-9♣-8♦

(wraparound straight draw + flush draw vs. open-ended straight draw + high cards)

This is the hand I wrote about in my article 'An interesting hand', published in 2001 for *Poker Digest* magazine, which forms part of the 'Classic Articles' section in my book *Secrets of Professional Pot-Limit Omaha*. At the time this hand took place I was known as a super-rock (I had just picked up pot-limit Omaha, being a typical limit hold'em grinder), playing only the nuts or close to it. However, in this hand I decided to go all-in on the flop when all I had was a draw. I had estimated my opponents to be rather weak in this hand and thought that I might be able to win the pot right away by making a semi-bluff all-in raise on the flop.

I was criticized though for playing my hand the way I did, not just by Kosta (the guy who lost the pot to me) but also by a few other players in the game, who claimed that I had been very lucky to win the pot. I had raised all-in against two opponents, figuring one of them for a set or two pair maybe and the other for some kind of draw (a higher flush draw probably, or some straight draw also). By doing so, I tried to get the draw out and play heads-up against the made hand, in which case my hand would probably be favourite. In fact, I figured that it was not unlikely that by raising I could win the pot there and then, by making my opponents fold hands that were currently better than mine. For instance, if they were in there with something like a small set or two pair, they could fear being drawing dead against one of my most probable hands (top set), and out of this fear it would be entirely possible that I might get them to lay down even fairly strong hands.

As it turned out, there was no set out there and my raise got called by a mere open-ended straight draw (no flush possible). High-speed simulations on Wilson's Omaha software show that my hand will win a whopping 69.8% of the time – not bad when all I have is a draw – as opposed to 30.2% for my opponent. However, when making my decision, I didn't know that I would be able to play my hand all-in against just an open-ended straight; I expected to be up against a far stronger hand than that. (Remember, people must figure *me* for a very good hand, considering my image.) I used Wilson's program to play my hand heads-up against either top set or the nut-flush draw, two of the most likely hands for one of my opponents to hold – especially if my raise gets called. To be specific, I did the following simulations:

Simulation A: 10♦-9♥-8♥-5♦ vs. J♠-10♣-7♠-7♣

(my hand up against top set; my opponent holds one blocker card for a straight)

Simulation B: 10♦-9♥-8♥-5♦ vs. A♥-K♥-5♣-3♠

(my hand up against the nut-flush draw; also gave my opponent a straight draw that is no good if he makes it, and of course he is currently in the lead with his ace-high)

Simulation A shows my hand is indeed a small favourite against top set: 53.8% vs. 46.2%. Analysis shows that for the times that I win, the winning hand will be a flush 54% and a straight 45% of the time; my opponent's wins come from a full house (69%), trips (18%), four of a kind (11%) and straight (2%). This data also shows that if my opponent *doesn't* improve (that is, if his hand remains trips), he will win only 8.3% (0.18 x 46.2%) of the time. He will therefore need to improve to win and it is for this reason that my hand – which to people new to Omaha may seem rather weak – is actually a tiny favourite over his, the temporary nuts.

Simulation B shows that my hand is in trouble when up against a higher flush draw: my opponent is a 56.8% to 43.2% favourite here. However, the dead money in the pot still gives my hand a positive expectation, meaning that if I play the hand time after time, I will still make money, despite being an underdog.

Some final words

In Omaha high it is very important to know the exact odds and percentages, especially when playing pot-limit. It is important to know exactly where you stand in a hand in order not to overestimate your cards (rather common for people who are relatively new to Omaha), but also to not *underestimate* them, so you might not recognize situations that are potentially profitable. In the second part of this article I will dig into this matter a little deeper, and analyse three more common match-ups, taken from live play.

A few Omaha simulations: part 2

In the first part of this article, I discussed the play of a pot-limit hand. I analysed my play on all streets, and with help of computer simulations I tried to figure out my chances against the most probable hands for my opponents. Here, I will discuss three more hands, taken from live play.

Hand No. 1: A♥-A♦-K♦-9♦ all-in before the flop in a three-way pot against A♠-A♣-9♣-6♣ and 8♥-8♣-7♥-7♣

This is a hand that I played a couple of years ago in a small pot-limit game in Vienna, Austria (while visiting my girlfriend, who used to live over there). I made it a habit to raise only three times the blind whenever I chose to raise preflop. That is: I never made a pot-sized raise before the flop but always made this small raise, regardless of position, to build the pot a little with my good hands without giving away too much information. If someone were to reraise pot, I would almost certainly be up against a big pair (most likely aces) and depending on the texture of my hand, my position, the other opponents and the depth of the money I could then decide whether or not to continue in the hand. If someone were to reraise me when I had a really big hand myself (quality aces or some other hand that I thought was best on the given deal) I would most of the time reraise the maximum to try to end the pot right there or to put maximum pressure on my opponents, depending on the exact stack sizes of course. (While this is a pretty good way to play against the rather inexperienced pot-limit players in Vienna, against more sophisticated, more aggressive opponents who might also reraise *without* aces, a different strategy is called for.)

In this hand, I was under-the-gun with A♥-A♦-K♦-9♦. Since I had raised before the flop with all sorts of cards (and therefore wasn't afraid that this action would give away my hand), I raised the blind here three times again. My neighbour on my immediate left reraised pot and someone in the middle cold-called this reraise before the action came back to me. Reraising once again would get slightly more than half of my stack in before the flop with a hand that figured to be best, so this is what I did. My opponent on my left reraised all-in, the cold-caller (after having thought for a long time) called all-in also, as did I. I had figured the opponent to my left for just big cards at first (he was obviously irritated that I made the same standard raises all the time, and I thought that at some point he would try to raise me off my hand with nothing), but when he reraised me once again, I knew that he had aces also.

When we all opened our hands, the cold-caller (with 8♥-8♣-7♥-7♣), who by the way is a very nice and friendly person, noticed: 'Hey, I might not be such a big dog after all.' I thought at the time that our pot equity would be something like this: me (with A♥-A♦-K♦-9♦) 33%, Herr Paul, the one with the double-suited pocket pairs 37% – because his cards were very live – and Hakan (with A♠-A♣-9♣-6♣) 30%. I figured his aces to be somewhat weaker than mine: his flush cards were rather dead and the sevens and eights he might need for a straight were in Herr Paul's hand. Hakan thought (as did most players at the table) that Herr Paul had made a mistake in calling all these raises, and that our aces were a big favourite over his small cards.

Simulations showed that the opposite was true: Herr Paul was an even bigger money favourite than I had thought, his 8-8-7-7 winning a whopping 47.1% of the time against 29.6% for my hand and 23.3% for Hakan's – food for thought for those who think that aces are unbeatable. Computer simulations like this show that aces *can* sometimes be very powerful, but also that the highly aggressive players, who like to play their small and medium cards against someone marked with aces, don't always have to be *completely* wrong – and, in fact, may sometimes be very right. By the way, for anyone interested, Hakan won the pot by making the nut flush in clubs.

Hand No. 3: A♠-A♣-Q♠-J♥ all-in on flop K♠-9♠-6♣ against A♦-K♦-J♦-9♣

Another hand I played in Vienna, Austria was this. I was in the blind (they play pot-limit Omaha there with only one blind) and everybody – yes, that's why I love playing in this game – had called the initial bet. I found A♠-A♣-Q♠-J♥, and even though I had made a pattern of making only small raises before the flop, I decided that in this case I would raise the maximum. Since I had a big stack, I thought that this might be the time to build a huge pot with this nice hand, even though I was out of position.[25]

---

[25] In all honesty, a huge mistake. Playing like this is one of the most awful ways one can play: making standard raises with all kinds of hands, yet raising pot with A-A. Especially from out of position, and with deep money, this pot raise with A-A was a classic beginner mistake on my part. The fact that players over there were so weak that they wouldn't automatically take advantage of the information that I had given away, doesn't take away the fact that a supposedly good player like me should never have made such a classic beginner's mistake.

We took the flop seven-handed, flop K♠-9♠-6♣. I had an overpair, the nut-flush draw and an inside straight draw. I thought that with so many draws or made hands possible on this flop, I might need to make the straight or flush (or trip aces) to win; coming out firing, I could expect to get called in a few places, since people over here don't fold easily. With so many dangerous cards on the turn, the last thing I wanted was to invest 15-20% of my stack now, and then have to release my hand if the turn card might have helped one of my opponents. So, I decided to check. Everybody checked to the button, who bet the pot like I expected him to. He is a very aggressive player who almost always bets the pot after everybody has checked to him, and *especially* when I am in. I figured that he didn't need to have a premium hand, let alone a premium *made* hand, and thought that this was a great opportunity to protect my aces and blast everyone else out of the pot. So, I made a pot-sized checkraise to try to play the hand heads-up against the button in a situation where I could easily hold the best hand *and* the best draw.

When everybody folded, he called all-in, showing A♦-K♦-J♦-9♣ for top two pair with one blocker card to my aces. I hadn't expected his hand to be this good, but I figured that my hand would still be at least even money against his. (He obviously didn't think so, by the way he reacted after a running pair gave me the pot.) Replaying the hand on Wilson's software showed the following results (simulation 100,000 hands): win rate for my hand 55.3% against 44.7% for my opponent. My wins: flush (62%), straight (17%), two pair (13%), trips (5%) and full (2%), his wins: two pair (57%), full (40%) and straight (3%).

All in all, after the flop I had definitely made the right decision in playing my hand the way I did. Even though I'd like to defend my hand, I don't want to put a substantial percentage of my stack in on the flop when it is probable that I will get called and the turn might easily give somebody else the nuts (or give *me* the nuts when I might not get any more action). This means that quite often with a hand like this (overpair/flush draw/gutshot) you would want to put all of your money in on the flop to see the turn *and* the river, or you don't want to put any money in the pot at all. The only time you're in real bad shape by making this checkraise all-in move, is when you're heads-up against a set, and even then you are usually not that far behind – especially if the money is not too deep and/or there is quite a fair amount of dead money in the pot.

Hand No. 4: A♥-8♦-7♥-6♦ vs. Q♠-J♦-10♠-9♣ on flop K♥-9♦-8♥.

The final example comes from my article 'An interesting hand (2)', included in the *Secrets of Professional Pot-Limit Omaha* book. It is a hand I played in Holland against a dangerous opponent (who had been affected by losing a big pot, however), who came out betting the pot from her big blind against the flop K♥-9♦-8♥. I had bottom pair, the nut-flush draw and an open-ended straight draw on the bottom end.

In the article I made an extensive analysis of the reasons to play my hand the way I did, and my motives for *not* making the play that would seem obvious: raising the pot. I was on the button and raising the pot would make me close to all-in with a hand that would be a favourite against almost any hand heads-up: even against a set this hand wouldn't be in terrible shape. Simulations show that my hand is a clear favourite over hers on the flop (61.5%-38.5%), and a pot raise would therefore have undoubtedly been the best course of action – especially since I expected her to be pushing a draw as well. I decided to just call, however, and raised her all-in after the turn 3♣, even though I hadn't improved. In fact, on the turn *she* had become the favourite to win (52.5%-47.5%).

Of course, because of the money that was in the pot already, it was still correct for me to go all the way to the river. Still, simulating this hand on the computer showed that I had made a mistake in playing my hand the way I did. Even though playing it the right way – raise pot on the flop – would probably have yielded the exact same result (she wouldn't have folded, I would have gone all-in and would have lost the pot, since I received no help on the river), that's not relevant here. Remember, professional players aren't supposed to think in a results-oriented fashion. It's making the right decision that's important, not getting the right results, and in this case there was no denying that I had played the hand *very* badly.

Some final words

In this article, and also in part I, I have tried to show you the right way to look at your game and to analyse the decisions that you make at the table. Computer simulations have become an important part of this analysis process, and I hope that these articles have given you a little insight into how to properly use them.

Play a night of poker with me: part 1

It is a busy Tuesday night in my regular cardroom. Because the weekly tournament is sold out, the cash game that I want to play cannot start until 9.30 p.m. Taking into account the closing time of the casino (3 a.m.), this means there will be only limited time to play what has become my favourite game: pot-limit Omaha, high only.

Despite the fact that on the very next morning my girlfriend and I are going on a poker cruise, and thus I will have just very little sleep, I decide that the game is well worth it. Usually, Tuesdays are the best days for playing this big game because all the gamblers are there, and giving up a little sleep seems like a small sacrifice to me. What I don't know is that this poker night will turn into a memorable one. Even though I am known for my consistency and for the fact that I hardly ever win big or lose big, on this day I am going to experience a *lot* more chip movement than I'm accustomed to. In this article, and also in its second part, I will guide you through this night and share with you the hands I played, the things that happened and the thoughts that guided the decisions I made.

The Ace gets off to a bad start

While sometimes I will buy into this game for quite a bit of money, because there are quite a few loose/aggressive players on my immediate left, I decide to buy in for the minimum (which is $500, blinds are $10 and $10). My reasoning: By letting the Action Men on my left do the betting and raising, I might well be able to win a very big pot, either by limp/reraising before the flop or by checkraising on the flop. While this strategy has given me tremendous success over the past few years, on this day I am in for some rough weather – I just don't know it yet.

After 15 minutes of play, I catch aces single-suited in the big blind. The opponent to my immediate left raises to $40 and gets called in a couple of places. I raise the maximum and get two callers. Because I have invested just over 50% of my stack already, I decide to bet the remainder of it blind. Even though the raggedy Q-7-3 rainbow flop doesn't seem that bad to me, when the player to my left moves in immediately, I know that I will need help. I don't get it, and my opponent's set of sevens scoops the pot.

Twenty minutes later, I play my second hand of the night. Under-the-gun with once again aces single-suited I make a minimum raise to $20, something that I do quite often. Three people call, and then the person on the button raises to $60. The big blind calls, and I once again raise the maximum with my aces – and once again I get two callers. As before, I put the remainder of my stack in without looking at the flop, and once again I get raised by a set: this time it is the button's K-K-7-4 that has improved over my hand. So, well within the hour I am down two buy-ins already, having moved in with aces twice – but little did I know about what was yet to come.

Some more losses

Another 20 minutes later, I play my third hand of the night. Under-the-gun, I once again raise to $20, holding K-Q-J-9 double-suited in hearts and spades. I get five callers and the flop comes 10-8-4 with two hearts. I check, the person to my left bets $100, gets called by the button, and I checkraise all-in to $460 with my wraparound straight plus king-high flush draw. The initial bettor now reraises all-in and succeeds in trying to shut out the button, and he also succeeds in beating me – his 10-8-x-x holding up against my monster draw.

Then, on the very next hand, I get aces in the big blind again. The person to my left raises to $40 again. He gets reraised to $120, and with one caller in the middle, I am able to get my entire stack in before the flop by reraising all-in. While the initial raiser folds, the reraiser does not, and he actually holds a great snap-off hand against my aces: 8-7-6-5 double-suited. He flops the nut straight to beat me once more.

All in all, the game has barely started and I am down four buy-ins already, with the people around me holding the chips – most notably the Action Men on my left. This means that not only will I have to fight hard to come back; it will also be pretty hard to do, because these Action Men tend to give *considerably* less action whenever they are in front. I don't like my position much, having gotten four premium hands already – *way* more than can normally be expected in just one hour of play – and having lost them all. This is bad not just from a financial point of view, but also because I have a lucky image that I just *love* to maintain – yet on this day it is clear that my opponents are starting to think that this might be the time to break me, that the Ace may now be more vulnerable than ever before.

Two more hands: Down to minus $3000

And vulnerable I am! Some 30 minutes later, I raise to $20 with the rather marginal J-9-9-8 double-suited. An opponent to my left makes it $40 to go and three people call, as do I. Having played with this player for many years, I know that in this situation (with him being in front quite a lot, and with me looking for an opportunity to build a big pot), he's got 100% pure aces – and on top of that, probably good aces as well. Now, the flop comes J-10-7 rainbow, giving me the nut straight, and the small blind comes out betting $120, slightly less than the pot. Now, while a lot of people might think that this is a great flop for my hand, it is not that good, actually. Even though I have the nuts, I have no redraws in case someone holds the same straight as me. What's more: I am not much of a favourite against the A-A-K-Q that the opponent on my left may well have, and also against a set I am not a big favourite by any means. If two or three people put their money in the pot, I will have to ask for not just one but two blanks – and even then I might still have to split.

So, in quite a few cases with my hand and this flop, one would simply flat call on the flop and wait for a safe turn card to make a move. But because I have a pretty good read on the bettor (I read him for a lot of hands, but not a straight), taking into account the person behind me who is marked with aces plus some other big cards, *and* because my stack is just a little too small to make the play suggested here, I decide to commit fully and raise all-in to $440. An additional reason for raising now is that the original bettor has a $2200 stack, so the player on my left will need a *very* strong hand to call here, because of the danger of getting popped again. Anyway, to cut a long story short, my two opponents are blocking each other quite a lot (the bettor holding K-Q-J-7, the person on my left A-A-K-Q), but an ace comes on the river to make this a split pot – with me once again getting nothing.

And then I lose my sixth buy-in as well. I am on the button with K-K-7-6 double-suited. An early-position player has raised to $30, gets called in three places and because it looks like my hand may well be best on the given deal, I raise the maximum to $200 total. Two people call, and then to my dismay the third caller pops it again. Now I know that I am up against aces for sure, and even though I hold quality kings, I am a big dog – but also too committed to fold now. When an ace flops, I know it's all over for me, and in less than three hours of play I have lost a (to me) unparalleled number of six buy-ins.

Down six buy-ins with the people around me in total control, I am thinking about the best way to try to recover. There is something to be said for trying to cover the table, meaning that I would buy in for so much that I would be able to break any player on a single hand. But seated to the immediate right of two highly aggressive and very experienced large stacks, I am still convinced that my small stack/move in early strategy is the right approach to tackle this game. But down no less than $3000, having had more good hands in a single session than normally in an entire week, and with the Action Men on my left in total control, I am not too confident that I can turn things around, actually. After all, this certainly looks like a *very* bad session to me – and with tomorrow's cruise ahead of me, I can think of better ways to start a holiday.

Some final words

In the second part of this article, I will describe the miracle turnaround that I *was* able to make, one of the biggest Houdini acts I have ever pulled. Fortunately, Lady Luck favoured me after all – but hey, I will share that with you now.

Play a night of poker with me: Part 2

In the first part of this article, I shared with you some hands I played and some decisions I made in my regular pot-limit Omaha game (buy-in $500, blinds $10 and $10). Playing a short-stack/move-in early strategy to take advantage of the somewhat overly aggressive players on my left, I lost six buy-ins in less than three hours of play and was down a rather significant amount: $3000. Not only had I received a bunch of hands that hadn't held up, I had also made one or two decisions that I wasn't really pleased with.

Perhaps just as importantly, it was clear that my opponents would fear me a lot less than they normally do (having seen me lose more pots in one night than usually in an entire week), and that my lucky image had been torn to threads – at least on this day. In fact, a friend of mine came over to me to with some genuine friendly advice. He said to me: 'Rolf, when it's not your night, and you just cannot win no matter what you do, then it may be better to simply give it up. I have never seen you lose so many pots, so if I were you I would simply go home and come back another day.' At the same time, I knew that my opponents at the table could smell my blood. They know that even when I'm buying in for a large stack, I am hardly ever down six buy-ins, and know this had happened to me by buying in for the minimum! But as it was, Lady Luck had some plans with me for the rest of the night – and as it happened, fortunately for me, she had some good intentions this time.

Lucky break for the Ace

I am in early position with A-8-6-4 double-suited, a decent but far from great hand, and I again make my standard raise to $20. Two players call and then the button makes it $100 to go. I don't really like this, but because I probably have a pretty good hand against some of his likely holdings (K-K-x-x, Q-Q-x-x, A-Q-J-9 or something similar), and also because I am getting quite good odds to see the flop, I decide to follow the small blind's example and call the raise. But then the player behind me reraises pot, and within seconds three or four players have their entire stacks in. With all this money in the middle staring me in the face, being in for $100 already and having to call 'only' $380 more, *and* because in a multiway pot against my opponents' most likely hands I am probably not in terrible shape, there is no way back for me now. I decide to put my money in, even though I don't really like it. But when I make the nut flush, I *do* like it, and with suddenly about $2400 in chips again, things look quite a lot better now than they did a few moments ago.

Then, on the very next hand, I get two red aces double-suited. Because I now have deeper money, I make it $40 to go instead of my usual $20, and three people call me. Flop: A-J-8 all spades, giving me top set with my three aces, but anyone with just two spades would be beating me already. I check, and then the person on my immediate left bets $120. Now, since this player has lost a significant part of his stack in this previous pot, I know him well enough to know that he will become a *lot* more liberal in both his calling and his betting requirements. So, I do not automatically give him credit for the nuts now – which I might have done just a few minutes ago. Everybody folds, and it is now up to me. If I decide to call, it will not be hard for my opponent to see that I've got three aces, meaning that it will be very easy for him to make the correct decisions on the turn and river. But because I feel that he doesn't have the nut flush, and because he knows that *I* might well hold the nut flush (after all, a raise with something like K-Q-J-9 double-suited would be common), I decide to put him to the test. I checkraise the maximum, and after a few seconds he announces: 'Well, then this is probably no good,' and folds his nine-high flush. I have semi-bluffed my experienced opponent off his hand and have won my second pot of the night, not just because of my cards but due to the way that I played them – even though with my opponent's current state of mind, it *was* a very dangerous move for me to make.

The Ace is on a roll now

Some 45 minutes later I manage to win another pot. With J-8-8-7, the jack-seven being suited in diamonds, I have flat called on the button and then paid off a large raise by the person on my immediate left – who I put on 100% pure aces this time. (I have a pretty good read on this player, and I almost always know whether or not he has a real quality hand or is just trying to represent one.) Because he has lost one or two other pots after our last encounter, he is now relatively short-stacked, and he bets all-in on the flop J-6-5 rainbow for about $300. When one player in the middle calls, I decide that I want this player out in order to play heads-up against the all-in player to see the turn and river card for free, so I raise the maximum. I don't succeed immediately, as the caller now calls my large raise too, but when an offsuit four comes on the turn he *does* surrender, and with a nut straight I win yet another pot. Suddenly, I am in the lead with more money in front of me than the $3500 I bought in for, something that I could only have wished for an hour ago, when I was completely down and out. So, proud as I am that I have been able to make this kind of turnaround without *really* pushing things – albeit by getting a bit lucky with two relatively marginal hands – I begin to think that I might be able to start my holiday in a more pleasant state of mind after all.

Preparing for the final battle

Little do I know that the climax of this night is yet to come! In the big blind, I pick up K-K-8-4 single-suited, and decide to flat call an early-position player's $40 raise. The player on my immediate left, who has obviously been affected by all the pots he has just lost, and who has called my $10 blind without looking at his cards, now reraises the maximum, trying to act very strong. Because I have played with him on so many occasions, I know that he would raise in this situation simply in order to build a big multiway pot, not necessarily because he holds a big hand – much less aces. When four(!) people call his big raise but no one raises all-in, I know that it is highly unlikely that *any* of the players is in there with aces.

I decide that calling is not an option and come over the top once more for a total of $1600. Because no one has more than $2200 in chips and because it is clear that everybody is pot-committed anyway, we all simply put all our chips in the middle, knowing that at least one of us is going to be *very* happy at the end of the deal. I ask the person who has made it $2200 if he has aces, and am relieved when he answers: 'No, queens'. I tell the dealer to just put a lot of kings on the board, and indeed the first card off the deck is a king. When the board pairs on the turn and indeed none of my opponents hold aces, I've got them all drawing dead and manage to win a massive pot with a hand that – although possibly best on the given deal – is certainly no monster. But it *is* a monster pot! With a total of well over $7500 (of which I have invested $2200 myself), this is one of the biggest pots I have ever won at this limit, and it completes probably the biggest turnaround that I have ever made.

Having eliminated four players on a single hand, the game is over immediately, and I have succeeded in coming back from very deep to book a massive win. (Well, a massive win for *me*, that is, because as I said I hardly ever win or lose big. Whenever I buy in for the minimum, a win or more than five or six buy-ins would be truly exceptional, and now I have won no less than twelve buy-ins after having been down six.) It needs to be said that I have gotten lucky when it mattered most, but you also have to *position* yourself to get lucky – which is exactly what I have done.

Some final words

I hope you liked this insight in a night of pot-limit Omaha, one of the biggest gambling games in poker. Even though on a single night it may often seem like there's not much skill to this game, the very best players in the world make *lots* of money playing it. Yes, it *is* a roller-coaster ride, and one single pot can make quite a bit of difference to your weekly, monthly and sometimes even your yearly results, but in the long run the very best players will always come out on top.

Fortunately for me, I also managed to come out on top on this particular night. Let's hope that after my holiday, once I get back in my usual playing routine again, I will be as fortunate as on this memorable day. And if I do… well, then I guess I will probably share it with you again.

Starting hand selection and stack size: part 1

Introduction

A lot has been written about the influence of the number of chips in front of you on the hands that you can and should play. Almost without exception, these writings are about tournament play. After all, it should be clear that in tournaments, those who only look at the quality of their cards when making the decision whether or not to play, and who don't take into account the size of their and their opponents' stacks, will perform significantly worse than the people who *do* make these adjustments.

But this article that you are reading now is not about tournament play – it is about the relation between stack size and hand selection when it comes to cash games. While in the past the majority of the cash games would always be limit, this meant that almost all cash game literature was written from the viewpoint of limit play, and the good big-bet strategies were almost always analysed from a tournament setting, not cash. But because of the recent growth of big-bet cash games, both in brick and mortar casinos as well as online, it is time to re-evaluate some of this old big-bet tournament literature and to dig into specific cash game strategies for big-bet play.

And that's exactly what I'll do in this two-part article series. I will discuss a couple of pot-limit Omaha starting hands, and I will try to analyse how the size of your stack can have a major impact on the playability and potential profitability of some of these hands. I will show that some hands are often playable with big stacks but not with small stacks – and sometimes the other way around as well. Note that the information I provide is not always easy to digest, and to my knowledge not too much has appeared in print about this specific issue before. But if you want to become successful in big-bet cash games, it is absolutely imperative to understand the concepts that I discuss here. In this two-part article, I will analyse three specific starting hands in my favourite game, pot-limit Omaha, and the impact of stack sizes on the best course of action – not just before the flop, but also later in the hand. It goes without saying that the underlying concepts I will share with you are not just for PLO; they are equally important for other big-bet games like pot- and no-limit hold'em.

Hand No. 1: K-K-8-3 rainbow (no suits)

Now, while most people who come from a hold'em background would think this is a premium hand, all good Omaha players know that this actually is a piece of cheese, because it has no suits and is totally uncoordinated – the pair of kings being just about the only value. Having said that, the hand *does* have some strength, and if you manage to flop a third king then you are usually in a very powerful position – especially when you are in a multiway pot and/or are up against relatively weak opposition.

This means that if you are holding a medium stack (say, between $500 and $700 in a game with $10-$10 blinds, or in other words with a stack size of 50-70 times the big blind) and the opposition is not too tough, there is nothing wrong with calling from middle or late position in an unraised pot to see the flop cheaply. After all, you know that if you *don't* flop a king, you will almost certainly be out, and you will not put a single chip in the pot from then on. But it is worth seeing this flop because if you *do* hit, you may very well win a big pot – as I said, especially if the pot is multiway and the opposition is rather weak.

But if you are playing a *small* stack (say anywhere from $150 to $250, or less than 25xBB), then this preflop call may not actually be so automatic. This is especially true if it is probable that the pot will be raised behind you. So, what this means is that with a small stack, holding this K-K-8-3 no suits, you *might* want to call on or near the button in an unraised pot, but not in early or middle position, because if you call now and the pot gets raised behind you, you will probably have to forfeit your bet – a bet that accounts to a fairly high percentage of your stack.[26] With a medium stack you *could* have made this call profitably, especially from middle position, because now if the pot gets raised behind you, the investment you will have lost is a much smaller percentage of your total stack. Remember, in big-bet poker you are always looking for opportunities to double through. Or to be more precise: especially with relatively shallow money, you should usually try to play for your entire stack when you decide to get involved. In other words, you should often play for all your money or not play at all. In cases like this, risking 5% of your stack with a very speculative holding is a definite no-no, especially if there is a reasonable chance that despite this 5% investment you may not even get to see the flop.

---

[26]   In some cases, when playing a short or very short stack, it may actually be worth going all-in preflop even with a hand this raggedy. This is especially true if you are in a game with highly aggressive players who may give you 'protection', either before or after the flop. They may bet very aggressively with marginal holdings to blast everyone out of the pot, in order to reach the river cheaply and maybe get lucky against the all-in player (you). What this means for you is that with, all the dead money in the pot, you are almost certainly a big money favourite – despite these crummy cards you are holding. In fact, heads-up against one player only, your K-K-8-3 may actually be a clear favourite over the hand that your opponent is betting and raising with!

What does all of this mean?

Now, what this means is that this exact same hand K-K-8-3 should often be *folded* with a short stack and can often be *called* with a medium stack – now, then logic dictates that we can almost always play it when holding a big stack, right? Well, not really. Because of the following conditions, playing this hand can sometimes be *profitable* if you have a medium stack – but actually *unprofitable* when playing a large stack (say, more than 100xBB):

♠ If you flop top set with a stack of 50xBB or so, you will almost never be making a terrible mistake by putting in your entire stack on the flop. Even if you are up against a made straight or a completed flush, you may well have up to seven outs on the flop and up to 10 outs on the turn to still win the pot. Especially with the dead money in the pot already, you will almost never make a serious mistake, and if you are up against more than one opponent, you are usually in a clear +EV situation – even if one, or even both, of your opponents have your three kings beat at this stage.

♠ But if the money is deeper, then the dead money in the pot accounts for a much smaller percentage of the total pot size. With a medium stack and a flop K-Q-J, you would not be that reluctant to put in all your money on the flop, knowing that even if you are up against the nut straight, you will still win the pot a significant percentage of the time, and in fact because of the dead money in the pot, putting in your money may actually be the mathematical correct play. But with a very large stack, it *will* worry you to put in all the money if you just have, say, anywhere from a 24 to 42% chance of winning! If you make a mathematically unsound decision when playing deep money, then the penalty will be very severe. So, flopping the third king with a large stack is not the same through ticket that it usually is with a short or medium stack. And because of this, an uncoordinated hand like K-K-8-3 – that has only one way to hit and that even when it hits has no back-up whatsoever – is usually a clear fold in deep-money play.

Some concrete examples of the problems/difficulties for this K-K-8-3 in deep-money play

Let's dig into this matter a little deeper, by analysing the troubles you may face when playing a big stack – even when you have flopped the hand you wanted: top set.

♠ Let's say the flop is K-10-6 with two of a suit. You bet the pot in middle position and get called by the button. The turn is an offsuit nine – a card that may or may not have helped your opponent. Let's say there is $220 in the pot, and both you and your opponent have $1200 left. It should be clear that this is a very tough situation for you. If your opponent is a good player, and has the hand reading abilities to put you on the hand that you actually have (top set), then he may be able to either make you fold the best hand by semi-bluffing you off your hand. Or when in fact he has made his straight, he may be able to lure you into calling or even raising with a hand that has only few outs to improve. From this simple example, it should be obvious that with deep money, the draw in position has some clear playing advantages against the made hand out of position. You should take these factors into consideration *before* your actual decision whether or not to get involved with your hand. After all, it makes no sense to play a crummy hand in order to flop a king – only to see yourself get into serious trouble once that third king has actually flopped.

♠ In the exact same situation, with the same two players and the same K-10-6 flop, let's say that something good happens for you now: the board pairs on the turn. Even though you probably have a lock, it may be hard for you to make any money now that your opponent knows that he may be drawing dead. While checking might work against some players in order to induce a bluff, if your opponent has a good read on you and knows you probably have top full, you may not get much more money out of him.

♠ If the turn is what you want (a blank), you bet the pot ($220) and get called, well then on the river you will face the same unpleasant situation as in the first example. Almost any river card will be scary with all the straight and flush possibilities, and if your opponent is a good player then he may very well lure you into making the wrong decision. And if the board pairs on the river, well then again you may not make a lot of money if your opponent reads you correctly. Because of all this, you may end up winning a relatively small pot in this situation when your hand remains good, but when the final pot gets extremely large, then you will *lose* a rather high percentage of the time.

Conclusion

With relatively deep money, this K-K-8-3 is usually playable only when you are in position, and when the opposition is fairly weak. You will usually need a hand like K-K-J-9 single-suited to make a profitable call when your position is not that great, because then you have the possibility to flop top set with redraws, which will allow you to play the hand more strongly. Also, if indeed you flop top set, you may now have at least some blocker cards against the straight draws that your opponents may well be holding. And having just one or two of these cards to block them, may actually make the difference between a profitable draw for your opponents and an unprofitable one. You should take all these factors into account *before* making the first, seemingly easy, decision whether or not to play. Knowing in advance the characteristics of a hand with regards to the size of your stack and the potential problems later in the hand, is *absolutely crucial* in order to play big-bet poker in a successful manner.

Some final words

In the second part of this article, I will analyse two more hands that can sometimes be played for a profit with certain stack sizes, but not with others. To be more concrete, I will analyse the medium rundown 9-8-7-6 with no suits, and the rather strange-looking A-A-A-x – a hand that causes quite a few Omaha players many problems.

Starting hand selection and stack size: part 2

In the first part of this article, I analysed that with a very marginal pot-limit Omaha holding like K-K-8-3 with no suits, it is sometimes correct to see a flop with a medium stack, but not always when playing either a small stack (<25 times the big blind) or a big one (>100 times the big blind). I will now discuss two more hands and the impact of stack size on the preferred play. Note that we are discussing cash game strategy, not tournament play.

Hand No. 2: 9-8-7-6 rainbow (no suits)

This is the sort of hand that good pot-limit Omaha players have come to appreciate, because under certain circumstances this type of holding can be very profitable. Again, just as in the K-K-8-3 example from last time, this is mostly when you are playing a medium stack, say in the range of 45 to 75 times the big blind in an unraised pot. In fact, with a stack of about 100xBB, you could even call a raise with this holding, especially if you are up against a weak player who a) almost certainly has a big pair, and b) has a tendency to overplay that big pair. But with a small stack, say anywhere from 20 to 30 times the big blind, you should not be too eager to get involved with this 9-8-7-6 – not even in an unraised pot. With a small stack, your goal should usually be to play for all your money, or not to play at all. An exception with this hand may be calling on the button in an unraised, multiway pot – that may actually be worth it. That is because this hand has quite a bit of nut potential, and can make quite a bit of money after the flop, provided you can see this flop cheaply. But in early and middle position it should almost always be folded, even when there's been no raise. Why? Well, I would say because the texture of your hand and the size of your stack just don't make for a very good combination:

♠ As in the previous article: You don't want to invest a relatively large percentage of your stack by calling the initial bet when you know you will have to fold if the pot gets raised behind you – and being in early or middle position, the probability of the pot getting raised behind you may actually be quite high.

♠ Even if the pot does not get raised, you will still get a lot of problem flops with this hand: hands like pair + gutshot, a good straight draw but against a two-suited board, trips with three low kickers, bottom two pair + straight draw on the ignorant end – all hands that are dangerous if many players have seen the flop cheaply. You will make a lot of second-best hands, especially if relatively weak holdings like J-10-8-6 double-suited are still in the pot – and in multiway, unraised pots it is very probable that these kinds of hands are still in.

♠ Because you are playing a short stack, you don't have enough strength (or better, not enough money) to seriously hurt your opponents and/or to pave the way for a successful bluff or semi-bluff. While with deeper money, this type of holding has a lot of playing advantages, for instance when up against a big pair (mostly because *you* usually know where you're at, while *your opponent* does not, and thus you can put lots of pressure on him even when you don't hold much yourself), with short money you don't have this luxury. Your opponent will simply put you all-in to see whether you have him beat or not, and the only way for you to win the pot is to have the best hand at the showdown.

So, it is clear that this type of holding (if it has no suits, that is; with suits you can play this hand *much* more strongly!) cannot be played very often with a short stack, and *can* often be played with a medium stack – now, how about deep money? Well, with deep money this can be a very dangerous and tricky hand that has quite a few actual playing disadvantages:

♠ You are often playing to make a straight, while your opponents may be drawing to a flush or a full house. This means that making your straight on the turn is *not* the same as winning the pot: Your opponents may have a bunch of redraws.

♠ What you would like most with this type of holding is to make your hand on the turn (most likely a straight) and then bet all-in to make your opponents pay to draw out, and to avoid headache on the river. But when the money is deep, there will usually be a lot of money left on the river even after a pot-sized turn bet. Now, it should be clear that if you make the nut straight on the turn with these small/medium cards of yours, that there will be a whole lot of possible river cards that will leave you without the nuts, creating higher straights, flushes and/or full houses. This carries the danger of either paying off with the worst hand, or throwing away the winning hand. (Both of these possibilities are even more likely to happen when you are in bad position with this type of holding. When playing deep money, you should be *very* reluctant to play these no suits small and medium rundowns if one or more opponents may have position on you. Reserve these hands strictly for on the button, and possibly the cut-off.)

All in all, what we have here is a situation where a hand is often playable with a medium stack, sometimes even against a raise, while this exact same hand should usually be folded with either very deep or very shallow money, sometimes even for just a single bet. Strange, yes – but undoubtedly correct.

Hand No. 3: A-A-A-J rainbow (no suits)

This is the type of holding that I have talked about before: three aces in the hand. Let's say you are playing a $420 stack and are in the $10 big blind. It gets raised to $30, one player calls, and now the button raises to $120. What should you do? Well, you should reraise all-in of course! Even though you have a bad and uncoordinated holding, if you can turn this pot into a heads-up contest, you will almost always be a favourite. What's more, against the most likely types of holdings for the button to hold (quality hands like K-K-10-10 or A-K-Q-J) you will even be a *big* favourite. Add to this the dead money in the pot from people folding, and it should be easy to see that this is a situation with a clear positive expectation.

With deep money, a hand like A-A-A-J with no suits can almost never be played. (Having said that, the three aces in your hand do provide you with a lot of bluffing opportunities after the flop. For instance, depending on the board cards you could credibly represent three different nut flushes, and also you can make a blocker play if three picture cards appear, trying to represent the ace-high nut straight now that is seems unlikely that any of the other players will have it. So, if your post-flop play is very good, if you excel at executing bluffs, and if everyone at your table is playing deep money, well then it may actually be worth it to play this A-A-A-J no suits out of freewill.) With a medium stack, you might occasionally want to call one bet to take a flop or to see if maybe a profitable situation will present itself. But usually, the more money you've got in front of you, the more you should try to protect it by avoiding marginal hands or situations that can easily get you into a lot of trouble.

So here, in contrast with the previous two hands, we have a hand that may sometimes be worth your entire stack when the money is shallow, yet not be worth even a single bet when the money is deep.

Conclusion

Playing a short stack

In general, things are simple when it comes to hand selection and finding profitable situations. To make a stand with a short stack, you should usually have a hand of at least some power like a big pair, or else hands that have some high-card potential *and* suits, meaning that you will have multiple ways to hit your hand. This second factor is usually more important than the nut potential of your hand – that is a factor that becomes increasingly important once the money gets deeper. Anyway, depending on both the looseness and the aggressiveness of your opponents, hands as weak as A-J-10-8 single-suited and K-J-J-8 double-suited may be good enough to go all-in before the flop with when you are playing a short stack. But at the same time, you should *avoid* hands like 6-5-4-3: speculative holdings that rely on implied odds and that don't hit very often, despite the fact that they do have quite a bit of nut potential. With these hands and a short stack, you should usually not even call the initial bet.

Playing a medium/large stack

With medium stacks, you can often play some more speculative holdings (for instance, the 6-5-4-3 mentioned above), especially when you are in position and/or are up against weak players who you can outplay easily. Because of this, hands like 9-8-7-7 are almost always playable when playing a medium stack, especially when your opponents have a tendency to overplay their big pairs. But this same 9-8-7-7 should be played with caution once the money is very deep. *If* you are actually playing it, you want to do it only in one of the following situations:

♠ In position, heads-up against a weak player who is marked with a big pair.
♠ On the button, and being the aggressor in the hand.

Note that with very deep money you will usually want to play these middle cards in raised pots only when you have a pretty good clue as to what you are up against. The reason to sometimes raise with these hands rather than call (remember, only when you have good position), is that your opponents may read you for a big pair/high card type of holding. You may profit from this either by a) bluffing or semi-bluffing them out of the pot because of a scary board, or by b) having them play back at you when it seems to them that the board may be bad for you – but when in fact you have hit the whopper.

Some final words

While quality hands like J-10-9-8 double-suited, K-Q-J-10 double-suited and aces with suits perform well in all cases, it is the marginal hands that may sometimes be profitable under certain circumstances, while being unprofitable under others. If you learn to distinguish between these situations, you will have a big edge over the (many) players who are oblivious to this, and who treat every single situation just about the same.

The power of protection

A while ago, I was in Barcelona to take care of the reports and updates for the annual European Poker Tour event over there. When I arrived back at my hotel room late at night, I was faced with the same kind of dilemma, the same trade-off as usual: Play poker or go to bed? Usually, I opt for bed. This time, I opted for playing. The $25-$50 blinds pot-limit Omaha games on a major site were just too juicy to pass on. Plus, the juiciest game of all had one seat open.

As I often do in loose-aggressive games, I bought in for the minimum $1000. I posted the big blind and was surprised to see no less than seven callers, including a late-position poster. I looked down and saw K-K-10-8 single-suited, a way above average hand for a big blind to have, and an even stronger one with all of these limpers around. After all, if I were to hit my king, I would very likely get action not just from drawing hands (that would have pretty much correct drawing odds to my top set), but probably also from weaker made hands that would be drawing thin or even dead.

However, this would all assume that I was to check down my hand, and decline my option to raise. But of course, this is not what I did. Having noticed that the early-position limpers were very loose (in Internet parlance: had a very high VP$IP) and thus were unlikely to have aces, I knew that there was only one way to play this hand: Raise pot. So, this I did. I made it $450 to go, and got called in no less than four places. All in all, a massive, multiway pot was in the making – and those who are familiar with my strategies know that this is exactly the way I like it.

The flop came down A-9-4 rainbow – without a doubt, an absolutely awful flop for my hand. I knew that in a pot this big, people would be very hard-pressed to lay down any ace after the flop, even if they reasoned that I could very well have flopped a set of aces. But calling a mere $550 with $2860 already in the middle would simply be *too* enticing for most people to 'sensibly' lay down even their mediocre hands.

Quite a few players in my position would therefore have reasoned: 'Hey, the ace is there. It is simply impossible for me to make them all lay down a better hand with this little money that I have, and there is literally zero chance that I have the current best hand. And with a draw to just two kings twice, on top of that cards that may not be in the deck anymore, I will simply have to give up. Betting here would be wasting my $550; it would be throwing good money after bad.'

While quite a few players would probably reason like this, my view is almost exactly the opposite. By making my pot-sized preflop raise, I have committed myself to the hand. This means that *not a single flop* should stop me from betting all-in here. I know that if against this A-9-4 flop I get called by one or two players who indeed hold a pair of aces or better, I will have made a slight –EV decision by moving in. However, as opposed to many other players, I usually don't mind making a slight –EV decision in extremely large pots, if there at least *some* chance that the hand could develop in such a way that I could get lucky by winning a massive pot, even while holding the worst hand going in. And as you can see later in this article – even in the seemingly hopeless situation that we have here with our kings, good things *are* definitely possible in this situation.

What happened was this. I bet all-in for $550, got called in two places, and then a highly aggressive player with a big stack moved all-in. While some players would imagine that this is a bad situation for me, it was exactly the situation I was hoping for. While the raiser *could* of course be raising with a hand like aces-up or a set and decide to end the pot right there, I was well aware of this player's betting and raising tendencies when there is a short-stacked all-in player. This player just loves to make huge raises in situations like this, either with big draws or with fairly weak made hands. By doing this, he hopes to shut out the field, keep his investments in the hand low, get to see both the turn and river card for a cheap price, and, probably most importantly of all, to get huge odds of 2-to-1 or even 3-to-1 on his money, while needing to beat just a single player who could have as little as just one pair.

So, what did this guy have, you ask. Aces-up, a set maybe? The answer is: No, my opponent didn't have that. He had a the truly awful 5-4-3-2 in his hand for a pair plus bottom wrap. Against my bare kings though, not a bad hand by any means. After all, now that the pot had risen to $3960, and because in the end he only needed to put $550 into the pot to reach the showdown, he would have needed just a little more than 12% pot equity to be in a +EV situation. Quite clearly, up against my hand he had much more than that. In fact, in this situation his horrible hand would win no less than 45% of the time, giving him an expectation of $2030 out of the $4510 pot – for a net gain of $1480 from the decision point on. (Net gain throughout the hand: $2030-$1000 = $1030.) Not bad at all when taking into account that in the end he needed to invest just $550 after the flop to get himself into this profitable situation. So, one could claim that by making this massive raise and shutting out the field, he had created a situation with a highly positive expectation for himself.

But at the same time, he had also created a highly profitable situation for me! What his raise had accomplished, was getting out all of the better made hands, meaning that my pair of kings was now suddenly the current best hand. This means that whereas up against a pair of aces *I* would require improvement to win the pot, now it was *my opponent* who required help. In the situation that I was in now, suddenly just two blanks would be good enough to win me an absolutely massive pot – holding a hand that on the flop had seemed dead in the water. Suddenly, my kings had an expectation of no less than $2480 out of the $4510 total pot – quite surprising when at first glance it seemed that I was drawing to just two outs!

Now, see here the Power of Protection. Even though I wound up losing the pot (a small card came on the river to complete my opponent's wheel), by going all-in on the flop and by inducing the highly aggressive player to protect me, I had turned a clearly –EV situation into a *very* +EV situation. Yet, if I would have ended up winning this five-way pot with an ace on the flop while holding just unimproved kings, well then I am certain that people would have called me a crazy lunatic who had absolutely no clue what he was doing – a sucker who regarded pocket kings in a multiway pot as the World's Fair.

However, if they read this article (or my *Secrets of Professional Pot-Limit Omaha* book), well then I guess they will know better. Or – probably just as likely – they may still not understand, or believe it.

Nice bluff!

Using my solid image in the end stage of a pot-limit Omaha tournament.

As readers know, my favourite poker game is *not* no-limit hold'em, the game that is always shown on TV. My favourite game is pot-limit Omaha. This being a four-card game where on average one needs a *much* stronger hand to win than in no-limit hold'em, some people claim that there is no bluffing, that it is just a nut-peddling game. In fact, nothing could be further from the truth. It *is* correct that at a showdown one will usually need a straight, flush or even full house to win – only rarely will a hand like two pair or even a single pair be enough. However, there are many common bluffing situations in PLO that are well known to the better players, and that I have also written about on many occasions. A few examples: betting someone off a better draw once the board pairs, playing the 'blockers' or executing the 'bare ace bluff' – every decent PLO player has knowledge of these concepts, and, perhaps more importantly, knows how to put these concepts to use at the tables.

As valuable and interesting as these bluff concepts are, the hand I will share with you here is – at least, to me – a much rarer bluff: It involves a checkraise bluff on the turn, with a hand that has absolutely no chance of winning in a showdown – yes, a hand that has absolutely no chance of even *improving* to the best hand on the river. In other words, a pure bluff with one card to come. This is one of the most dangerous types of bluff that one can make in PLO, because of the possibility of someone giving you action with either a very strong holding, or the combination of a decent made hand and a good draw. And it should be clear: When making a pure bluff, you don't want to get either one of those calls – as you will be drawing dead or close to it.

As I said, PLO is probably my favourite game. It offers an almost perfect combination of luck and skill and is usually action-packed – meaning that some of the biggest cash games in the world are indeed pot-limit Omaha. As much as I love PLO as a cash game, as a tournament game I don't like it as much. But still, it was at one of those – to me – rare PLO tournaments that I was involved in a remarkable hand, recently. The structure of this event was very slow, and I had succeeded in building a very tight and solid image. That was the good news; the bad news that with about 40 out of 240 players left, I had only a below-average stack. That's when this hand came up.

In the big blind, I woke up with K-5-2-2 no suits, one of the worst possible starting hands in Omaha high. As there has been no raise, I got to see the flop for free: Q-10-9 rainbow. I checked, obviously planning to fold to whatever bet someone would make – after all, all I had was a mere pair of deuces. It got checked around, and then an offsuit 7 came on the turn. Of course, I checked again, the limpers also checked, and then it was up to the button, the strong and solid Mickey Wernick. He bet 4000 into the 8000 total pot.

Knowing that Mickey would never have checked this flop with a straight or even two pair, this could mean only one thing. Either he had just made the understraight on the turn with the 8-6 or a small set of sevens maybe, or else he was simply trying to pick up the pot with nothing much. Being close to 100% certain that neither Mickey nor any of the other players was in there with the nuts, I chose to make a move that I make only on very rare occasions: a checkraise on the turn with absolutely nothing, as a total bluff.

Without a doubt, a highly dangerous play, even more so because my stack was not very large in relation to the others – and thus calling me down would be relatively cheap to them. But I was saved by the power of my image. All the other players folded, and Mickey also quickly threw away the 8-6 that I feared he might have, and that he would probably have paid off with against most other players. So, I won this pot on a total bluff, on a – for PLO – very rare move, and gained valuable ammunition to get further in this event. The reasons for success: a good read of the hands that were out there and a proper analysis of the psychology of the situation – plus of course, the correct exploitation of my tight and solid image.

A questionable pot-limit Omaha play

A while ago, I released the book about what by many is perceived as my specialty game, *Secrets of Professional Pot-Limit Omaha*. A book that for a large part focused on how to beat the $10-$20 online PLO games, and that fortunately for me has received some exquisite reviews.

Right after I released this book, I was fortunate enough to make a successful transition into the online $25-$50 games. Possibly as a result, but also simply because of my big ego, a relatively high number of my recent articles have discussed some good moves, expert plays, or just my successes in general.

But the fact that things have been going well for me lately, doesn't mean that I never make mistakes. Quite the contrary, I would say: Much more than in the past, I sometimes do things now that are outright stupid. I figured that it was time to also share these mistakes and errors with you, hoping that you may find some valuable lessons in them. Here I will analyse a questionable pot-limit Omaha play that I have made. And in fact, the term 'questionable' with its slightly negative connotation may actually be a bit too mild: the terms 'outright stupid' and 'stubborn' may be more suitable.

The situation

I find a juicy $25-$50 game on a major site. As I often do, for reasons that I have explained in my book, I buy in for the minimum $1000. After 20 minutes of play and one successful (uncontested) checkraise from the big blind with a rather marginal draw, I am up to $1220.

As those who have read my book know, I usually choose between two or three different strategies/game plans to tackle a game. If, as I have done here, I opt for a short-stack approach, this would mean that almost always I try to go for the limp-reraise before the flop, or the checkraise after. This of course to take advantage of any overaggressive players that are seated to my left. So, once I find A-K-Q-Q single-suited as the first one in from early position, I choose to limp – entirely in line with the recommendations from my book. This in the hopes of limp-reraising a loose-aggressive player behind me, or else – if the action really gets crazy – maybe fold my hand, having made just a fairly limited investment. So far, so good.

In contrast to the loose-aggressive nature of this specific table, all the players seem to respect or fear my under-the-gun limp – because everyone behind me folds. The small blind calls and the big blind checks, meaning that we take the flop three-handed, pot size $150.

The flop then comes A-8-2 rainbow and it gets checked to me. Taking into account that I am up against just the two players in the blinds, and considering the ill-coordinated nature of the board, this seems like a simple case of betting and picking up the pot. Right?

'Fancy play in the making

Well yes, that would probably be the correct move. However, as most readers of my works are aware of, I hardly ever make the standard 'book' play – not even in situations that seem to clearly warrant it. For instance, in this situation I know that if I bet anywhere between $100 and $150, the combined factors of the board, my fairly big bet and my limping from under-the-gun as a short stack, will probably lead my opponents to a simple conclusion: that there's a good chance that I am in there with A-A for top set.

However, I choose not to go for the obvious play of picking up the pot with the pair of aces/king kicker that I actually have. I choose to do something different, betting an unusually small $50. This is a bet that may either be perceived as a very cheap steal attempt with absolutely nothing (say, a Q-J-10-9 or so), or else as a very small bet with an absolute monster hand, designed to get my opponents to play back at me with holdings that are drawing very thin or even dead to mine. I know that almost anyone in this situation, with my decent-but-not-great holding, would not have made this small bet that I have made, as they would have tried to avoid the situation where this small bet could cause their opponents to doubt the strength of their hand. But because unusual betting patterns fit well within my overall style of play, I decide to play the hand in this strange, rather unconventional manner.

The small blind instantly checkraises the pot to $300. This is a player that I know very well, and he is not someone who makes a lot of checkraise moves with nothing. So, it is clear to me that he has a hand that in his mind may very well be best. With him being in the small blind, with this uncoordinated board, and taking into account his fast checkraise that is almost certainly designed to represent more strength than he actually has, I read my opponent for a two-pair type of hand, most likely A-8 or A-2. The big blind folds, and it is up to me. What do I do?

Analysing the psychology of the situation

Knowing that my opponent is highly unlikely to be holding top set himself, and knowing that *he* should know that for a tight short-stacker like me, A-A would be a typical limp-reraising hand from under-the-gun, I decide that this is a great time to represent the three aces that I may very well have. So, I raise the pot, right?, you say. Well, again: No, not really. I again choose to do things differently.

I decide to play my hand the exact same way that I would play it if I *really* had three aces against this rainbow flop: I make another minimum reraise to $550. Taking into account the psychology of the situation, it should be clear to my opponent that he now has a decision to make for at least the remainder of *my* stack – knowing that if he calls now, I will definitely bet the remainder of my stack, and he will simply have to call that bet. Plus, he knows that if indeed I have the hand that I am representing, almost certainly his hand will be a *very* big dog to mine. In fact, up against aces he could very well be drawing dead.

However, things turn sour for me. After long deliberation, my opponent chooses to reraise me all-in. This means that I now face a $1170 total bet for a total pot of $2490 – assuming that I call the $670 more. I still read my opponent for an A-8, A-2 or even 8-2, and against this range of possible holdings I would be getting the correct odds to call. In other words: Because I have misplayed my mere top pair/top kicker grossly by giving way too much action, I have now made it correct to also put the remainder of my stack in the middle, in just an unraised pot, and with a typical hold'em hand.

I indeed make the call – and it turns out that even my read is wrong, as my opponent shows me 8-8 for middle set. I am drawing to just two outs twice for a higher set, plus some remote runner-runner straight, flush and full house potential – but I fail to improve. In the end, the entire table sees I have given away $1170 after the flop in a situation where it was *clear* that my opponent had to have had a better hand than mine. Not the best of all plays, no question about it – and quite possibly, one of the best (or worst) examples of the 'fancy play syndrome' that you will ever see.

Some more doubtful pot-limit Omaha plays

I had just experienced one of my best-ever sessions online. Having stepped up to the $25-$50 blinds pot-limit Omaha games, and multi-tabling those games, I had experienced one of my smoothest sessions ever. Having bought in for the minimum $1000 at almost all the tables I played, I had managed to win $14,000 in just two hours of play. Not a shocking amount to the true high rollers, of course, and in fact less than just three times the *maximum* buy-in for this game. But to me – the tight, conservative player who hardly ever loses big but who also has very few massive wins – this $14,000 win was not to be sniffed at.

In line with my usual routine, regardless of whether I have been winning or losing, I took 60 minutes off to relax, to have breakfast, to shower and to get dressed – so that once I returned to the game I would again be fresh, prepared and relaxed. When I logged in again, I was pleased to notice that two overaggressive players had entered the $25-$50 games – players that in fact are big winners and cause problems to many players, but that for my shortstacking/sandbagging style of play can be considered rather ideal opponents. I was even ecstatic when I got the exact seats that I wanted, as on no less than two tables, I was able to sit to their immediate right. And those who are familiar with my strategies know what this means: it was time for the usual 'Rolf show' with limp-reraises before the flop, or check-raises afterwards. While in a different seat, I may have opted for a maximum buy-in to try and break the weaker players, I actually love to exploit the good players' overaggression by playing in a manner that most 'good' players don't appreciate: by buying in short, and by playing a sandbagging, move-in-early, 'no headache' type of game. It is a rather risk-free strategy if you know how to use it, that requires relatively little advanced thought, and that is very well suited to multi-tablers like me.

So, still thinking about my previous winning sessions, and happy about getting my preferred seat on no less than two tables, I actually started thinking: 'Rolf, this is your lucky day. How much better than this can things get?' I posted my big blind (in the big blind position; when shortstacking in a full-ring game with overaggressive players to my left, I hardly ever wait until behind the button as so many people think is best), and action got under way. I got A♠-J♥-10♣-8♥, and to my surprise the two loose-aggressive players to my left both folded. In fact, *everyone* folded to the button, who made it $175 to go. The small blind folded, and it was up to me.

Now, people who are familiar with my writing know that when employing my shortstack approach, I usually adhere to the simple system 'play for my entire stack, or don't play at all'. So, in this case my options were basically limited to either folding, or else reraising pot to $550. (Calling was not being a serious option, being out of position with a hand that has too many holes, little nut potential, and having invested 17.5% of my total stack already after this call.) Knowing that this opponent is quite aggressive, especially when he is in steal position, and mostly as a way to vary my play, I decided that for once I would make the play that I almost never make in this spot – calling. Knowing that my opponent didn't need to have much, and would make an automatic bet after the flop against my perceived weakness, I decided to just call the raise and then check to him, planning to checkraise on every flop that might have given me just the slightest bit of help.

The flop came 3-3-8 rainbow, giving me a typical hold'em hand: two-pair eights and treys with an ace kicker. I checked, and as expected my opponent instantly bet pot, $375. I realized that my opponent now either had me terribly beat (say, with something like A-A), or if he *didn't* have me beat, well then because of the A, J and 10 that I had, my opponent could almost never have that many outs to improve over me. In fact, there was some chance that even though I just had two pair, my opponent would be drawing extremely thin (say, with a hand like A-7-6-5 or A-10-6-4). And in fact, the betting sequence of him raising pot before the flop and then again betting pot after the flop against this non-threatening board were indications to me that my opponent *didn't* have aces but was making a move. After all, betting pot with aces on a 8-3-3 rainbow flop against a lone opponent with short money is usually not the smartest way to play – both from a maximizing wins, as well as minimizing losses, point of view.

After some deliberation, I decided to deviate from my initial plan to simply checkraise all-in, and I simply called – more than anything to give my opponent the chance to bluff an additional $450, and also to not *always* just checkraise or check-fold. So, when on the turn a jack came that gave me jacks and eights, I again check-called, and in fact felt rather good about my prospects of winning the pot. So far for the quality of my read: When the hands were shown down, my opponent turned out to have the exact hand that he had been representing all along: aces. So, he scooped the pot, having played his hand in an absolutely ABC manner that should never have been rewarded – yet I had convinced myself on every street that only ABC players or total donks would play their aces this way. As a result, I had deviated from my plan that instead of doing the obvious (just folding my problem hand before the flop and going on to the next hand), I had check-called my entire buy-in away with a hand that was in dire straits to begin with. Or, as we call it in big-bet play: I had simply donated my money by outthinking myself and by fancy-playing my way to the river.

When on the very next hand, I got kings in the small blind and then got it all-in before the flop to lose against yet another very obvious A-A hand, I had pissed away $2000 – having misplayed my first two hands of this new session terribly.

Of course, I knew that over the entire day, I was still up $12,000 – a more than decent win by all accounts. But I also knew that by playing the way I did, I probably didn't deserve any of it.

So, I pulled myself together, lifted my game again, and ultimately would end *this* session with a more than decent win too. But despite this, I was still mad at myself for the way I had played those two hands right after my return. Any top player would *not* have let his previous good results affect both his mindset and his decisions at the table – and at least in this case, I had shown that I was not the top player that I want to be.

The size of the buy-in: same game – different approach

While on my travels, I recently bumped into two very juicy online pot-limit Omaha games. Quite frankly, the $25-$50 blinds games that I some-times play nowadays were not very interesting, while at another site the $100-$200 and $200-400 games seemed very tough: with some very good players, and shorthanded too. Not exactly the type of composition I was looking for.

But then I noticed the $10-$20 games at yet another site, in what used to be my bread and butter game. I noticed that these games were unusually good – and it didn't take me long to find out the reason. A friend of mine, who is actually a more than decent player when it comes to reading hands but who is simply a bit too overaggressive both before and after the flop, was what is considered to be 'throwing a party'. However, this time he was throwing a party at the other players' expense. Knowing that he hardly ever buys in for the full $2000, he now had $5800 in one game, and $3700 in another – so it was quite clear that he was on a roll.

Of course, I immediately put myself on the waiting list for both games. Despite the fact that normally when a table is on fire it could take quite a while for a waiting player to get a seat (now that the game is so good, no one wants to leave), in this case I was fortunate. Within five minutes seats became available, and I could enter these two very juicy games both at the same time.

Now, while most players always buy in for the same amount, regardless of the texture of the game, I am one of the few players who varies these amounts. As people should know by now, I am actually one of the few 'good' players who often buys in for the minimum, rather than the full amount. But 'often' isn't exactly the same as 'always'. Some tables simply require a different approach to others.

Table one – approach A

At the first table, I got the seat to the immediate right of my friend. Now, knowing that despite his many strengths he also has some exploitable weaknesses (as said, especially his overaggression early in the hand), it was quite clear to me which strategy would be best here. I bought in for the minimum $400, in the hopes that I could either limp-reraise him before the flop with my good hands (the premium pairs of course, but also the double-suited coordinated hands), or else checkraise him after the flop when the situation seemed right. In fact, I was now in the exact position that nowadays is often referred to as 'Rolf's seat' – the seat to the right of a maniac that in the past most people tried to avoid, but that – as I have shown – can actually be one of the most profitable seats in the house. When playing short money, you may not only be able to trap the overaggressive player to your left, but by doing this you will also be bagging the entire field. This means that you can create lots of dead money for those times when you come over the top, giving you extra EV when your hand is good, and also making up somewhat for the times where you have misjudged the situation, and your hand is *not* good. But that's not all there is to it. Because you've got everyone caught in the middle, you will often get a reliable response from them to 'see where you're at'. Let's say that you limp with a relatively marginal A♠-Q♥-Q♦-8♠, your loose-aggressive friend raises, and then no one reraises – well, then it should be clear that this relatively marginal hand could be worth playing for all your money. So, by always letting him do the betting for you, you will have found an excellent checkraise station where, once the action gets back to you, the best decision should be quite clear, and where you will be in perfect position to both maximize your wins and minimize your losses.

Now, those who are familiar with my works know that this is one of my favourite game plans, one of the strategies that I frequently use. And therefore, I am often referred to as someone who advocates a short-stack approach. But nothing could be further from the truth. If you are a really good player, you would more often than not do even better by buying in for the maximum – which is exactly what I did at the second table.

Table two – approach B

Also at this second table, I got offered a seat next to my overaggressive friend – but this time, it was the seat to his immediate *left*. A seat that in general I like to avoid, as it carries the danger of getting sandwiched, squeezed or sandbagged by the other players who are using the overaggressive player's tendencies to their advantage – and thereby putting me in the middle. With anywhere from a small to fairly large stack in this position, it is entirely possible to lose a significant percentage of your stack cold-calling or reraising the maniac before the flop with your decent hands, only to get faced with an over-the-top reraise that you cannot call.

Still, because the waiting list behind me had grown, I took the seat – and obviously, this time I bought in for the maximum $2000. The reason was simple. I would now be trying to break my opponent in a heads-up situation by trying to isolate him either before or after the flop, knowing that he would give lots of action with sub-optimal holdings. In other words: I would now be trying to get as much money as possible off this one player, with the ultimate goal of trying to break him on one single hand. This is opposed to the situation at the first table where I would be using my mini-stack to get myself all-in early, almost certainly in a multiway pot or else heads-up with lots of dead money. In this situation, I would probably be getting a clear overlay despite the fact that I would not necessarily be an *absolute* favourite, but rather just a *money* favourite.

The end result

Fortunately for me, both approaches worked. On table one, I managed to turn my $400 into $1260 with my fairly marginal A♠-J♥-10♥-8♠. I had gone all-in before the flop in a three-way pot, and had gotten protection after the flop because my friend had bet the eventual winner out of the pot. And at table two, I was able to break my opponent just like I had planned to. Having flat called his raise while holding crappy kings, a loose-aggressive short-stacked player behind us went all-in. When my friend then just flat called this all-in raise, I knew for a fact that he didn't have aces – so I moved all-in with my kings. As it happened, my unimproved kings would scoop both the main and the side pot, meaning that in the space of just ten minutes I had won two major confrontations.

As I had been using two entirely different approaches to win these pots, I am certain that some of my opponents might reason something like this: 'Gee, this player is strange. At one table, he buys in small, yet at another table he buys in big. Strange player – probably doesn't have a clue.' Well, now they know the reasoning behind it, I guess. Same game, different approach – yet in both cases, clearly correct.